Beyond
Counseling
and Therapy

Beyond Counseling and Therapy

Second Edition

ROBERT R. CARKHUFF
BERNARD G. BERENSON

Carkhuff Institute of Human Technology
Amherst, Massachusetts

Holt, Rinehart and Winston
New York   Chicago   San Francisco   Atlanta
Dallas   Montreal   Toronto   London   Sydney

771085

Library of Congress Cataloging in Publication Data

Carkhuff, Robert R.
  Beyond counseling and therapy.

  Includes bibliographies.
  1. Psychotherapy.   2. Counseling,   I. Berenson,
Bernard G., joint author.   II. Title.
RC480.C3 1976   616.8'914   76-16184

ISBN 0-03-089812-9

Preface to First Edition

As committed counselors and therapists, we feel that we have something to say concerning theory and practice, training and research in counseling and psychotherapy. In the following pages, we attempt to say it.

We have organized the book around our own experiences in counseling and training and our research and theorizing concerning facilitative interpersonal processes in general. In the first section we attempt to describe the present state of conditions for the human in trouble, the person in need of help. The hope that we see is in the attitudinal disposition of the whole counselor, a whole person who views counseling as a way of life.

In the second section, we describe our attempts to develop a comprehensive model of facilitative interpersonal processes, a model in which both therapist and client are assessed on the same core dimensions of interpersonal functioning. A variety of potential preferred modes of treatment are constructed around these core dimensions. The potential preferred modes of treatment are studied in the third section in order to determine the unique contributions of each; that is, the contributions that each might make to constructive client process movement and outcome over and above those changes accounted for by the central core of facilitative conditions.

In the fourth section, we attempt to make application of the model of core conditions and preferred modes of treatment to clinical practice. Of necessity, any theoretical model does not translate easily to clinical practice. Therefore, attention is given to what is unknown to us as well as what is known. Phases of therapy are hypothesized and described. The implications of crisis therapy, "the crossroads for both client and therapist," and the need for confrontation at the crisis point in counseling and real life are described and the preferred modes of treatment blended fully into therapeutic processes. Finally, the thread which holds the entire book together, the whole person—"the goal of training and counseling" is considered.

In the last section, counseling and therapeutic processes are viewed again in their relation to society at large, and a summary and overview of the book is presented.

We have written this book with all persons concerned with effective human relations in mind. In particular, we have been concerned with those in the helping and teaching professions: counselors and psychotherapists; guidance and rehabilitation specialists; educators, psychologists, and social workers, as well as the intelligent, interested and concerned lay public.

R. R. C.
B. G. B.

Buffalo, N. Y.
June 1967

Preface to Second Edition

It is a privilege to respond to the request for writing a second edition of *Beyond Counseling and Therapy*. This gives us the rare opportunity of up-dating readers on the developments that have taken place over the past decade.

Most important have been the extensive research and application projects that have refined and sharpened the model for helping. That model is based upon the learning phases of exploration, understanding, and action in which a helpee engages in order to change or gain constructively in his or her life. The helping skills that are required to facilitate the helpee's movement through these phases are the sharpened theme of this scond edition.

In this context, the book examines the development of the helping model in six sections:

    I. Developing the dimensions of the helping model.

    II. Developing the skills of the helping model.

   III. Developing the unique contributions of traditional therapeutic approaches.

   IV. Developing the clinical applications of the helping model.

    V. Developing the training applications of the helping model.

   VI. Developing the learning implications of the helping model.

This book is meant for the same but expanded audience of helping professionals. We have coined the term "functional professional" to connote all of those people—staff personnel, lay personnel as well as indigenous helpee populations—who are concerned with helping, whether they have credentials or not. All functional professionals can discharge professional responsibilities. All credentialed professionals are not functional professionals!

We are pleased to say that we are still helping practitioners. We are also trainers. And consultants. And technology developers. Each level of development does not preclude but rather incorporates every previous level of development. Privilege is the reward for the immature. Responsibility is reward enough in itself for the mature.

We are also pleased to say that we are still optimistic, angry young men: young in spirit, at least—we have not lost our energy and vitality; angry in the respect that we see so little real change in the world around us, especially the helping world; and optimistic in the sense that we know so much more about how to change the world and the people in it.

We are not innocent for we know we can be killed. But we are growing—and that is the privilege of life. In a world where so many around us have given up and are merely going through the motions of living out the roles that others have assigned them, we are building steps to our dream of humankind's fulfillment of its humanity—its full development of its human resources. We continue to think there is no more worthwhile cause to which to give ourselves.

We wish to acknowledge the continuing stimulation and support of our colleagues in the Institute, Dr. William A. Anthony, Dr. David N. Aspy, Dr. George Banks, Dr. David H. Berenson, Dr. David H. Bland, Dr. John R. Cannon, Dr. Tom Collingwood, Dr. Ted W. Friel, Dr. Andrew H. Griffin, Dr. Richard M. Pierce, and Dr. Flora Roebuck. Finally, we wish to acknowledge the administrative assistance of Bernice Carkhuff and, in general, the support and encouragement from our wives, students, clients, and colleagues.

A very large measure of gratitude goes to our editor, Brian M. Heald, who contributed corrections, observations, and valued insights in addition to his patience, hard work, and sensitivity.

R. R. C.
B. G. B.

Amherst, Massachusetts

Contents

Section Six   Toward a Teaching-Learning Model   277

section one

HELPING
AND LIFE

All helping and human relationships may be "for better or for worse." Any time that we intervene in the lives of people we love or people whom we are paid to serve, our effects may be constructive or destructive. It depends in part upon the level of interpersonal skills that we offer. Those of us who offer high levels of interpersonal skills help people. Those who offer low levels of interpersonal skills harm people. Those who offer moderate levels do not make a difference. The purpose of this first section is to explore and understand the interpersonal skills we need to help people. The use of these interpersonal skills is guided by the phases of helping in which people being helped engage in order to learn and change constructively. These phases of helping involve exploring, understanding, and acting.

EXPLORING ──────▶	UNDERSTANDING ──────▶	ACTING ──
Where you are	Where you are in relation to where you want to be.	To get from where you are to where you want to be.

FIGURE I   People explore, understand, and act in order to change and gain.

1

. . . our children are lost
because we are lost.

Dimensions of Human Nourishment

Twenty years ago, Dorothy Rogers (1957) pointed out that in any random sample of 100 typical children, 1 or 2 children would commit major crimes and serve time in jail; 3 or 4 would be too retarded to become self-supporting unless they received specialized training; 30 to 50 would be sufficiently maladjusted to add to the statistics of petty crime, vocational failure, chronic unemployment, emotional instability, marital unhappiness or divorce, and other incidents of failure in our social system.

In response, as a nation we have poured more than $30 billion a year into mental health programs.

This cost starts with the more than $2.5 billion dollars a year of direct public outlay for services in treating the mentally disabled. To this must be added the cost of maintaining police, courts, penal and probation systems, the costs of alcoholism, accidents, absenteeism, medical care, and welfare. These costs, plus the loss of manpower due to all of these factors, amount to more than $30 billion per year, making difficulties in living the most costly sickness in society today.

This directly measurable economic cost is equalled, if not surpassed, by the immeasurable costs of personal tragedies and the loss of personal productivity and talent of individuals handicapped or crippled because of mental problems.

What did we get in return for our heavy investment in mental health?

Whereas Dorothy Rogers's data indicated that two out of three children could be expected to evidence symptoms of maladjustment, today—two decades later—we can expect that more than four out of five will lack the life skills necessary to enable them to function effectively in their worlds (Carkhuff, 1976c; Carkhuff and Berenson, 1967).

These are our children.

And through it all, our children will feel left out of things and less and less in control of their destinies, indicating that what they think does not count, that the people running the country really do not care, and that the rich get richer and the poor get poorer.

Our children are lost.

How did we get to such a human crisis? No doubt the pressures of our industrialized and urbanized society have taken their toll. The Bomb, to be sure! Drugs! Overpopulation! Automation! Pollution! Crime! The fragmentation of knowledge!

All of these things and much more!

But, mostly, our children are lost because *we* are lost.

Our children are undernourished because we do not know how to nourish them. We cannot provide human nourishment because we do not have the skills to do so.

The clients and patients who seek out our inpatient and outpatient treatment centers are largely people who cannot find sources of human nourishment in their everyday lives. Indeed, they are often the broken and disabled products of a social system that has often disallowed or made difficult their emergence as constructive and potent persons.

The clients and patients who seek our treatment are so desperate for nourishment that many of them are willing to (and must) pay for the devoted attentiveness of another human being. They seek parenting where there was none, teaching where there was little, and helping because it promises much.

Often in their desperation they turn away from what they need most, the communication that would free them to become truly human, the specialty area skills that they must learn to live effectively in their lives. They continue in this desperation not only to seek out treatment but to turn it into a destructive habit.

Sometimes, they turn from the only thing that will save them: contact with a healthy person.

The "more knowing" roles prescribed by society, those of parent, teacher, minister, guidance counselor, coach, and perhaps even spouse, while seemingly incorporating the notion of providing human nourishment, have obviously left their principal functions undischarged. They have left their "less knowing" counterparts impotent and unfulfilled. They have ceded their own special voids to their children, students, and partners, for they have very little to offer.

HELPING DIMENSIONS

Human nourishment is made up of commitment, discipline, skills, and strategies. Mostly, human nourishment is dependent upon hard work and the acquisition of skills.

The *commitment* is to grow, to be our best physically, emotionally, and intellectually so that we may make it possible for others to be their best physically, emotionally, and intellectually.

The *discipline* enables the person to do what needs to be done without temper tantrums and self-indulgence. More than that, discipline provides control over our temperament and insures awareness of others at least at some basic level.

Skills provide the response repertoire that enables us to live, learn, and work effectively.

The systematic *strategies* provide the means to achieve physical, emotional, and intellectual goals for ourselves and others.

Historically, we made an intensive and extensive effort to bring together a large body of evidence suggesting that all interactions between helpers and helpees have a "for better or worse" effect upon the helpee (see Figure 1.1). In counseling and therapy, teacher–student, or parent–child relationships, the consequences may have constructive or deteriorative effects on intellectual and physical as well as on emotional functioning. In perspective, the facilitative or retarding effects can be accounted for by a core of dimensions that are shared by all interactive human processes, independent of theoretical orientation. Patients, clients, students, and children of persons functioning at high levels of these dimensions improve on a variety of criteria, while those of persons offering low levels of these dimensions deteriorate on indexes of change or gain (Berenson & Carkhuff, 1967; Carkhuff, 1969; Rogers et al., 1967; Truax & Carkhuff, 1967).

Those core dimensions that have historically received the most imposing support are those involving the levels of empathic understanding, positive regard, genuineness, and concreteness or specificity of expression, offered by those persons designated as "more knowing" or the helpers. In turn, these dimensions are related to the degree to which the "less knowing" person, or the helpee, can explore and experience himself in the relationship, a dimension also shared by all interactive processes between "less knowing" and "more knowing" persons. Additional dimensions, such as those involving the levels of appropriate self-disclosure, spontaneity, confidence, intensity, openness, flexibility, and commitment of the "more knowing" persons, have been incorporated. However, the empirical evidence in support of these dimensions is sparse and, in a very real sense, movement toward these dimensions represents movement to the unknown from the known—a very necessary movement but one for which at present we have very little demonstrable effects.

It is useful for us to review our learning and definitions of

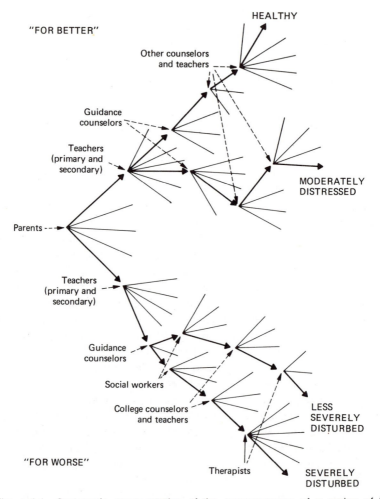

Figure 1.1   Systematic representation of the consequences of a series of "for better or worse" relationships.

the core dimensions in order to gain historical perspective as well as to point out that these scales are of continued use in research.

HELPER DIMENSIONS

While techniques may be learned and employed to communicate the primary core of facilitative dimensions, the dimensions themselves are integrated parts of the human personality. Although we attend to the dimensions as individual and distinctive units, the dimensions converge at high levels in the healthy personality and at low levels in the unhealthy person. In more moderate ranges, the individuals may function at relatively high levels on some dimensions and low levels on others.

In general, we might hypothesize that the levels at which an individual functions with others reflect the levels of his or her attitudes and comprehension of himself; that is, the individual is as empathic, respectful, and genuine concerning a wide range of feelings and experiences in others as he or she is concerning a wide range of feelings in herself. The individual's understanding and attitudes toward himself underscore the need for levels of minimally facilitative conditions. The individual's understanding and attitudes toward others underscore the need for training in the discrimination and communication of high levels of conditions, even for those individuals who have healthy attitudes and understandings of themselves, and especially for those who wish to function in a helping role.

Five-point scales have been developed to assess the core dimensions (Carkhuff, 1969).[1] On all scales, level 3 is defined as the minimally facilitative or effective level of functioning.

---

[1] The scales themselves have many limitations, most obviously a high degree of subjectivity on the part of the raters or judges. This subjectivity could not be avoided, even if it were undesirable. In actuality, counseling and psychotherapy are highly subjective experiences, and the scales are merely attempts to assess the levels of the dimensions involved in these experiences. In operation, research emphasis is placed upon a high degree of relationship between the ratings and reratings by the individual raters as well as a high degree of relationship between the ratings of different raters. Only the verbal material of therapy can be rated, and often unorthodox communications by the therapist may have a constructive impact upon the client. The communications which do not fall within the range of definitions of the scales may not receive high ratings. In the end, heavy reliance is placed upon the overall average levels of conditions throughout therapy as assessed by the ratings of random selected excerpts. For example, at a crises point in helping, responses by both helper and helpee may be made which are rated at low levels, but which, nevertheless, enable the helpee to become further involved in therapeutic process movement. If both helper and helpee function at high levels during the ensuing process, the overall average ratings will be much higher. The scales and those from which they are derived (Truax & Carkhuff, 1967), with all their limitations, emerge as important instruments with repeated replication in the same and different settings.

Empathy

With empathic understanding, where the first person or helper strives to respond with great frequency to the other person's deeper feelings as well as to his or her superficial feelings, we find a number of important dynamics that emphasize the underlying understanding of the individual therapist of himself and others and de-emphasize the techniques employed to communicate this understanding. We find, for example, that the helper's final, not his initial, level of empathic understanding is related to patient improvement in therapy (Cartwright & Lerner, 1963). The implication is that, ultimately, the helper's effectiveness is related to his continuing depth of understanding rather than to his ability to "technique it" during early phases of therapy. Indeed, too much empathy too early in helping may have a deleterious effect upon patient development (Carkhuff, 1969), because it may create too much tension or anxiety in the helpee. On the other hand, there is a direct suggestion that there exists an optimum amount of empathy beyond which too little psychological tension will exist to initiate a process of constructive change (Bordin, 1955; Wolberg, 1954). Thus, as the helper proceeds with her helpee to explore previously unexplored areas of human living and human relationships, it is her communication of her ever-growing awareness of the helpee, and of herself in relation to the helpee, which provides the helpee with the experimental base for change. With communicative skills, the helper's self-understanding will translate directly to his or her ability to "tune in" on the helpee's wavelength and thus overcome the alienation and isolation characterizing the person in need of help. In the context of an understanding relationship, the helpee is helped to clear up distorted perceptions and their underlying assumptive bases and ultimately, one hopes, to effect corrective action and constructive change. We must emphasize that empathy is not the client-centered mode of reflection with which it is most often confused. Concerning the effectiveness of techniques of communication in general, it is important to note that a convergence of client-centered and psychoanalytic thinking has produced the measures of empathic understanding most highly related to the relevant indexes of client change or gain (Truax & Carkhuff, 1967); that is, the measures of empathy most highly predictive of change integrate the client-centered notion of the reflection of feelings and the analytic emphasis upon diagnostic accuracy. In this regard, there is evidence to suggest that the mode of communicating empathic understanding which approximates the depth reflection of the client-centered school and the moderate interpretation of the psychoanalytic orientation appears to be of the greatest potentially demonstrable efficacy.

The emphasis, then, is upon movement to levels of feeling and experience deeper than those communicated by the helpee, yet within a range of expression that the client can constructively employ for his or her own purposes. The helper's ability to communicate at high levels of empathic understanding appears to involve the helper's ability to allow himself to experience or merge with the experience of the helpee, reflect upon this experience while suspending his own judgments, tolerating his own anxiety and communicating this understanding to the helpee (Fox & Goldin, 1964; Katz, 1963; Truax & Carkhuff, 1967). It is the manner of the helper, not his theory or technique, that communicates understanding and fosters growth. The helper can best convey his understanding of the helpee's situation by being fully human and not reacting mechanically by reflecting the helpee's words or merely understanding problems intellectually.

At level 3 of the empathic understanding scale, the verbal or behavioral expressions of the first person, the helper (counselor, therapist, teacher, or parent) in response to the verbal or behavioral expressions of the second person, the helpee (client, student, or child), are essentially *interchangeable* with those of the second person in that they express essentially the same affect and meaning. Below level 3, the responses of the helper detract from those of the helpee. Thus, at level 1, the lowest level of interpersonal functioning, the helper's responses either do not attend to or *detract significantly* from the expressions of the helpee in that they communicate significantly less of the helpee's experience than the helpee has communicated. At level 2, while the helper does respond to the expressed feelings of the second person, he or she does so in such a way that it *subtracts noticeably* from the affective communications of the helpee. Above level 3, the helper's responses are additive in nature. Thus, at level 4 the responses of the helper add noticeably to the expressions of the second person in such a way as to express feelings a level deeper than the helpee was able to express. Level 5, in turn, characterizes those helper responses that add significantly to the feelings and meaning of the helpee in such a way as to express accurately feelings some levels beyond what the person himself was able to express or, in the event of ongoing deep self-exploration on the helpee's part, to be fully with him in his deepest moments.

Respect

Respect or positive regard, in turn, has its origin in the respect that the individual has for himself. He cannot respect the feelings and experiences of others if he cannot respect his own feelings and experiences. If the significant adult figures of his or her early environment did not communicate this respect, often the individual must, in adult years, move through a process of therapeutic personality change involving the communication of respect to attain high self-regard. In addition, the communication of respect appears to shatter the isolation of the individual and to establish a basis for empathy. There are strong indications that the communication of human warmth and understanding are the principal vehicles for communicating respect (Carkhuff, 1969).

In this regard, Raush and Bordin (1957) suggest that there are three critical components involved in the communication of warmth: (1) the helper's commitment, (2) her effort to understand, and (3) spontaneity. They present evidence to indicate that it is the helper's effort to understand which communicates respect and is the major tie between the helper and the helpee. The work of Norvas and Landfield (1963) indicates that those helpers whose communications of warmth incorporate understanding have the greatest success in helping. The very deep respect for the other person's worth as a person and his or her rights as a free individual is often subsumed under terms such as "unconditional positive regard" or "nonpossessive warmth." However, these constructs appear to be superfluous, at best, and most to be misnomers. In this regard, Spotts (Rogers et al., 1967) has presented evidence to indicate that positive regard accounts for all of the variability of effectiveness of unconditionality. Unconditionality would, instead, appear to be nothing more than the initial suspension of potentially psychonoxious feelings, attitudes, and judgments by the helper in all significant interactions with helpees. If the person does indeed have respect for his or her own feelings and experiences and those of others, he or she will communicate this respect over a continuing period of interaction. In this context, Waskow (1963) has established that under some circumstances with some helpee populations, the more "judgmental" helpers elicit the greater depth of helpee self-exploration and experiencing. Again, respect can be communicated in many modalities. We must emphasize that it is not always communicated in warm, modulated tones of voice; it may be communicated, for example, in anger. In the final analysis, it is the helpee's experience of the expression that counts, and the helpee may experience the helper's attempt to share his or her own experience fully as an indication of the helper's respect for the helpee's level of development.

Respect or positive regard in interpersonal processes is defined at minimally facilitative levels by the helper's communication of a positive respect and concern for the helpee's feelings, experiences, and potentials. Levels below 3 are characterized by a lack of respect or negative regard. Thus, at its lowest level 1, there is a communication of a clear lack of respect or negative regard for the helpee, whereas at level 2 the helper responds to the helpee in such a way as to communicate little respect and concern for the feelings and experiences of the helpee. Levels above 3 are characterized by the communication of deepening levels of respect. Thus, level 4 describes helper communications carrying a deep respect and concern for the helpee, while level 5 characterizes a helper who communicates the very deepest respect for the helpee's worth as a person and his or her potential as a free individual.

Genuineness

The distinction between how a helper says what he says and how much of his own personality is revealed through his statements is made by Barrett-Lennard (1962), and underscores the degree to which the helper's statements appear to reflect his true feelings. "The degree to which one person is functionally integrated in the context of his relationship with another, such that there is an absence of conflict or inconsistency between his total experience, his awareness and his overt communication is his congruence in the relationship." In short, the base for the entire helping process is the establishment of a genuine relationship between helper and helpee (Truax & Carkhuff, 1967). The degree to which the helper can be honest with herself and, thus, with the helpee, establishes this base. However, the construct of genuineness must be differentiated from the construct of facilitative genuineness (Carkhuff, 1969). Obviously, the degree to which an individual is aware of his or her own experience will be related to the degree to which he can enable another person to become aware of his or her experience. However, many destructive persons are in full contact with their experience; that is, they are destructive when they are genuine. The potentially deleterious effects of genuineness have been established in some research inquiries (Truax & Carkhuff, 1967). Hence, the emphasis upon the helper's being freely and deeply himself in a nonexploitative relationship incorporates one critical qualification: when his only genuine responses are negative in regard to the second person, the helper makes an effort to employ his responses constructively as a basis for further inquiry for the helper, the helpee, and their relationship. In addition, there is evidence to suggest that whereas low levels of genuineness are not related to additional increases in helpee functioning (Truax & Carkhuff, 1967); it is important to avoid the conscious or unconscious facade of "playing the therapeutic role." The necessity for the helper's expressing himself or herself fully at all times is not supported. Again, genuineness must not be confused, as it so often, with free license for the helper to do what he will in therapy, especially to express hostility. Helping is not for the helper. The helper does not operate *in vacuo*. When she crosses the threshold of the conference room, the helper serves the helpee and must be guided by what is effective for the helpee. With a very brittle helpee leading a very tenuous existence, the helper may withhold some very genuine responses. Nevertheless, in his helping, she or he is continually working toward a more equalitarian, fully sharing relationship. *If there can be no authenticity in therapy, then there can be no authenticity in life.*

Facilitative genuineness in interpersonal processes is defined at minimally facilitative levels by the helper's providing no discrepancies between what he or she verbalizes and what other cues indicate he or she is feeling, while also providing no positive cues to indicate really genuine responses to the helpee. Below level 3, there are cues indicating discrepancies in the helper's expressions and cues for ungenuine responses. At level 1, the helper's expressions are clearly unrelated to what other cues indicate he or she is feeling at the moment, and/or the helper's only genuine responses are negative in regard to the helpee and appear to have a completely destructive effect upon the helpee. At level 2, there are indications that the helper's responses are slightly unrelated to what other cues indicate he is feeling at the moment, or that when his responses are genuine they are negative in regard to the helpee; the helper does not employ his negative reactions constructively as a basis for further inquiry. Above level 3, there are indications of deepening genuine responses. Level 4 characterizes the helper when he or she presents positive cues indicating genuine responses (whether positive or negative) in a nondestructive manner to the helper. At level 5, the helper's expressions indicate that he is freely and deeply himself in his relationship with the helpee; he is completely spontaneous in his interaction and open to experiences of all types, both pleasant and hurtful; in the event of hurtful responses, the helper's comments are employed constructively to open further areas of inquiry for both the helper and the helpee.

Concreteness

Concreteness or specificity of expression, a variable that is largely under the therapist's direct control, involves the fluent, direct, and complete expression of specific feelings and experiences, regardless of their emotional content, by both helper and helpee. This dimension appears to serve at least three important functions. First, the helper's concreteness ensures that his or her response does not become too far removed emotionally from the helpee's feelings and experiences. Second, concreteness encourages the helper to be more accurate in his understanding of the helpee, and thus misunderstandings can be clarified and corrections made when the feelings and experiences are stated in specific terms. Third, the helpee is directly influenced to attend specifically to problem areas and emotional conflicts. In at least one study, concreteness emerged as the most significant contributor to effective helping, far outweighing the contributions of empathy, positive regard, and genuineness (Truax & Carkhuff, 1967). Perhaps the most significant qualification applying to this variable is that the material must be of personally meaningful relevance to the client. In addition, while concreteness is of significant value during the early phases of helping, it may be of less or little value when less conscious material is dealt with later. In this context, Pope and Siegman (1962) suggest that helper specificity may be anxiety-reducing when the content area is neutral but anxiety-arousing when the material is emotion-laden. Of all the dimensions, it would appear that we could most easily train therapists to function at high levels of concreteness because it is less tied to the personality or life style of the therapist.

Personally relevant concreteness, or specificity of expression in interpersonal processes, is defined at minimally facilitative levels by the helper's enabling the helpee to discuss personally relevant material in specific and concrete terminology. Below level 3, varying degrees of vagueness and abstractness dominate the conversations. Thus, at level 1 the helper leads or allows discussions with the helpee involving only vague and indefinite generalities, while at level 2 the helper frequently leads or allows discussions that may even involve material personally relevant to the helpee to be dealt with on a somewhat vague and abstract level. Above level 3, specificity and concreteness dominate the problem-solving activities. Level 4 describes the helper's frequent helpfulness in enabling the helpee to develop fully in concrete and specific terms almost all instances of concern; level 5 characterizes the communications of the helper who is always helpful in guiding discussion so that the helpee may discuss fluently, directly, and completely specific feelings and experiences.

Depending upon the levels of the facilitative dimensions offered by the helper, the helpee may engage in a variety of activities.

HELPEE DIMENSIONS

The activities of the helpee are, in reality, much the same as those in which the helper engages. Thus, the helpee, facilitated by the helper's role as both model and agent, becomes openly and deeply himself or herself in the relationship. These dimensions are related to the genuineness and self-disclosure dimensions of the helper. With them, the helpee feels increasingly free to explore where he or she is in relation to his or her world.

Similarly, with the exploration of experience, the helpee comes increasingly to understand the dimensions of his experience—where he is in relation to where he wants to be in his world. In a very real sense, the helpee, like the helper in relation to him, is learning to become empathic and respectful of his own experience.

Finally, with the understanding of the experience, the helpee becomes disposed toward developing a direction and acting upon what he understands about his problems and his goals. This is related to the dimension of concreteness. The helpee, like the helper in relation to his task of helping, develops concrete and specific steps to achieve his or her goals.

The process by which the helpee is helped involves exploration, understanding, and action (see Figure 1.1).

The helpee explores where he or she is in relation to the world. He does this so that he can understand where he is in relation to where he wants to be. With this understanding, he can act to get from where he is to where he wants to be.

Exploration

The dimension of exploration as a phase of learning leading to understanding is well documented in the therapeutic literature (Carkhuff, 1969). It is perhaps the most significant activity of the helpee in the helping process. The exploratory process gives both helper and helpee the opportunity to get to know the helpee's experience of where he is in the world. In this respect it is, for the helpee, a kind of self-diagnostic process: a process by which the helpee will, with the helper's responsiveness, come to have a more complete and intense grasp of his or her experience. In addition, with exploration, the helpee is freed to experience and experiment with himself and thus get to know himself in different ways in relation to his world. Exploration is in part under control of the helper and in part under control of the helpee (Carkhuff, 1969; Truax & Carkhuff, 1967). When the helper raises or lowers the level of his interpersonal skills, most helpees raise or lower the level of their self-exploration. The exception is the high-level functioning helper whose high-level functioning helpees tend to continue independently of the level of conditions that the helper offers. On the other hand, when the helpee raises or lowers his or her level of exploration, most helpers tend to raise or lower their level of interpersonal skills. The exception is the high-level functioning helper who tends to upgrade his or her interpersonal skills level at the point where the helpee's exploration drops precipitously.

Self-exploration in interpersonal processes is defined at level 3 by the voluntary introduction by the helpee of personally relevant material concerning *where he or she is in relation to his or her world and the people in it*, although he or she might do so in a mechanical manner without the demonstration of emotional involvement. Below level 3, the helpee either does not voluntarily introduce personally relevant material or responds only to the introduction of personally relevant material by the helper. Thus, at level 1 the helpee does not discuss personally relevant problems or material, either because he has had no opportunity to do so or because he actively evades the discussion even when it is introduced by the helper. At level 2, the helpee responds with discussion to the introduction of personally relevant problems or material by the helper but does so in a mechanical manner without the demonstration of emotions. Above level 3, there is a voluntary introduction of personally relevant problems or material by the helpee with increasing emotional involvement. Thus, at level 4 the helpee voluntarily introduces discussions of personally relevant problems or material with both spontaneity and emotional involvement, and at level 5 the helpee actively and spontaneously engages in an inward probing to discover feelings or experiences about himself and his world.

Understanding

Exploration is a necessary but not sufficient condition of understanding. It allows the helpee to participate in the learning process and thus motivates the helpee to understand himself or herself (Lewin, 1951). What he or she wants to understand is where he or she is in relation to where he or she wants to be. The basic foundation for understanding rests upon insights as discriminative stimuli which increase the probability that related behaviors will occur. However, action does not usually follow insight. For one thing, the insights are usually not developed systematically. Each piece of explored material is not utilized as a base for the next level of understanding. Therefore, the individual does not "own" them and cannot act upon them (Hobbs, 1962). We have been plagued with insight therapy approaches with patient products who have "understood" but have been

unable to act upon their understanding. Some studies of professional training in the helping professions suggest the sources of
these discrepancies. While the clinical trainees improve over the
course of training in their ability to discriminate effective helper
responses, they tend to deteriorate in their ability to communicate these responses while they evaluate their self-ratings of that
ability (Carkhuff, 1971). Thus, there is a discrepancy between
insight and action.

Self-understanding in interpersonal processes is defined at
level 3 by the helpee's ability to add to his exploration of where
he is an *understanding of where he wants to be or needs to be
in relation to his world and the people in it*. Below level 3, the
helpee either does not respond to his or her problems or cannot
translate them to goals. Thus, at level 1, the helpee does not respond to the personally relevant problems or material he has
explored, either because he had no opportunity to do so or because he actively evades the further discussion of problems even
when the helper introduces it. At level 2, the helpee responds
with discussion to the introduction of personal problems by the
helper but does so in a mechanical manner without searching
for solutions or goals. At level 3, there is a voluntary attempt to
develop goals that would resolve the problems by simply flipping
the problems over to develop the goal (the goal is the reverse
side of the problem—"where I am deficient in an area, I want to
develop assets"). Thus, at level 4, the helpee of her own initiative
adds to her understanding by developing alternative courses of
action for achieving the goals for where she wants to be. At level
5, the helpee chooses the preferred courses of action for achieving the goals for where he or she wants or needs to be.

Action

The discrepancy between insight and action is also a function of
the lack of systematic action programs that flow from systematically developed insights (Carkhuff, 1971). Thus the helpee is
provided with the opportunity to acquire experience in developing a relevant course of action and in trying out new behaviors to
implement that course of action. McClelland (1961) has developed
insights related to achievement motivation and followed them
with the opportunity for the development of behaviors flowing
from the insights. The implications are important for training in

the systematic development of action programs to follow understanding or insights. Thus, understanding does not translate into
behavior change unless both insights and action are systematically developed. Behavior change may effectively precede the
insights, provided the behavior is consolidated with the insights,
allowing the helpee to make the discriminations necessary to use
his or her responses.

Action in interpersonal processes is defined at level 3 by
the helpee's ability to operationalize a course of *action to get
from where he or she is to where he or she wants to be in his or
her world.* Below level 3, the helpee either does not respond to
his goals or cannot take action steps to achieve them. Thus, at
level 1 the helpee does not respond to goals concerning where he
wants or needs to be. At level 2, he responds with discussion to
the introduction by the helper of steps to achieve the goals but
does so in a mechanical manner without searching for new
steps. At level 3, there is a voluntary attempt by the helpee to
develop steps to achieve goals that would enable him to resolve
his problems by simply defining the goal in terms of the steps
needed to achieve it. Thus, at level 4 the helpee of his own
initiative adds to his direction by developing all of the steps
necessary to get him to his goals; and at level 5, the helpee
initiates the action steps by implementing them in order to get
from where he is to where he wants to be.

Experimental exploration, then, initiates the helping process for the helpee. Understanding provides the mediating process
which, in turn, leads to behavior by the helpee. With the feedback from that behavior, this helping or learning process is
recycled: concrete feedback stimulates further exploration which
leads to more accurate understanding and, thus, more effective
action.

The helping process of exploration, understanding, and
action constitutes the basis for the development of a helping
model. If we understand how a helpee gains or changes over the
course of helping then we must develop the helping skills we
need to bring about this change or gain.

For the helpee, then, being helped is learning. The helpee is
guided through the phases of learning: exploration, understanding, and action. It remains for us to understand the helping skills
required to facilitate this learning.

We do this because we are committed to improving upon

our 20 percent success rate. We do this because we want to help five out of five of our children rather than one out of five.

We also do this because we are disciplined in achieving the goal of helping all our children grow; because acquiring the skills to help someone else to grow involves growing ourselves; and because we can develop the strategies to help our homes, schools, and business—our communities—to become places in which to grow.

REFERENCES

ASPY, D. N. *Toward a technology for humanizing education.* Champaign, Illinois: Research Press, 1972.

BARRETT-LENNARD, G. T. Dimensions of therapist response as causal factors in therapeutic change. *Psychological Monographs,* 1962, *76,* No. 43.

BERENSON, B. G., & CARKHUFF, R. R. *Sources of gain in counseling and psychotherapy.* New York: Holt, Rinehart and Winston, 1967.

BORDIN, E. S. Ambiguity as a therapeutic variable. *Journal of Consulting Psychology,* 1955, *19,* 9–15.

CARKHUFF, R. R. *Helping and human relations. Vol. I: Selection and training.* New York: Holt, Rinehart and Winston, 1969.

CARKHUFF, R. R. *The development of human resources.* New York: Holt, Rinehart and Winston, 1971.

CARKHUFF, R. R. *The art of helping communication and discrimination* (audiotape series). Amherst, Massachusetts: Human Resource Development Press, 1976. (a)

CARKHUFF, R. R. *The art of helping training* (videotape series). Amherst, Massachusetts: Human Resource Development Press, 1976. (b)

CARKHUFF, R. R. *The promise of America.* Amherst, Massachusetts: Human Resource Development Press, 1976. (c)

CARKHUFF, R. R., & BERENSON, E. G. *Beyond counseling and therapy* (1st ed.). New York: Holt, Rinehart and Winston, 1967.

CARTWRIGHT, R. D., & LERNER, B. Empathy, need to change and improvement with psychotherapy. *Journal of Consulting Psychology,* 1963, *27,* 138–144.

FOX, R. E., & GOLDIN, P. C. The empathic process in psychotherapy: A survey of theory and research. *Journal of Nervous and Mental Disorders,* 1964, *138,* No. 4.

HOBBS, N. Sources of gain in counseling and psychotherapy. *American Psychologist,* 1962, *17,* 18–34.

KATZ, R. L. *Empathy: Its nature and uses.* New York: Free Press, 1963.

LEWIN, K. *Field theory in social science.* New York: Harper & Row, 1951.

McCLELLAND, D. D. *The achieving society.* Princeton, N.J.: Van Nostrand, 1961.

NORVAS, M., & LANDFIELD, A. Improvement in psychotherapy and adoption of the therapist's meaning system. *Psychological Reports,* 1963, *13,* 97–98.

POPE, B., & SIEGMAN, A. W. Effect of therapist verbal activity level and specificity on patient productivity and speech disturbance in the initial interview. *Journal of Consulting Psychology,* 1962, *26,* 489.

RAUSH, H., & BORDIN, E. S. Warmth in personality development and in psychotherapy. *Psychiatry,* 1957, *20,* 351–363.

ROGERS, C. R., GENDLIN, E. T., KIESSLER, D., & TRUAX, C. B. The therapeutic relationship and its impact: A study of psychotherapy with schizophrenics. Madison: University of Wisconsin Press, 1967.

ROGERS, D. *Mental hygiene in elementary education.* Boston: Houghton Mifflin, 1957.

TRUAX, C. B., & CARKHUFF, R. R. *Toward effective counseling and psychotherapy.* Chicago: Aldine, 1967.

WASKOW, I. E. Counselor attitudes and client behavior. *Journal of Consulting Psychology,* 1963, *27,* 405–412.

WOLBERG, L. *The technique of psychotherapy.* New York: Grune & Stratton, 1954.

section two

TOWARD A HELPING MODEL

The dimensions of helping may be factored into responsive and initiative dimensions. The responsive has as its antecedent the attending behaviors upon which responding is based. The initiative dimension incorporates the transitional dimension of personalizing understanding, which is based upon responsiveness. Together, these interpersonal skills facilitate the helpee's movement through the phases of helping. Attending is a precondition of helping that facilitates the helpee's involvement in helping. Responding facilitates helpee exploration. Personalizing facilitates helpee understanding and initiating facilitates helpee action. The purpose of this section is to explore and understand where we are functioning in helping and where we want to be in our functioning.

FIGURE II Helping skills help people to explore, understand, and act in order to change or gain.

2

. . . counselor and counselee make
a mutual nonexposure pact.

The Levels of
Human Nourishment

Functionally, most counselors suffer from the same problems with the same intensity as do their counselees. Most basically, both possess a limited repertoire of responses or skills in living, learning, and working.

Both counselors and counselees have low levels of physical energy. They have fluctuations of energy only within a depressed range. They are energized only in a periodic eruption that is not under their control. They express little vitality because they have little life. Take a good look at them within and without the counseling session.

Both counselors and counselees communicate in such ways as to increase distance rather than intimacy. They are at their best the first day of school, the first hour of counseling, the first minute of the session. Thereafter, they deteriorate. They counsel for years without the accurate communication of the feelings expressed by others or the spontaneous expression of their own feelings. They withhold love because they cannot experience people ouside their own skins. Indeed, they cannot experience themselves fully, for if they did they would know that it was not love at all that they were withholding. Listen to them as they interact with their counselees.

Both counselors and counselees are egocentric and resistant learners. They say, "Don't teach me anything that I don't already know." They fight every step of the way to prevent new input—to distort new goals and to refuse new steps. They have only concepts of what they are to do and make every effort to avoid learning new principles—let alone new skills. They are one-dimensional people who, in the middle of crises for others, ask only stupid questions and, in the middle of crises for themselves, answer them. Watch them as they are asked to learn new approaches.

Both counselors and counselees invest little of themselves in their jobs. Instead of human accountability, they are preoccupied with the appearance of survival. They acquire language instead of skills. They emphasize irrelevance in lieu of productivity. They focus on fantasies (without steps) rather than goals with steps. In the end, counselor and counselee make a mutual nonexposure pact: "You don't expose me and I won't expose you."

In the process, they also make a nonnourishment pact in

the respect that one cannot nourish the other if he or she does not deal with the shortcomings of the other.

ILLUSTRATIONS OF LEVELS OF
HUMAN NOURISHMENT

The following examples will serve to illustrate the levels of functioning in the helping process. As the reader will note, each excerpt begins with the helpee's expression of a similar problem or experience. The excerpts demonstrate and can be rated on all helper-offered dimensions as well as on factors of these dimensions.

The first excerpt involves a somewhat depressed helpee in her initial helping contact with a helper functioning at low levels of the helping skills.

> *Helpee:* Sometimes I just get so depressed, I don't know what to do.
>
> *Helper:* Everyone feels that way once in a while.
>
> *Helpee:* Yes, but—but—this time I'm really—really as low as I think I can ever get.
>
> *Helper:* Everybody has their ups and downs.
>
> *Helpee:* Well, I don't know—I don't think it can get worse.
>
> *Helper:* Tell me more.
>
> *Helpee:* I really don't feel much like it right now.
>
> *Helper:* I understand.
>
> *Helpee:* I'm just—just—hitting bottom.
>
> *Helper:* Perhaps we can talk more about it next time.

This brief excerpt would be rated at the lowest levels. The helper responds passively with homilies that are not accurate reflections of the helpee's experience. In no way does the helper even communicate any attentiveness to the helpee's experience. Indeed, his responses are calculated to prevent helpee exploration rather than to facilitate it. There is no empathy, no respect, no genuineness, and no concreteness. The helper functions at the lowest levels of responsiveness and initiative. Consequently, there is no exploration. The helper—and perhaps the helpee—never finds out what the problem is really about. Both helper and helpee are functioning around level 1.

This second excerpt indicates a similar kind of helpee with a helper still functioning at low levels.

Helpee: I'm really down—I don't think I can handle things any more.

Helper: Is there a particular area where you feel this way?

Helpee: Well, I guess my exams are pressuring me most.

Helper: Have you prepared for your exams?

Helpee: In a way—but not really—I don't know.

Helper: How many do you have?

Helpee: Five, I guess, but its more than that. . .

Helper: When do you take them?

Helpee: I don't know. . . I've got the schedule here somewhere.

This brief excerpt serves to illustrate that there are an infinite variety of ways to fail in helping. The helper responds to material with questions that become increasingly more stupid. We never do find out for sure whether this is the problem or not because the helpee never really explores himself beyond the initial introduction of the exam pressure. Even if the helpee answers all of the helper's questions, the helper will have no diagnosis or prescription. He will simply resort to one of the homilies like "You have to solve your own problems." This helper is, indeed, one and the same as the first helper. He is rated at level 1 because he does not respond or initiate effectively. His helpee is rated at level 1 because he really does not explore his experience.

The third excerpt illustrates a helper who is trying to involve the helpee in the helping process but does so at moderately low levels.

Helpee: I don't know if I can make it.

Helper: Things don't look too good, huh?

Helpee: Right! I don't think I'm going to make it in school this semester.

Helper: That's important to you—and to others.

Helpee: Yeah! I guess it is—at least it is to my parents.

Helper: Then we're going to have to work on ways to make it happen.

Helpee: I don't know what they are.

Helper: Well, the first thing we're going to do is find out where all your teachers think you are.
Helpee: O.K.! But I don't think they're really happy.
Helper: Just have your parents sign this and I'll get a progress report from each of your teachers.
Helpee: I guess nobody's really happy with me—including myself.

The helper is really trying to get the helpee involved in activities that will lead to helping him. But she only knows about school because that is all she responded to. She has not really fully entered the helpee's frame of reference. Although she does respond to the content of the helpee's expression, she does not respond to the feeling or the meaning. She proceeds prematurely, albeit concretely, to set about on developing a course of action. There is minimal introduction of new material under the helper's guidance. Overall, the helper is rated at level 2 in terms of both the responsive and initiative dimensions and the helpee is rated at level 2 in terms of his exploration.

The fourth excerpt involves a similar helpee expression of experience and a helper who responds at minimally effective levels to that experience.

Helpee: I just don't know where I'm at.
Helper: You're really confused.
Helpee: Yeah—but it's more than that because I don't know if I can handle things.
Helper: You're feeling down because things are getting hard to. . .
Helpee: Especially chemistry. I don't know if I can handle old Dr. B———'s exams. And if I can't, I'm done here.
Helper: You're really scared because it will be all over for you.
Helpee: Yeah—and that's not good for me because my parents and my girl will be let down.

This helper responds accurately with empathy to each expression which the helpee makes. As a consequence, the helpee introduces more and more personally relevant material. The helper is rated at level 3 for her overall responsiveness and the helpee is rated at level 3 for his overall exploration.

The fifth excerpt involves a helper who responds at moderately high levels to a similar experience expressed by the helpee.

Helpee: Everything is piling up. School and other things.

Helper: It's all pretty overwhelming for you.

Helpee: I think I'm going to flunk out and that sets off a lot of other things.

Helper: You're really upset because of all the things that could happen.

Helpee: Yeah! I'm most upset for my girl. If I flunk out of school, she's really going to be hurt and my parents are going to be hurt, too.

Helper: You're really hurting because you will hurt a lot of people by letting them down.

Helpee: I just get all disoriented. I let all the people down who matter to me—most of all myself. I don't know if I can make it in life.

Helper: You're really scared because you can't handle things.

Helpee: I've got to learn to be a man.

Helper: You're scared because you can't handle things but you really want to learn how to.

Helpee: That's it exactly! That's why I'm here. First of all, I want to learn how to handle school. If I can do that, I'll have a first step toward handling myself.

The helper begins by responding at the level that the helpee is expressing himself and moves gradually to personalizing this understanding of the helpee's experience. Gradually, the helpee comes to understand where he is in relation to where he wants to be. The helper is rated at level 4 overall in terms of her responsiveness and initiative and the helpee is rated at level 4 in terms of his exploration and understanding.

In the sixth excerpt, the helper responds and initiates at the highest levels.

Helpee: Things are really falling apart.

Helper: You're feeling pretty low.

Helpee: I never felt lower. I don't know where I'm at in school.

Helper: You're feeling down because things are not clear in school.

Helpee: I think I'm flunking and that's going to mess me up good.

Helper: You're really worried about what's going to happen when you flunk.

Helpee: I can't seem to get up for it and if I don't, it's curtains for me—I'll be drafted.

Helper: You're scared because you can't get motivated.

Helpee: I just can't seem to study—I really don't know how.

Helper: You're scared because you can't study and you really want to find out how.

Helpee: You know, I got this far and I don't even know the first thing about studying.

Helper: You'd really be relieved if you could learn how to study. There is a study program called SQ3R. I'd like to try to introduce you to it. The S stands for survey. The Q for question. The 3 R's for read, recite, and review. I'd like to show you how it works.

Helpee: Wow! You mean I can learn how to study? Thank you! I'd really like to get going.

The helper not only responds with a personalized understanding of the helpee's frame of refrence but initiates to help the helpee to do something about his understanding. She is rated at 5 in terms of her interpersonal functioning and the helpee is rated at 5 in terms of his acting upon his understanding.

These illustrations serve to highlight the different levels of functioning of helpers. The helpers can serve to facilitate or retard the helpee's development by facilitating or retarding his or her exploration, understanding, and action. Even in these brief excerpts you can see the difference in helpee process movement and outcome. Helping may truly be "for better or for worse."

LEVELS OF GENERAL NOURISHMENT

There is little functional difference among the modal levels of interpersonal functioning of the general public (see Table 2.1). In

TABLE 2.1 Modal Levels of Interpersonal Skills of General and Professional Populations

Population	Modal Level of Functioning
Inpatients	1.2
Welfare populations	1.5
General public	1.5
College freshmen	1.5
Community volunteers	1.6
Nurses	1.7
Teachers	1.7
Upper class students	1.8
Dormitory counselors	1.8
Guidance counselors	1.9
Inpatient therapists	2.0
Graduate students (psychology)	2.1
Outpatient counselors	2.1
Trained helpees[a]	2.6
Trained subprofessionals	2.7
Trained subdoctoral	2.7
Advanced training (functional professionals)	4.0

[a] Trained in the same helping skills as helpers.

general, they range between levels 1.5 and 2.0, with a standard
deviation about the means of less than one-half level (Carkhuff,
1969; Carkhuff & Berenson, 1967).

As can be seen, inpatient populations do function at lower
levels than do outpatient populations, who, in turn, are not different from the general public, welfare populations, or college
freshmen. All are essentially oblivious to the experiences of the
people around them. In effect, they are immune to constructive
human encounters. Functionally, the only real difference between
the inpatient populations and the general public is the fact that
the inpatients encountered some experiences that they were
unable to handle with their extremely limited repertoire of interpersonal responses. The general public, on the other hand, has
yet to encounter these experiences and then be reinforced for
their inabilities by a restricted environment that punishes initiative and encourages dependency.

While college freshmen are similarly out of it, there is a

trend toward improved functioning with education and/or when the students or others are oriented toward helping or choose to major in one of the helping professions. Thus, sophomore dormitory counselors and upper class students demonstrated slightly higher levels of responsiveness as they peak in their interest in humanity and pass on to becoming part of the general public, and perhaps eventually part of the inmate population. In this regard, it is an interesting note that in one of our assessment programs we assessed activist student leaders and found them generally to be functioning at levels lower than the general public and their fellow students when cast in the helping role with a fellow human being. It seems the political types try to appear more responsive than they behave in practice.

In addition, community volunteers and hospital attendants and nurses and other people associated with helping are functioning at slightly higher levels than the general public, although not quite as high as the upper class students or dormitory counselors (Carkhuff, 1969). The direct suggestion is that through interest and experience, these people have learned some of the responses that prove to be more effective than others.

However, the typical human relationship at all of these levels peaks with the first contact and declines thereafter. Many "marriages" are balanced precariously upon the memories of the "love at first sight" experiences. Some of the couples hold on to each other like two drowning swimmers because they have nothing else to hold. But whether together or apart their minds are elsewhere, desperately hoping for the life preserver that someone might throw to them.

The typical human relationship in life involves ignoring each other, especially the experiences that each goes through, ignoring feelings, displaying a lack of interest or concern in and negatively relating to the expressions of personally relevant material by the other person. At "best" the parties to a relationship use cheap and efficient "role" homilies and subtract only subtly from each other as each struggles desperately to keep afloat. At worst, they detract visibly and significantly as they scramble to tread water by resting—temporarily—on their drowning partner.

It is significant that from within the general public, the highest levels of facilitative conditions a person under duress can receive averages 2.0, from a best friend. The implication, then, is that an individual in trouble seeks out a good friend in order to have a less retarding experience than his everyday encounters provide.

Among nonprofessional populations, the levels of functioning are highest for beginning graduate students in psychology, although somewhat lower for students in other helping professions. From among these graduate students, those functioning at the highest levels appear to be in most jeopardy. Typically, in graduate training programs as in life, the best and the worst are eliminated as the great horde in the middle rolls on.

In our first edition, we concluded that those students who communicated the highest levels of understanding and whose clients and patients had the greatest opportunity to change or gain constructively received the lowest grades in their training programs. The past ten years have confirmed that conclusion.

We have just passed through a decade where training has consisted either of learning a few limited conditioning techniques (with incredibly little practice) or of encouraging the trainee to "do your own thing." In the former condition, there was little attention to the client's experience other than as a behavior that was to be manipulated. In the latter condition, helping was based upon the helper's expression of his or her experience.

The past decade has not been, as some would have us believe, a period of experimentation and exploration. It was a period of psychopathic self-indulgence with no standards, full of temper tantrums and contempt for helpees and trainees.

Even where attempts have been made to incorporate training in interpersonal skills, the emphasis has been upon concepts and language rather than upon delivering to the helper the skills that he or she needs to deliver to the helpee.

Those students who demanded some kind of systematic skills training and/or attempted to employ helping skills for the benefit of their clients received the lowest grades and were judged as having "hang ups."

It may be appropriate for us to stop pointing an accusing finger at society and begin instead to monitor the helping professions and hold their members accountable.

LEVELS OF PROFESSIONAL NOURISHMENT

The thesis that training is deteriorative is supported by the base rate data on professional helpers (Carkhuff, 1969;

Carkhuff & Berenson, 1967). There is a direct suggestion that professional teachers, counselors, and therapists never again achieve the level of functioning on relevant helping skills that they had upon entering graduate school.

While helpers may sound different and ask apparently intelligent (but irrelevant) questions, they are not functionally different from the general population. As a whole, they cannot deliver—even for money—because they have a limited repertoire of responses.

Teachers function well below minimally effective levels of helping skills even though the basic principle of learning dictates that they cannot teach a child unless they have entered that child's frame of reference and related the subject matter to that frame of reference.

Guidance counselors do not function at much higher levels than teachers. Even though many of them have been exposed to the concepts of helping skills, they have not learned and applied the skills themselves due to the inadequacy of the training they received and their capitulation in an environment that does not support the use of the skills.

Both the teachers and guidance counselors exhibit poor attending, observing, and listening skills, in addition to responding inadequately to the experience of the student. Too frequently, the students, like the teachers and counselors before them, are asked to act without understanding or to understand without exploring.

Together, the teachers and counselors provide the essential ingredients of a retarding educational experience for the student.

Although there is some evidence that outpatient counselors and therapists function slightly better than do inpatient counselors and therapists, the difference is irrelevant in terms of client and patient gain. Both inpatient and outpatient practitioners function significantly below minimally effective levels and, as a consequence, usually provide "for worse" relationships and outcomes. The same conclusions can be drawn when we compare prominent and less prominent therapists as well as therapists representing major orientations to helping, such as existential, client-centered, psychoanalytic, and vocational counselors, and behavioristic-oriented therapists during their efforts to establish themselves as potent reinforcers. Again, even when people are desperate enough to pay for help they receive in return the same relative levels of human nourishment that made them desperate in the first place. Perhaps too many helpers never get over wanting or needing to be a helpee.

The traditional roles of the therapist as either a self-denying, warm, accepting parental surrogate or an aloof, analytic superior provide absurd choices and have, over the years, constituted the basis for many absurd arguments. These roles, from one extreme to the other, are as silly as suggesting that the therapist should only be assertive or only be understanding. The advocates of both extremes in roles and technique never tie their arguments to what is relevant: effectiveness. Professionals choose to defend one extreme or the other only when they are in doubt about their essential contributions and their skills to make them.

There is growing awareness that our society's designated experts have not provided either the nutrition or the direction to sustain human emergence in general and individual emergence in particular.

The professional helpers to whom we turn because human sustenance is not available in the general environment are themselves functioning at ineffectual levels of those dimensions related to constructive change or gain. Beyond their counseling and psychotherapy, their distorted perceptions and communications lead to the deterioration of their own significant human relationships. They find the same lack of personal fulfillment in their daily living that their clients do. Perhaps most important, they cannot allow the clients to find more in life than they themselves have found.

The crises of counseling and psychotherapy may be likened to those of the person floundering in the water several hundred yards off shore. Perhaps the distressed person does not know how to swim or, knowing how, simply does not have enough strength to make it to shore. Our professional lifeguards, it seems, do not know how to swim themselves. To be sure, they have been given extensive training in many lifesaving techniques, all of which they have tested in the children's shallow pool. They know how to row a boat; they know how to throw out a ring buoy; they know how to give artificial respiration. But they do not know how to swim themselves. They cannot save another because, given the same circumstances, they could not save themselves.

In their desperate search for means to be effective, young counselors and therapists move from one fad to another. In their desperate search for help, the person at the crisis point turns to one professional helper, then another, losing hope with each empty experience. The young therapist plunges into theory and technique and ends up asking the same stupid questions his mentors (regardless of orientation) asked their patients. The patient answers the stupid questions and ends up resigned to his or her inevitable deterioration. The therapist attempts to apply theory and technique to encourage behavior change without fully understanding what the patient needs or wants.

Without understanding what the patient needs, the therapist compounds the confusion by not realizing the impossibility of defining therapeutic goals without first fully comprehending where the patient is physically, emotionally, and intellectually; and this can only be done if the therapist has the skill to respond accurately to the patient.

Most often the responses or reflections of the therapist are inaccurate because the therapist lacks listening skills. The therapist cannot listen because the therapist cannot or does not choose to observe the patient. It is not possible for the typical therapist to observe the patient because the average therapist does not physically or psychologically attend to the patient. Therapists and helpers in general rarely attend fully to their helpees for many reasons. They are not always sure they wish their patients well, which, in turn, makes it difficult at best for the therapist to greet the patient politely or with kindness. Therapists do little about the poor dispositions of their patients because the therapists are no better off. The theory and technique are represented by an interrelation in the complex mazes of the roles, not the "beings," of counselor and client. The theory and technique are calculated to prevent direct and honest communication between two parties. Indeed, there is no communication at all unless the client fits his or her prescribed role. No human being, client or counselor, can be incorporated in a role. The communication in counseling and therapy is from the role of the counselor to the role of the client and vice versa, with each groping not so much to "touch" the other as to protect himself or herself.

The most effective communication between two persons encourages decency and responsible honesty. Effective communication encourages both parties to risk their best rather than accepting the certainty that comes with being less than they can be with one another and themselves.

Responsible honesty does not translate to impulsive self-indulgence but rather to doing what is effective. Responsible honesty translates to a disciplined use of helping skills for the benefit of the client, not a "do your own thing" exercise for the helper. It is out of the disciplined use of skills that the sounds of life emerge.

Too often counseling, therapy, and graduate training deteriorate into a mutual nonexposure pact where the client is almost honest and the counselor is most often dishonest. Helpers with a limited response repertoire can create nothing better than dishonesty and the human toll left in the wake of unfulfilled promises. If the client were fully honest, he or she would acknowledge the dishonesty of the counselor and would not engage in the lifesaving game.

In their lifesaving training, our counselors learn the game of therapy, an elaborate game involving numerous mazes, many of which are dead-end. The object of the game is to find that path which allows the counselor and client to communicate in some indirect way. In the less fortunate cases, the game takes the form of a counselor's soliloquy, since the counselor already knows which route is the correct one, and the client does not. In the more fortunate cases, the client moves into proper position and receives the benefits of the particular orientation and techniques that are available to him.

If counselors and psychotherapists functioned in real life the way most of them do in the therapeutic hour, they would be patients.

REFERENCES

CARKHUFF, R. R. *Helping and human relations. Vol. I: Selection and training.* New York: Holt, Rinehart and Winston, 1969.

CARKHUFF, R. R., & BERENSON, B. G. *Beyond counseling and therapy* (1st ed.). New York: Holt, Rinehart and Winston, 1967.

3

. . . only powerful swimmers can free
and teach another person to swim . . .

A Model for Helping

When the critics issued the challenges to the efficacy of the helping professions, there was a mixed reaction. On the one hand, there was the discomforting data that suggested that groups treated by professional practitioners fared no better on the average than groups not treated by professional practitioners. On the other hand, there was the comforting suggestion of the base rate data that approximately two-thirds of the clients and patients seen by the professional practitioner got better.

Now Dr. William Anthony (1972) comes along and indicates that the suggestion of the data is comforting only in appearance. Where we have assumed that two-thirds of our helpees will get better whether we treat them or not, Anthony indicates that these figures cast inflationary images of the success of our efforts. Within six months, 40 percent to 50 percent of institutionalized patients will return to the institution. Within three to five years, 65 percent to 75 percent of the ex-patients will once again be patients.

In other words, of the two-thirds of the patients who appeared to get better, more than two-thirds got worse after treatment.

If we continue to multiply our results of a two-thirds institutional success rate times a two-thirds recidivism rate for each three-to-five year period, we get a much more accurate approximation of helping effectiveness: around 20 percent. This figure jibes with other indices of effectiveness in research studies of over fifty helping programs.

This rate does not warrant the extraordinary investment in helping and mental health programs, both in terms of helper and helpee—in time, money, and effort. No other profession in human history has survived with a 20 percent success rate.

THE GAME OF LIFE

Society's umbrella extends over all areas of human endeavor and even protects a profession that does not hold its members accountable for failure to deliver what they promise. It maintains the group identity, power, and influence while sacrificing full individual growth and emergence. Power often lies in the hands of those who have sold the greatest portion of their integrity.

They pose as the leaders of the profession, knowing full well they can no longer help another person emerge. On the contrary, they ask, even demand, that the price for a share in the power is apparent effectiveness. They insist upon training the next generation of helpers just as they have been trained, fully aware that the training they received did not make them effective and fully aware that it will not make the next generation of helpers effective. Society often tolerates the substitution of the individual experience with the collective lies we often call society's collective experience.

The collective experience contains enough truths to ensure society's survival. As helpers and helpees grow physically, emotionally, and intellectually, they learn to discriminate the myths of life from life itself.

As a profession we have not, in any detail, spelled out what we want our product to look like: the helper or the helpee. Our goals have been poorly defined and, as a consequence, the programs designed to achieve those goals have been poorly defined and thus have been ineffective and too frequently deleterious. The confusions of goals with substance, technique with outcomes, and theory with intelligence are products of a profession with few functional standards. Perhaps it would be useful to explore some of the myths perpetuated by the helping profession.

The myths tell us that what is neutral is good; what is marginal is bad; what is vulnerable and sensitized is sensitive; what is communicated in low, modulated tones is warm and respectful; and what is rational is genuine. When we look at our collective product, we find only a weak and impotent person no more capable of helping another than he is of helping himself.

The myths tell us that counseling and psychotherapy are most likely to rehabilitate the troubled person. They provide us with impotent role models—the shadowy figure of the analyst and the reflective mirror-image or alterego of the client-centered practitioner. They provide us with tests which have answers about people, so that the individual takes personality, aptitude, and interest tests in order to determine where he should go and what he should do, and satisfaction inventories in order to find out whether he has made the appropriate choice, all of which should enable him to conclude at the end of his sixty-eight years of existence that he has lived a "reasonable life." When we look at the data, we find that troubled people, both children and adults, are as likely to be rehabilitated if they are left alone as if they are treated in professional counseling and psychotherapy.

The myths tell us that clients can only benefit from experienced and professional practitioners in the human relations areas. When we look at the data, we find that counseling and psychotherapy can have constructive or deteriorative consequences for clients; and these changes can be accounted for by the level of the therapist's functioning on facilitative dimensions, independently of the therapist's orientations; therapeutic processes may be "for better or for worse."

The myths tell us that in order to become effective practitioners we must spend many years and thousands of hours learning all that is learnable in the areas of counseling and psychotherapy. The trainee proceeds to invest himself or herself in a highly intellectual, ritualistic or completely leaderless and unstructured experience, learning by rote the jargon and techniques of one theory or another.

Yet with all those hours the experience culminates in few if any skills relevant to helping the trainer, helper, or helpee. Little of the experience translates to functional helping skills because trainers do not define their training goals, compound their technique with outcome, possess a limited helping response repertoire, and hence do not themselves have the discriminations to determine the difference between constructive and deleterious interpersonal relationships. When we look at the data, we find that *there are no training programs which have demonstrated their efficacy in terms of a translation to client benefits and that on those dimensions related to constructive outcomes trainees deteriorate in functioning.* Training experiences based upon systematic skills programs enjoy good success (Carkhuff, 1969).

The myths tell us that psychology is the science most concerned with human relations and with discovering the answer to man's problems. Instead of human problems in search of an answer, when we look we find methodology in search of content and working machinery in search of questions to ask.

The myths tell us that our students can only grow intellectually with intellectually resourceful and knowledgeable teachers. When we look at the data, we find that high-level—functioning teachers elicit as much as two and one-half years intellectual or achievement growth in the course of a school year, while teachers functioning at low levels of facilitative conditions may allow only six months of intellectual growth over the course of twelve months: students may be facilitated or they may be retarded in their intellectual as well as emotional growth, and these changes can be accounted for by the level of the teacher's functioning on the facilitative dimensions, independent of his knowledgeability; education may be "for better or for worse."

The myths tell us that academic achievement equals creativity. The teacher, taking the school child by the hand, always says explicitly or implicitly, "I am only trying to help you to become a more creative and productive member of society." When we look at the data, we find that academic achievement is independent of all other real-life indexes of creative achievement and leadership (Holland & Richards, 1965).

We could go on. There are many other fraudulent myths, some less harmful than others. However, the necessity for seeing and breaking through the myths of counseling and psychotherapy is of life and death urgency.

TOWARD A MODEL FOR HUMAN NOURISHMENT

Perhaps the central occurrence in any helping relationship is the transformation of a person with a limited repertoire of responses (the helpee) into a person with an extensive repertoire of responses (the helper). In other words, the business of helping is changing helpees into helpers.

It is his limited repertoire of responses that gets the helpee into trouble in different situations. It is his extensive repertoire of responses that gets the helper out of trouble and frees him or her to emerge as a fully functioning, truly human being.

If our helpees are to make it in life, then we as helpers must make it first. We must expand the quantity and quality of our responses in all areas of living, learning, and working. We must acquire the responses that enable another person to expand the quantity and quality of their responses.

The identification, definition, and testing of the core dimensions provided the basis for establishing a comprehensive model for helping and, thus, training. It is based upon the phases of helping or learning that the helpee goes through: exploration, understanding, and action. The skills that the helper offers are guided by the helpee's movement through these phases (see Figure II, Section Two).

In other words, with a change or gain in behavior as the goal of helping, the helpee must act in some way to demonstrate the change or gain. Whether the helping process begins with the behavior and is recycled through exploration and understanding in order to consolidate the behavior change or begins with exploring and proceeds through understanding to action is not critical. What is critical is that the phases of helping are recycled in an on-going learning process and that the helper has the skills to facilitate the helpee's movement through these phases (Carkhuff, 1972).

In order to demonstrate a change or gain in behavior, then, the helpee must first explore where he or she is in relation to his or her world. This means exploration from within her frame of reference as well as exploration in terms of reality testing and diagnosis in the real world. The real world includes people as well as things: the helpee in relation to the people in it, himself, authority figures, peers, the helper; as well as things such as learning materials and working experiences.

The functional purpose of exploration is understanding. The helpee explores where she is in relation to the world in order to understand where she wants to be in relation to her world. This phase of learning includes defining and operationalizing objective goals from an external frame of reference as well as developing values and desires that dictate the goals.

Finally, understanding is instrumental for action. The helpee explores and understands so that she may act to get from where she is to where she wants to be. This phase of learning emphasizes the development and implementation of the steps of an action program that enables the helpee to achieve her goals.

Again, the helpee's behavior provides feedback from the environment, particularly the human environment. This feedback is recycled to stimulate more expanded exploration which, in turn, facilitates more accurate understanding and, thus, more effective action.

In developing a model for human nourishment, then, we must focus upon the helping skills that the helper needs to facilitate the helpee's movement through the phases of helping. Helpee exploration, understanding, and action become the process criteria that serve to guide the helper's efforts in helping. He must draw upon his helping skills only as he has successfully completed each one of these phases of learning, both within the helping sessions as well as between helping sessions.

The helping model for human nourishment was based initially upon extensive factor-analytic studies of the dimensions of helping (Berenson and Mitchell, 1974; Carkhuff, 1969). What emerged in these factor analyses were the two sets of activities that helper and helpee engage in during helping.

The helpee, as we have indicated, engages in the exploration, understanding, and action necessary to achieve a desired change or gain in behavior.

The helper, in turn, utilizes two principal sets of helping skills in facilitating the helpee's movement through exploration, understanding, and action (Carkhuff, 1972). We may call these responsive skills and initiative skills. The helping process, we find, begins with the responsive skills and then antecedent attentive skills and culminates with the initiative skills and the transitional personalizing skills.

Responsiveness is based totally upon the helpee's experience and the helper's skills to discriminate and communicate accurately his or her understanding of that experience.

Initiative is based upon the helper's experience of the helpee's experience. In other words, the helper filters the helpee's distorted perception of his experience through the helper's undistorted perception of the helpee's experience.

One is not possible without the other. At the highest level, responsiveness is initiative because it helps the helpee to do something about his or her experience. There is no accurate understanding without action.

At the highest level, initiative is responsiveness because action programs are not helpful if they are not based in understanding. There is no effective action without understanding.

Responsiveness incorporates dimensions such as helper empathy and respect. The responsive factor emphasizes responding to the helpee's experience at the level at which the helpee expresses his experience. In other words, responsiveness means responding to where the helpee is in relation to himself, his world, and the people in it.

Initiative incorporates dimensions such as helper genuineness and concreteness as well as emphasizing other interpersonal dimensions such as confrontation and immediacy of experiencing and, most importantly, program development skills (Carkhuff, 1972). The initiative factor emphasizes initiating from the helper's experience. In other words, the helper takes the helpee's experience into consideration in developing his or her own experience of the helpee and, in conjunction with the helpee, in developing goals and action steps to help the helpee get from where she is to where she wants or needs to be (Carkhuff, 1973, 1974).

Human nourishment in the form of helping, then, is a function of the helper's ability to attend and respond to the helpee's experience to personalize the helpee's understanding of his goals and to concretize the helpee's action steps to achieve the goals (see Figure II).

The helping skills needed to facilitate the helpee's movement through the phases of learning may be broken down with a more global rating scale of the levels of human nourishment.

At level 1, the helper is not even attending to the helpee, either because he has not had an opportunity to do so or because, consciously or unconsciously, he has chosen not to do so. Nothing constructive can happen under these conditions.

At level 2, the helper is attending or giving his attention to the helpee in order to involve the helpee in the helping process. Giving attention means attending physically to the helpee, observing him and listening to him. Attending is a prehelping skill that is necessary but not sufficient for helping.

At level 3, the helper uses her attending to respond to the experience of the helpee in order to stimulate and reinforce the helpee's exploration of where he or she is in relation to his or her world. The helper responds to the content, feeling, and the reason for the feeling (meaning) of the helpee's experience at the level that the helpee expresses it.

At level 4, the helper uses his responsiveness to personalize the helpee's understanding of where she is in relation to where she wants or needs to be in her world. The helper personalizes the feeling, meaning, and problems that enable the helpee to establish goals in her world.

At level 5, the helper uses the personalized understanding of goals to assume initiative in the steps to achieve the goals. The helper develops the primary and secondary steps to enable the helpee to act to get from where she is to where she wants to be.

Obviously, each set of helping skills—attending, responding, personalizing, initiating—breaks down into many more subsets of skills. For example, attending physically breaks down to squaring with another person, leaning forward or toward them, and making eye contact with them. In turn, squaring with another person involves facing the other person, assuming an erect posture and squaring your right shoulder to the other person's left shoulder.

Each step becomes a goal in a smaller program (Carkhuff, 1974).

Similarly, the entire set of helping skills culminates in larger efforts for human resource development. For example, helping skills lay the basis for teaching skills and then planning and working skills. These, in turn, demand, in order, management, community development, and ultimately, social planning skills.

Each goal becomes a step in a larger program (Carkhuff, 1974).

The helpee seeks help for problems or goals that he is unable to handle on his own or in conjunction with someone else. The helper shatters the client's experience of isolation and hopelessness with a "hovering attentiveness" which involves the helpee in the helping process. Here, at a minimum, the principle of reciprocal affect may operate: the helpee is inclined to invest himself in the helping process to the degree that the helper is disposed to investing in him. The helpee begins to involve himself in the helping process. The helpee involves himself by introducing personally relevant material. The helper both stimulates and reinforces the exploration of material by responding to the helpee at the level the helpee has explored himself. Increasingly, the helpee explores himself with emotional proximity to the material being shared. In the highly facilitative atmosphere, the helpee's anxiety about his problems is counterconditioned and reduced. The helpee gets the first clear picture of where he is in relation to his world.

In the context of his understanding relationship, hope is introduced for the helpee: there is an improved prospect for the reestablishment or establishment of positive experiences. Goals are set and courses of action to achieve the goals are considered.

The helpee understands where he is in relation to where he wants to be in his world.

Finally, the helper, through the accuracy of her understanding, becomes a potent reinforcer for the helpee. She becomes both model and agent for the helpee's change or gain. The helpee finds in the helper things that he wants or needs for himself. The helper helps the helpee to achieve these things by developing programs to implement the preferred courses of action to achieve the helpee's goals. The helpee knows how to act to get from where he is to where he wants to be in his world.

Helping, it can be seen, is hard work and requires high levels of energy. Attending to someone constructively requires that we wish them well. Accurate observing requires attending. Listening requires observing, and responding requires listening. Personalizing goals in helping requires accurate responding and constructive behavior change requires personalizing goals. Effective helping is more than hard work that requires personalizing goals; it is more than hard work that requires energy; helping requires skills. Helping requires decency: the skills to attend and respond. Helping requires responsibility: the skills to understand and act upon that understanding. Helping requires discipline: the orderliness skills to use what we know for the benefit of helpees.

At another level, it is possible to conceptualize effective helping at a very simple but programmatic level. Professional helping proceeds and is sustained by four basic programmatic phases: recruiting, teamwork, fundamentals, and inspiration. Recruiting in the sense that when the effective helper responds to where the helpee says he or she is, that response is an invitation to learn how to respond effectively to the world the helpee lives in. Learning how to prepare to respond and responding accurately constitutes the first steps required to move from loser to winner. Teamwork between helper and helpee is a blend of the helpee's experience of where he or she is physically, emotionally, and intellectually and the helper's experience of where the helpee wants or needs to be physically, emotionally, and intellectually. Teamwork blends helpee and helper experience into personalized helpee goals. Acting to achieve personalized goals requires fundamental life skills. The inspiration for continued growth as well as the basic means for continued growth are rooted in the helper's ability to blend responsiveness and initiative such that the most empathic responses are the most highly initiative.

TOWARD A DEMONSTRATION OF
HUMAN NOURISHMENT

Given a model for human nourishment, then, our goal is to equip helpees with a large repertoire of effective physical, emotional-interpersonal, and intellectual responses so that he or she can live, learn, and work effectively and hence be a helper. In order to do this, those designated as trainers must acquire a large repertoire of effective physical, emotional-interpersonal, and intellectual responses along with the specialty skills needed to design and implement effective training programs. But first, we must truly believe it is possible to be effective not only as a helper but in our own private lives. The helper, after all, is asking the helpee to live as the helper lives.

We can do better than we have done personally and professionally because we have the programs to teach the skills needed to grow. We can do better than we have done personally and professionally because we have the technology that spells out the goals, substance, and strategies necessary to grow and sustain growth. We can do better than we have done personally and professionally because we have the means to be the models of and agents for constructive change. We have only to choose life over death.

The data on the levels of human nourishment might not be so imposing were it not for contrasting data based upon the selection and/or training of potent and constructive lifesavers. The fact is that we can select and train potent therapeutic agents.

The most potent therapists we have been able to bring together average out around level 4 or above on the five-point scales. It is significant that each of these persons was either thrown out of their graduate training programs or led a very tenuous graduate school existence. These therapists have evolved toward higher levels of effective functioning, in large part, through a continuing open and honest, mutual sharing and discovering process with each other. Each therapist has somehow, through his experiences, learned to swim on his own and in turn has contributed and received a sharpening of true lifesaving skills. He or she does not, however, participate in the game of lifesaving, for he knows too deeply the life and death urgency of his counseling encounters. He knows that if counseling is not an effective way of life for him he will be unable to enable the client to choose life and find fulfillment in it.

In addition, there is extensive evidence to indicate that in relatively short periods of time both professional and nonprofessional trainees can be brought to function at minimally facilitative levels. The effective training programs incorporate a heavy experiential emphasis with a focus upon the trainee's own constructive change or gain. The trainees learn first to discriminate the levels of the dimensions involved and finally to communicate at high levels of these conditions. The difficulties the trainees encounter in learning to implement and make operational these dimensions in role-playing and clinical encounters and those that are induced by the discrepancies between their evaluations of their own levels of responding and the feedback of the ratings of others constitute the basis for many therapeutic inquiries.

A contrast with the apparent deterioration in functioning in the four or more years, or several thousand hours, of the usual graduate training is provided by the results of these training programs. In less than twenty-five hours, both prospective undergraduate dormitory counselors and experienced guidance counselors, who were functioning as groups at less than level 2, were brought to function modally at almost level 3. In the case of the college students, the improvement in interpersonal functioning was significantly greater than that in a training-control group which met for the same number of hours and did everything that the training group did with the exception of incorporating the therapeutic experience and employing the previously validated research scales. Significant gains were reflected on a variety of indices beyond those involving objective tape ratings. The trainees saw themselves as having changed more constructively than the other groups. The "standard" clients whom they saw before and after training discerned the same significant differences between groups. Furthermore, in this case the dormitory roommates felt that the members of the training group were functioning at significantly higher levels following training than did the dormitory roommates of the members of the training-control group or those of a control group which did not meet at all. Thus, there was a generalization of the training to all areas of interpersonal relationships. In addition, trainee self-change was reflected in a variety of other ways in both programs, including, for example, constructive change as reflected on the MMPI.

There are, in addition, a large number of projects based upon systematic training in interpersonal skills that demonstrate highly significant constructive outcomes. These projects reflect positive gains for helpers and helpees in a wide variety of settings including large-scale social action programs, race relations, education, adult and youth corrections, and family life.

Longer-term programs with both clinical psychology graduate students and lay hospital attendants established that both groups could be brought to function at minimally facilitative levels in less than 100 hours, and these conditions translated directly to patient benefits as assessed by outcome indices such as ward ratings and hospital discharge rates. The gains accomplished by the trainees here were retained longer than the shorter-term programs, in large part because not enough opportunity for practice has been incorporated for the short-term trainees to have transferred the conditions as a way of life. Furthermore, the levels of interpersonal functioning accomplished will be modified by whether or not the environment supported or reinforced the continued communication of these conditions.

These programs have been extended into all areas of credentialed and noncredentialed helper programs (Carkhuff, 1969, 1971). These include extensive functional professional training programs where lay personnel are trained to discharge professional responsibilities. These programs have been related to extensive outcome indices, including indices of physical, emotional, and intellectual functioning as well as indices such as institutionalization and recidivism rates. All functional professionals can discharge their professional responsibilities in helping their clients. All credentialed professionals are not functional professionals.

All this is not to say that unselected and/or untrained lay personnel can discharge professional responsibilities. They can not. It is to say that, with selection, healthy people can be taught to function in facilitative ways in relation to other people.

The functional professional programs have included successfully training staff members such as nurses and attendants in hospitals, teachers in schools, correctional officers in institutions, and policemen in communities.

In turn, people indigenous to the population being helped have been selected and trained to function effectively in relation to the populations they are servicing. This includes previously unemployed persons learning to help unemployed people to obtain jobs; human relations specialists learning to help students to learn; and parents learning to help their children to live effectively in their homes and communities.

Finally, the recipient populations themselves can be taught the skills they need to service themselves. Thus, patients can be directly taught the skills they need to "make it" effectively, first inside and then outside the institution. Students can be taught directly the skills they need to live and, most importantly, learn effectively in the schools because those who have the skills to stay in school will not tend to get in trouble, while those who do not will tend to get in trouble. Parents can be taught the skills they need to effectively rear their own emotionally disturbed children.

TOWARD OTHER SOURCES OF
HUMAN NOURISHMENT

An integral part of the systematic training effort has been the incorporation of the potential contributions of a variety of potential modes of treatment.

Many of the effects on a variety of outcome criteria, which we employ to assess our counseling and psychotherapy, may be accounted for by the primary core dimensions of interpersonal functioning. Although the weights of these dimensions may vary with therapist, client, and contextual variables, preliminary evidence suggests that in the general case we may be able to account for from 20 percent to 50 percent of the variability of a variety of outcome indices (Truax & Carkhuff, 1967).

Secondary dimensions may, for some therapists, clients, and situations, singly or in their various interactions, operate to facilitate or retard the effects of the primary conditions (see Figure 3.1). Many of the dominant and currently available treatment approaches incorporate these secondary dimensions. When these treatment approaches are appropriately employed in the context of the facilitative core dimensions, they may contribute significantly to the efficacy of the counseling and therapeutic proc-

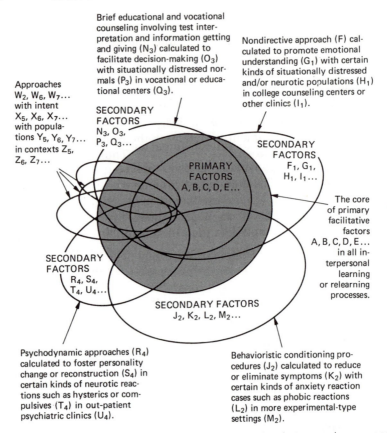

Brief educational and vocational
counseling involving test interpretation and information getting
and giving (N_3) calculated to
facilitate decision-making (O_3)
with situationally distressed nor-
mals (P_3) in vocational or educational centers (Q_3).

Nondirective approach (F) calculated to promote emotional
understanding (G_1) with certain
kinds of situationally distressed
and/or neurotic populations (H_1)
in college counseling centers or
other clinics (I_1).

Approaches
W_2, W_6, W_7...
with intent
X_5, X_6, X_7...
with popula-
tions Y_5, Y_6, Y_7...
in contexts Z_5,
Z_6, Z_7...

SECONDARY
FACTORS
N_3, O_3,
P_3, Q_3...

SECONDARY
FACTORS
F_1, G_1,
H_1, I_1...

PRIMARY
FACTORS
A, B, C, D, E...

The core
of primary
facilitative
factors
A, B, C, D, E...
in all in-
terpersonal
learning
or relearning
processes.

SECONDARY
FACTORS
R_4, S_4,
T_4, U_4...

SECONDARY FACTORS
J_2, K_2, L_2, M_2...

Psychodynamic approaches (R_4)
calculated to foster personality
change or reconstruction (S_4) in
certain kinds of neurotic reactions such as hysterics or com-
pulsives (T_4) in out-patient
psychiatric clinics (U_4).

Behavioristic conditioning procedures (J_2) calculated to reduce
or eliminate symptoms (K_2) with
certain kinds of anxiety reaction
cases such as phobic reactions
(L_2) in more experimental-type
settings (M_2).

Figure 3.1   The interpersonal core of primary facilitative factors and some possible examples of secondary factors.

esses; that is, given a particular interaction pattern of therapist,
client, and contextual variables, brief educational or vocational
counseling, nondirective therapy, behavioristic conditioning,
psychoanalytic therapy, or any one of the many other available
approaches, with their full implications concerning goals and
techniques, might be "preferred modes of treatment."

On the other hand, inappropriate application of these
approaches may retard the effectiveness of the treatment. For
example, a nondirective approach may work very effectively,
especially during initial contacts, with a highly motivated college
student and not at all with an inpatient psychotic patient. Thus
the appropriate application of the approach may increase the

accountable effectiveness about 10 percent or more, while the inappropriate employment of the approach may contribute nothing or actually detract from the process and in some way contribute to the deterioration of the helpee. In the context of high levels of helper-offered facilitative dimensions, given a meaningful interaction of relevant variables, a variety of treatment approaches may be employed. Figure 3.1 illustrates the core dimensions and several notable potential preferred modes of treatment. As can be seen, a great part of the effectiveness of any one orientation can be accounted for by the central core of facilitative conditions that each of these orientations hold in common (Carkhuff, 1969; Truax & Carkhuff, 1967). Thus, trait-and-factor-oriented vocational and educational counseling involving information giving and receiving may (with an otherwise functioning client) facilitate and contribute additional effectiveness to a treatment process that involves the need for choice or for decision-making to relieve situational stress. A behavioristic approach involving systematic counterconditioning may be the treatment of choice for the person with an isolated anxiety reaction, such as a phobia, which presents an obstacle to his or her effective functioning. In other cases, such as with severely disabled inpatients, environmental manipulation with a behavioristic orientation may contribute most effectively. The nondirective and the psycholoanalytic approaches seem to make their principal contributions in correcting the distorted perceptions and communications that lead outpatient neurotic-type populations into continual difficulty. An attempt to enumerate the dimensions of the unique contributions as well as the limitations of each of these approaches will be made in Section Three.

It is important to note that almost all training programs in the helping professions have been built around the secondary dimensions of one or another orientation to counseling and psychotherapy. Most clinical psychology, psychiatric, and social work training centers have focused upon psychodynamic thinking and treatment. Very recently, a few psychology and psychiatric programs have come to emphasize the behavioristic approach. Some of the guidance and counseling programs have mistakenly followed one or the other suit. Others have variously concentrated upon the nondirective approach or the trait-and-factor approach to counseling that involves personality, interest, and aptitude testing and interpretation, and "theories" of vocational choice. Given the relevant interaction of variables, each of these orientations may indeed have a unique contribution to make. However, none of these orientations has at this stage demonstrated that it is likely to account for a major part of the variation in the change indices of most treatment cases.

In addition, while all of the programs must make passing mention of the therapeutic relationship, few devote systematic attention to the primary core dimensions both in (1), the didactic teaching and shaping of behavior, and (2), providing the experiential therapeutic base for change in their trainees. Again, the intent is not to negate but rather to discern the potentially significant contributions of the various orientations to counseling and psychotherapy and to put them in proper perspective in building systematically around a common core of interpersonal conditions.

In summary, then, personal difficulties evolve in large part because of a social system that precludes the potent and constructive emergence of the individual and reinforces the provision of only the lowest levels of human nourishment in the individual's environment. In his distress, the individual cannot turn to anyone in his environment, simply because even his best friends are functioning at less than effective levels of living. He turns finally, in his urgency, to professional helpers who have themselves not yet recovered from the severely handicapping experience of graduate training and life in an empty society. The professional helpers invite the pospetcive client to become involved in the game of lifesaving, which, if successful, offers the client no more benefits on the average than if he were not treated at all and which, if unsuccessful, can have severely retarding effects upon the overall functioning of the client. Providing the client with an honest experience, the very experience the client requires to free himself, is prohibited because the helpers can no longer be honest and open with themselves.

In contrast, we know that with selection and/or training we can produce potent therapeutic agents who can effect significant constructive client change or gain. We know also that our training programs are only as good as the therapists who conduct them. We know that only persons who are themselves powerful swimmers can manage the burden of a drowning person—one who often has to be helped against the currents of a social system which would prefer the drowning to potent emergence. We know that only persons who are themselves powerful swimmers can free and teach another person to swim by himself, to enable him to live creatively and productively with his own experience and perhaps at a later point to help another person to shore. We draw upon all systems to make this possible.

REFERENCES

ANTHONY, W. A.   Efficacy of psychiatric rehabilitation. *Psychological Bulletin*, 1972, *28*, 447–456.

BERENSON, B. G., & MITCHELL, K. M.   *Confrontation.* Amherst, Massachusetts: Human Resource Development Press, 1974.

CARKHUFF, R. R.   *Helping and human relations. Vol. I: Selection and training.* New York: Holt, Rinehart and Winston, 1969.

CARKHUFF, R. R.   *The development of human resources.* New York: Holt, Rinehart and Winston, 1971.

CARKHUFF, R. R.   *The art of helping.* Amherst, Massachusetts: Human Resource Development Press, 1972.

CARKHUFF, R. R.   *The art of problem-solving.* Amherst, Massachusetts: Human Resource Development Press, 1973.

CARKHUFF, R. R.   *How to help yourself: The art of program development.* Amherst, Massachusetts: Human Resource Development Press, 1974.

HOLLAND, J. L., & RICHARDS, J. M.   Academic and non-academic accomplishment: Correlated or uncorrelated? *Journal of Educational Psychology*, 1965, *56*, 165–174.

TRUAX, C. B., & CARKHUFF, R. R.   *Toward effective counseling and psychotherapy.* Chicago: Aldine, 1967.

section three

POTENTIAL PREFERRED MODES OF TREATMENT

The core dimensions comprising the responsive and initiative factors account for from 20 to 50 percent of the variance of a variety of outcome indices. Secondary dimensions may, for some counselors, clients, and situations, singly or in their various interactions, operate to facilitate or even retard the effects of the primary core dimensions. The purpose of the next section is to further explore the potential preferred modes of treatment in order to determine the unique contribution which each might make over and above those effects accounted for by the core conditions. Our conclusion is that these modes of treatment emphasize one phase of learning to the exclusion of others rather than putting the helping process together.

EXPLORING		UNDERSTANDING		ACTING
Client-Centered		Psychoanalytic		Behavior
Existential		Trait-and-Factor		Modification

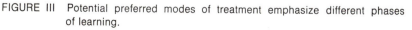

FIGURE III   Potential preferred modes of treatment emphasize different phases of learning.

. . . a highly verbal transaction, emphasizing words about feelings, rather than the more direct expression of feelings themselves between a self-denying, middle-class parental surrogate and his initiate.

Apparency in Search of a Person

The Unique Contributions of the Client-Centered Approach

All therapists are client-centered in the sense that they serve for the benefit of their clients. To the degree that any therapist is not client-centered, he is not doing therapy. However, the term "client-centered" must be differentiated into members of the client-centered school and those who are shaped by what is effective for their clients. In the hope that these groups might become one, we will attempt to discern and describe the potentially unique contributions of the client-centered system as it has evolved in its identification with Carl Rogers and his work (1951, 1954, 1957). By "unique contributions," we mean those over and above the ones the client-centered approach shares with other interview-oriented therapeutic approaches. Thus, we will attempt to discern where and under what conditions this approach accounts for practices more effective than those accounted for by the central core of facilitative conditions common to all therapies.

This central core of conditions, involving the communication of counselor dimensions such as empathic understanding, positive regard, genuineness, and concreteness or specificity of expression, is shared by almost all well-known counseling approaches, and evidence for the relationship of high levels of these dimensions to successful client process movement and outcome has been summarized elsewhere (Carkhuff, 1969; Truax & Carkhuff, 1963, 1964, 1967).

Disclaimers notwithstanding, the greatest part of the unique identification of the client-centered approach must be attributed to its nondirective disposition. While outsiders may not be attuned to the subtle nuances in client-centered practice as, for example, the increasing emphasis upon the congruence of the counselor or therapist (Gendlin, 1962; Rogers et al, 1967), they continue to identify the client-centered process with many of the nondirective techniques such as reflection (Truax & Carkhuff, 1967).

In order to explore the unique contributions of the "client-centered" approach, we might perhaps first view that approach in encapsulated form.

THE CLIENT-CENTERED OR
NONDIRECTIVE STANCE

The client-centered approach is built around two central theorems. First, inherent in the individual are the capacity to understand the factors in his life that cause him unhappiness and pain and the capacity to reorganize his self-structure in such a way as to overcome those factors. Second, the individual's inherent powers will operate if a congruent therapist can establish with him or her a relationship involving a depth of warm acceptance and understanding. The process of therapy which follows is one by which the structure of the client's self is relaxed in the safety and security of the relationship with the therapist, previously denied experiences are perceived and, by means of a verbal, symbolic analysis, integrated into an altered self (Rogers, 1951, pp. 66–74).

One of the effects that these theorems accomplish is an absolution of the therapist from the responsibility for effects other than the creation of a therapeutic atmosphere or relationship. In reaction to the distortions inherent at the other extreme, where the therapist is the sole focus of evaluation, the relationship is one where the therapist endeavors to keep himself out, as a separate person, and where his whole endeavor is to understand the other so completely that he becomes almost an alter ego of the client (Rogers, 1951, pp. 42–43). Rather than the interaction of two persons, each committed to experiencing and understanding himself in relation to the other and the other in relation to him, "the whole relationship is composed of the self of the client, the counselor being depersonalized for purposes of therapy into being 'the client's other self.'" It is precisely "this warm willingness on the part of the counselor to lay aside his own self temporarily, in order to enter into the experiences of the client, which makes the relationship a completely unique one, unlike anything in the client's previous experience" (Rogers. 1951, p. 208). Recent innovations in client-centered thinking have modified this typical middle-class self-sacrifice to allow for a kind of defensive congruence of the therapist (Rogers, 1957; Rogers et al., 1967), a genuineness which is employed at particular points in therapy, rather than for a full, open, and spontaneous emergence of the therapist's person.

The second aspect of the relationship is the safety and

security the client experiences as a consequence of the therapist's consistent and deep acceptance. "It is this absolute assurance that there will be no evaluation, no interpretation, no
probing, no personal reaction by the counselor, that gradually
permits the client to experience the relationship as one in which
all defenses can be dispensed with—a relationship in which the
client feels, 'I can be the real me, no pretenses' " (Rogers, 1951,
p. 208). We might add, "I can be the real me, no pretenses, while
you, the therapist, are unreal, in all your pretenses." It is as if
one person cannot be both real and constructive, as if another
person cannot dispense with his defenses in interaction with a
"real" person.

Rogers (1957), in a theoretical statement, organized what
he termed "the necessary and sufficient conditions of therapeutic
personality change." On the basis of his own clinical and research
experiences as well as those of his colleagues, Rogers extra-
polated six conditions which were:

> . . . necessary to initiate constructive personality change,
> and which, taken together appear to be sufficient to inau-
> gurate the process:
> 1. Two persons are in psychological contact.
> 2. The first. . . , the client, is in a state of incongruence or
>   not integrated in the relationship.
> 3. The second. . . , the therapist, is congruent or integrated
>   in the relationship.
> 4. The therapist experiences unconditional positive re-
>   gard for the client.
> 5. The therapist experiences an empathic understanding
>   of the client's internal frame of reference and endeavors
>   to communicate this experience to the client.
> 6. The communication to the client of the therapist's
>   empathic understanding is to a minimal degree achieved
>   (Rogers, 1957, pp. 95–96).

It should be noted that condition 6 was modified by Rogers
(1959) to emphasize the client's perception of the communication,
whether intended by the therapist or not. Nevertheless, Rogers
(1957) emphasized that "No other conditions are necessary. If
these six conditions exist and continue over a period of time, this
is sufficient. The process of constructive personality change will

follow" (p. 96). While evidence in support of these hypotheses has been presented (Rogers, 1962; Rogers et al., 1967; Truax & Carkhuff, 1963), the theoretical statement has not yet opened itself up to further and necessary refinements. For example, no provisions have been made for the differential weightings of the primary dimensions due to particular interactions of relevant therapist, client, and contextual variables. Second, no provisions have been made for the possibility that additional or secondary dimensions may, for some therapists, clients, and situations, singularly or in their various interactions, operate to facilitate or even retard the effects of the hypothesized necessary conditions or simply account for an additional degree of effectiveness themselves (Carkhuff, 1969). Furthermore, there are the studies, such as that by Spotts (Rogers et al., 1962), which indicate that the variability of unconditionality is accounted for by the communication of positive regard alone and suggest that the constructs involved must be open to further modification and delineation.

Concerning technique, says Rogers, "the sincere aim of getting 'within' the attitudes of the client, of entering the client's internal frame of reference, is the most complete implementation which has thus far been formulated, for the central hypothesis of respect for and reliance upon the capacity of the person" (Rogers, 1951, p. 36). In the therapist's reflections, clarifications, summarizations, and reformulations of the client's expressions, the client is able to see his own attitudes, confusions, ambivalences, and perceptions accurately (hopefully) expressed by another person ("who is only partly another person"), but with a new quality stripped of the complications of emotion. The client can see himself or herself objectively and the way is paved for the integration of more clearly perceived aspects of the self. "In this attempt to struggle along with the client, to glimpse with him the half understood causes of behavior, to wrestle with feelings which emerge into awareness and slip away again, it is entirely possible that the simple concept of 'an accurate reflection of feeling' no longer fits the therapist's behavior. Rather than serving as a mirror, the therapist becomes a companion to the client as the latter searches through a tangled forest in the dead of night" (Rogers, 1951, pp. 112–113).

In recognizing that the techniques of the different approaches to counseling and therapy are relatively unimportant except insofar as they serve as channels for fulfilling one of the conditions, Rogers (1957) acknowledges that the therapist's technique of the reflection of the client's feelings (Rogers, 1954, pp. 26–36) is not per se an essential condition of therapy: "To the extent, however, that it provides a channel by which the therapist communicates a sensitive empathy and an unconditional positive regard then it may serve as a technical channel by which the essential conditions of therapy are fulfilled" (Rogers, 1957, p. 102).

The outcome of counseling and therapy, in turn, is closely related to the process of therapy in the sense that the therapist must be completely willing that any outcome, any direction, may be chosen by the client. Only then will the potentiality of the individual for constructive action be realized. "It is as if he is willing for death to be the choice that a healthy normality is chosen" (Rogers, 1951, p. 49). The client's self following therapy "functions smoothly in experience, rather than being an object of introspection" (Rogers, 1951, p. 129). Furthermore, ". . . there is a change in the valuing process during therapy, and one characteristic of this change is that the individual moves away from a state where his thinking, feeling and behavior are governed by the judgements and expectations of others, and toward a state in which he relies upon his own experience for his values and standards" (Rogers, 1951, p. 157).

HISTORICAL CREDITS

The client-centered position must be considered a traditional one in that its adherents follow and implement well-defined and prescribed modes of functioning in counseling and therapy, often independent of the ensuing process and outcome. We should note that a difficulty in assessing the contributions of traditional stances, in general, is the sense in which the position has made contributions which were once substantive and innovative but are no longer functionally related to the position of the original contributor (that is, many subsequent positions have incorporated those principles of the previous positions which have proved effective). These "historical contributions" deserve brief attention.

Perhaps the major historical contribution of the client-centered approach has been the impetus it has given to the growth of the idea of the central core of facilitative conditions. Rogers, in 1957, following on the heels of Shoben in 1949 and others, attempted to discern and describe "the necessary and sufficient conditions of therapeutic personality change." Unfortunately both positions, as well as many others that have followed them, have been tied (in the perceptions of their audiences) to the techniques of the communication of attitudes and sensitivities.

In addition to the focus it brought to the client's feelings, the client-centered approach in general provided fuller attention to the whole person of the client, including in particular a fundamental belief in his constructive capacity. This position holds that something critical intervenes between the stimulus and the response and that this intervening variable really can only be understood in the present, subjective state of the individual involved. In so focusing upon the client's present feelings, the position has to a great degree rendered the past irrelevant.

In his emphasis upon freeing the individual's capacity for growth, the client-centered therapist will often institute the conditions of empathy and unconditionality, quite independent of the client and his needs in any given instance for direction or dependency. These historical contributions have further limitations in the very respect that the conditions are often related to techniques. There is little proviso for the untrained teacher or ward attendant whose students or patients improve on a variety of relevant indexes of constructive change. In addition, whereas client-centered therapy brought more complete attention to the whole person of the client, it has neglected the whole person of the therapist and the two-way flow of communication. Lastly, the position has emphasized the present and reality as the individual sees it to the exclusion of a very often relevant past and external world impinging upon the present functioning of the client.

In summary, seen for its stimulus value, the client-centered contribution is a most profound one: "If a theory could be seen for what it is—a fallible, changing attempt to construct a network of gossamer threads which will contain the solid facts—then a theory would serve, as it should, as a stimulus to further creative thinking" (Rogers, 1959, p. 191).

Historically, client-centered helping started out as a stance that represented great strength based in its capacity to tolerate and accept the widest range of human behavior. It became weak when its promulgators did not look beyond how little people asked for and how little they settled for.

THE UNIQUE CONTRIBUTIONS

Many of the unique contributions of the client-centered process must be tied to specific techniques such as the reflection of the client's feelings and attitudes by the therapist. Most of the remaining contributions can be accounted for by the facilitating effects of the central core of conditions of all effective human relations. To the following list of unique contributions we must add two important qualifications: (1) the client-centered mode is one of many possible modes or vehicles for making these contributions and, in some cases, it may be the most effective mode; (2) in most cases, we must add the expression "within limits" to qualify the effects of the approach in general. Given a desirable interaction of the relevant therapist, client, and contextual variables, the appropriate application of the "client-centered" approach would appear to make the following unique contributions:

Process Contributions to the Client

1. The client-centered approach provides the client with an opportunity to find his own mode of expression.

The essential direction in the communication process comes from the client and he has the opportunity to find his own words for his own feelings.

2. The client-centered approach provides the client with immediate and concrete feedback of what he has just communicated.

The therapist's reflection offers the client an opportunity to hear a playback of what he has just communicated and allows him to judge the impact or adjust the communication.

3. The client-centered approach provides the client with an opportunity to experience previously denied experiences.

In the client-centered atmosphere, the client may relax his defenses in the secure knowledge that no judgments or punitive action will follow.

4. The client-centered approach draws the client's attention to many things to which he has not attended or which he has not communicated.

In expressing himself and in rehearing his own messages, the client has the opportunity to attend to previously unattended areas.

5. The client-centered approach provides the client with the opportunity for the discovery and correction of faulty generalizations.

In being provided the opportunity for his own systematic construction of his communications, the client can discover the inadequacies of his reasoning and generalizations.

Process Contributions to the Therapist

1. The client-centered approach provides one vehicle for the communication of the therapist's sensitivities and attitudes.

The atmosphere created by the client-centered approach offers the client the promise of full acceptance and the apparency of freedom.

2. The client-centered approach allows the therapist an opportunity to gauge the client's level of affective expression or assertive behavior.

Simply because he is oriented to listening and hearing the client's expressions, the client-centered therapist, at least initially, has the most complete opportunity for understanding the level at which the client is functioning.

3. The client-centered approach provides the therapist a means of knowing whether his perceptions and communications are congruent with those of the client.

The therapist is able to gauge whether his responses are related (and how highly related) to those of the client from the feedback which he gets from the client.

4. The client-centered approach provides an opportunity for therapist's communications to be freed from professional jargon and interpretation, which often are not understood by the client.

Since the therapist's messages are, in large part, restatements of feelings expressed by the client, he is constrained from employing many of the constructs he might otherwise express.

5. The client-centered approach defines the therapist's responsibilities within safe ranges.

The therapist who wishes to avoid responsibility for the condition or life of the client has fairly well-defined rules and regulations to guide him.

6. The client-centered approach keeps the unique and personal aspects of the therapist out of therapy.

This constitutes a contribution since it minimizes the potentially destructive impact of some therapists while giving therapy the facade of being personal.

THE LIMITATIONS OF THE CLIENT-CENTERED APPROACH

The limitations of the client-centered approach can be noted in a manner similar to the contributions. It may be seen readily that most of the limitations center around the therapist's inability to employ himself or herself fully in the two-way communication of therapy.

Process Limitations for the Client

1. The client-centered approach does not provide the client with real-life conditions for functioning.

The apparent conditions are simply not lifelike and make it difficult for the client to generalize from a relationship with an alter ego to other areas of human functioning.

2. The client-centered approach provides no opportunity for the client to have an impact upon the therapist.

The therapist does not relate to communications that involve him as a person and thus communicates the following message to the client: "No matter what you do I will remain the same."

Process Limitations for the Therapist

1. The client-centered approach is unable to provide a vehicle for the therapist to give fully of himself or herself.

In the highly personalized depersonalization process, the therapist is discouraged from a fully personal sharing of and relating to the client's very personal problems.

2. The client-centered approach does not provide the therapist with an opportunity for the translation of his or her commitment to action.

Neither within therapy nor out of therapy can the therapist act upon the client or his environment in the manner which he feels will, in the end, be most effective for the client.

3. The client-centered approach prescribes an apparency in the therapist's communication which elicits an apparency in the client's communications.

The client's responses will be as apparent as those of their elicitors and, thus, nonfunctional in lifelike situations.

4. The client-centered approach channels communication in a regression of expression toward a more socially acceptable mean or mode, one that makes no real and lasting difference.

When the client's responses are superficial, the therapist responds at deeper levels; and when the client's responses are deep and inflammatory, they are modulated by the therapist's words about feelings, whether or not the more socially acceptable response is helpful to the client.

5. The client-centered approach does not leave the therapist free to explore feelings in a wide range of affect and intensity.

This is perhaps not so much the fault of client-centered theory as it is of the mode of functioning of most client-centered therapists; that is, the emphasis is upon words reflecting depression and distress to the exclusion of all other feelings (depressing responses may be handled at level 3 of five-point scales assessing therapeutic functioning (Carkhuff, 1969) and joyous, elated, excited, and hostile feelings at level 1).

6. The client-centered approach does not provide the therapist with an opportunity for the employment of other and more directive techniques.

The client-centered therapist is denied the opportunity of employing more directive techniques, such as systematic counterconditioning, when these techniques appear appropriate to the conditions of the case.

THE CONDITIONS OF SUCCESS
AND FAILURE

The question "where and under what conditions can the client-centered approach most effectively make these contributions?" leads us into several areas of inquiry. The condition that looms largest before us is that involving the initial or early stages of counseling or therapy. When the therapist does not know who and where the client is or where he or she (the therapist) is in relation to the client, as is the case in initial encounters, it appears most facilitative to reflect the feelings of the client. When the therapist has not known the client long enough to really care about him or her as an individual and when no basis of mutual concern has in fact been established, it might be most facilitative to employ techniques for communicating warm acceptance. When the therapist has been unable to establish communication or has lost communication with the client, then the client-centered approach appears efficacious, although even here a more direct and honest approach often appears most effective. However, as therapy continues and the client has experienced freedom and acceptance and has explored his perceptual field, he seeks a more and more equalitarian relationship in which he has impact upon the therapist.

In general, there is some research evidence and a great deal of experiential evidence to suggest that the client-centered approach is most effective with a population characterized as follows: depressed neurotic outpatient or level 2 individuals (Carkhuff & Berenson, 1967) who bring extremely distorted perceptions to bear in all of their human interactions, distorted perceptions which ultimately lead to the deterioration of all of these relationships; persons who nevertheless possess a sufficient degree of ego strength and other resources to function in many of the roles society has prescribed for them; persons who supply their own motivation and are sophisticated, psychologically attuned and verbally facile; in sum, patients who have the potential for, and are indeed striving for, middle-class status. The client-centered approach appears to work best when the client's inner resources are really enough and when his greatest need is to understand and trust his own experience, and when the therapist's need is to understand the client's experience but he does not trust his own (the therapist's) experience. The client-centered approach works most effectively when the client's response is enough and the therapist's response is appropriate.

The client-centered approach would appear to be least effective in its more traditional form with low-level functioning or level 1 persons, such as hospitalized psychotics. An attempt has been made to employ the client-centered method with inpatient schizophrenics (Rogers, Gendlin, Kiessler, & Truax, 1967). The success of this application has been in large part contingent upon the therapist's ability to define himself and the boundaries of his therapy in his interaction with the patient. These success contingencies with psychotics have led to the growing emphasis within client-centered thinking upon therapist congruence.

Furthermore, for a variety of reasons, the client-centered method does not appear to be an effective mode of functioning with high-level functioning or level 3 persons. The constant emphasis upon the reflective mode of communication, for example, is unnecessary with higher-level functioning persons. Once the high-level functioning client is aware that his counselor is functioning at high levels and is genuinely sensitive and respectful, the client can continue on his own independently, whether or not the counselor continues to function at high levels (Holder, Carkhuff, & Berenson, 1967). The level 3 person is already functioning at effective levels of interpersonal dimensions: the distorted perceptions and communications, to the clarification of which the client-centered method is dedicated, are not dominant; his existence is not a miserable one aside from periodic episodes of situational stress.

It is interesting to note that when client-centered cases are viewed by theorists and therapists from differing orientations, the following generalities emerge:

1. The reflective method of communicating the therapist's empathic understanding is the ingredient most frequently pointed to as dominating the client-centered therapeutic process.

As seen by outsiders, reflection may dominate alone or in combination with other ingredients (Carkhuff & Truax, 1967). However, the expectation that the success or failure of the case is tied to the success or failure of reflection is not met.

2. The success or failure attributed to the client-centered

cases appears independent of the effectiveness or ineffectiveness of the method of reflection.

Reflection succeeds as often as it fails in client-centered cases
designated as successes by outsiders; reflection fails only slightly
more than it succeeds in cases that are seen as failures. The
suggestion, then, is that the success or failure of client-centered
cases is not (or only minimally) related to the success or failure
of its principal method.

3. The ingredient most highly related to success in client-
centered cases involves the therapist's active, personal
reaching out and involvement with the client.

It is significant that, while these acts of caring appear only infrequently and do indeed go beyond the prescribed role, this ingredient was seen as the principal source of effectiveness in several
successful cases. Only in one case, in which no improvement was
discerned, did the therapist successfully communicate a giving
of himself.

4. In relatively few client-centered cases, the effectiveness of dimensions such as structuring the client's
comments has been related to successful outcome, and
the ineffectiveness of these dimensions has been related to unsuccessful outcomes.

5. None of the "necessary and sufficient conditions" of
the client-centered approach are ever operationalized
beyond reflection. None of the conditions are ever
developed beyond concepts.

Because none of these concepts is defined in terms of specific
behaviors they never develop into goals or means to achieve goals
for the helpee as well as helper. The resulting impotence for both
must result in mutual frustration.

6. Building the relationship on the "self of the client" is
not only impossible but its statement communicates
that the helper is without positive direction in his or
her life.

This saintly attitude does not reflect the process or the outcomes
of the client-centered approach. The helping process can begin
with the "self of the client" if the helper is capable of making an
accurate reflection of the client's full experience. Client-centered

helpers always seem to just miss the mark by responding only to superficial feelings.

7. The notion of warmth is also never really operationalized in terms of the helper's posture or words. Modulated tones of simple reflections hardly reflect warmth, but are "give-aways" for psychopathic attempts at seduction.

8. Keeping the unique and personal aspects of the helper out of helping may be *the* means to protect the helpee from the helper who knows how destructive he or she really is. Keeping the personal character of the helper out of the helping process makes it only momentarily more difficult to see how withholding and destructive the helper is and wants to be.

9. The client-centered approach promises to respond fully to where the helpee is and fails. Because of this failure, if the helpee is to determine where he or she needs to be and gets there, the helpee truly must do it alone: a remarkable as well as a strange definition of helping. The client-centered helper seems to be saying "I help best when I do nothing to help."

10. If the helpee acts, he or she is most likely to do so without a plan and, even worse, without a goal!

11. Responding to only the superficial aspects of the helpee's experience is the beginning *and* the end of client-centered helping.

12. Among other reasons, the client-centered approach fails because it communicates that the helper really does not give a damn because he or she is not willing to engage in the real work of helping.

13. The client-centered approach fails because it cannot help people to be more sensitive with a helper who is only sensitized to a very minute aspect of human experience.

14. In this system, the helper deals only with the obvious and limits the helpee's learning to only the obvious.

15. The client-centered approach has not provided its

trainees and helpees with skills training because the approach simply does not provide opportunities for *actively* helping anyone.

16. The client-centered helper provides the apparency of the opportunity for the helpee to find his or her own mode of expression because the conditions of helping have no direction, no personal involvement, no standards, no program, no action, and no learning.

17. The client-centered helper trains the client to confuse superficial and often empty responding with action, setting up a benign process within which life offers less and less.

18. Shallow reflections of how helpees present themselves hardly qualify a helper as a professional or as a helper. The fact is, the simple skill of client-centered reflection can be taught *and* learned *in less than three minutes* if it is taught systematically.

19. The client-centered approach fails because, in order to practice it, one must experience himself or herself as a failure and ask, not so nondirectively, that others experience themselves as failures.

20. If the client-centered helper believes the six "necessary and sufficient" conditions are truly necessary and sufficient to initiate constructive personality change, then such a helper has twisted and distorted human experience into a cruel and contemptuous pathology.

Thus, it appears that successful client-centered outcomes can be attributed to techniques quite antithetical to the client-centered stance, although it should be noted that just as many failure cases as success cases may be attributed to structuring (Carkhuff & Truax, 1967). The effective employment of structuring, however, would seem to suggest that the therapist must break free of his nondirective orientation in order to function effectively.

It appears, then, that the success or failure of client-centered therapy is independent of its principal mode of communication but is in large part related to the communication of the therapist's personal involvement and giving of himself—a communication certainly unintended and, at the minimum, limited by the position. If the acts of personal involvement account largely for the effectiveness of client-centered therapy, then we might consider how much more successful these therapists might be if they had a more open and spontaneous vehicle for communication—themselves.

Alternate theories of the effectiveness of client-centered process and outcome have, of course, been postulated. Frequently, however, the sources of effectiveness would seem to function in spite of the avowed intention of the client-centered therapist. Among the most creative of these are those posited by Whitaker (Carkhuff & Truax, 1967), who suggests two principal dynamic sources of change: (1) the therapist by his impersonal, dispassionate, self-denying example teaches the client to become uninvolved and detached from life's exigencies and mischances; (2) the client finally must "break free" of an unreal relationship with his "alter ego," and, in breaking free, affirm his own identity and existence.

SUMMARY AND CONCLUSIONS

Beyond the initial phases of therapeutic encounters, the technique of client-centered therapy appears to make no significant contribution to constructive change over and above that change accounted for by the central core of facilitative conditions. To be sure, its philosophy is not only in keeping with but also gave great impetus to the development of thought concerning a central core of conditions. Perhaps most importantly, its founder, Carl Rogers, found the client-centered mode of functioning most effective for himself. The central message, then, is that others must find a mode appropriate for themselves. Today we have the opportunity to learn to use our own personalities most effectively, in part because Rogers dared to break free of the psychoanalytic tradition in finding the method by which he, personally, could be most effective.

The major limitation, then, would appear to be in those phases beyond the introductory, exploratory experience. At some point along the line in therapy the therapist must move from technique to person. Since by its nature all therapy is client-centered, it is more than understandable that the therapist starts out client-centered. However, we would hypothesize that it is also understandable, and indeed necessary, that therapy become relationship-centered and finally, in truly therapeutic cases, become a kind of existential sharing in an equalitarian relationship.

The repeated, limited, and apparently sole statement of the client-centered helper is "Look, look, see how special I am; see how good I am. I am truly a good person. I am the only good person."

The real inner statement is: "If I limit my techniques, I stand a good chance of never being exposed for my hatefulness in withholding everything and producing nothing."

To the extent that all therapeutic processes are inherently client-centered in that they occur for the benefit of the client, none are truly client-centered in the sense that the conditions they institute are often independent of the client's needs and attitudes. However active or passive the client-centered therapist, there are many not-so-subtle indications that the process is a rather precise reflection of a polite middle class and will function most effectively with persons who share the attitudes, the values, and the potentials of this polite middle class.

The system relies upon the "capacity of the person" while the helper, if he or she persists, must become ulcerated, numb, or both. The withholding of everything beyond low-level reflections is analogous to slowly starving the helpee to death. Such "helpers" have never experienced being fully appreciated for being special, and make their clients, who need more than reflections, experience the same denial.

In summary, *the client-centered approach is a highly verbal transaction, emphasizing words about feelings rather than the more direct expression of the feelings themselves (that is, "I am angry," rather than angry expressions) between a self-denying, middle-class, parental surrogate and his initiate.* The approach suffers not so much because of the clarification of communication which it is able to achieve during initial phases as because of what it excludes: the full personalities of all parties to a relationship; persons who do not share in the same tradition and values; persons, both client and therapist, who cannot be defined by any set of techniques and cannot relate role to role; persons to each of whom benefits can only accrue in a full communication process between full humans.

The notion that helper congruence is communicated by

reflecting the expressed feelings of the helpee is limited at best and absurd at worst. Such a limited vehicle for helper expression can only culminate in denial of helpee experience and debilitating modes of passivity for the helpee. The degree of helpee self-denial is a blatant clue to the helper's limited skills, his ability to employ his or her experience, and finally, the helper's disregard for the helpee's welfare.

The production of reflection as a concept does not constitute a delivery to the helpee but a need to look helpful while never being responsible.

In summary, the client-centered approach is calculated to make an apparent difference while requiring the therapist to make only an apparent effort.

REFERENCES

CARKHUFF, R. R. *Helping and human relations (Vols. I and II.)* New York: Holt, Rinehart and Winston, 1969.

CARKHUFF, R. R., & BERENSON, B. G. *Beyond counseling and therapy* (1st ed.). New York: Holt, Rinehart and Winston, 1967.

CARKHUFF, R. R., & TRUAX, C. B. The client-centered process as viewed by other therapists. In C. R. Rogers, E. T. Gendlin, D. Kiessler, & C. B. Truax (Eds.), *The therapeutic relationship and its impact.* Madison: University of Wisconsin Press, 1967.

GENDLIN, E. T. Client-centered developments and work with schizophrenics. *Journal of Counseling Psychology,* 1962, *9,* 205–211.

HOLDER, T., CARKHUFF, R. R., & BERENSON, B. G. The differential effects of the manipulation of therapeutic conditions upon high- and low-functioning clients. *Journal of Counseling Psychology,* 1966, *14,* 63–66.

ROGERS, C. R. *Client-centered therapy.* Boston: Houghton Mifflin, 1951.

ROGERS, C. R. The necessary and sufficient conditions of therapeutic personality change. *Journal of Consulting Psychology,* 1957, *22,* 95–103.

ROGERS, C. R. A theory of therapy, personality and interpersonal relationships, as developed in the client-centered framework. In S. Koch (Ed.), *Psychology: A study of a science* (Vol. III). New York: McGraw-Hill, 1959.

ROGERS, C. R., & DYAMOND, R. F. *Psychotherapy and personality change. Chicago:* University of Chicago Press, 1954.

ROGERS, C. R., GENDLIN, E. T., KIESSLER, D., & TRUAX, C. B. The *therapeutic relationship and its impact: A study of psychother-apy with schizophrenics.* Madison: University of Wisconsin Press, 1967.

SHOBEN, E. J.   Psychotherapy as a problem in learning theory. *Psychological Bulletin,* 1949, *46,* 366–392.

TRUAX, C. B., & CARKHUFF, R. R.   For better or for worse: The process of psychotherapeutic personality change. In *Recent advances in the study of behavior change.* Montreal: McGill University Press, 1963.

TRUAX, C. B., & CARKHUFF, R. R.   Significant developments in psychotherapy research. In L. E. Abt & B. F. Riess (Eds.), *Progress in clinical psychology.* New York: Grune & Stratton, 1964.

TRUAX, C. B., & CARKHUFF, R. R.   *Toward effective counseling and psychotherapy.* Chicago: Aldine, 1967.

5

. . . Those who fear death must face
death before they can live life;
those who do not fear death live life.

Man for Each Other

The Unique Contributions of the Existential Approach

The essential task of all therapy is to enable man to act and to accept the awesome freedom and responsibility for action. Although in its origins existentialism described the condition of modern man rather than his therapy, it alone addresses itself directly to the feelings of loneliness and alienation that incapacitate man and disallow his action. Even in its application in therapy, the existential approach concentrates upon the philosophical assumptions underlying therapy rather than upon "the technique of therapy." In this sense, the existential approach to therapy deserves a unique treatise: it does not involve "unique contributions to treatment" as much as it involves a philosophical base for man in his human relationships, some of the dimensions of which we have attempted to specify. Of all the major therapeutic approaches, the existential approach alone focuses upon the crucial questions concerning the nature of man; its answers are sometimes poetic, often confusing, but always stimulating.

THE EXISTENTIAL APPROACH IN ITS RELATION TO THERAPY

The currently popularized existential approach to therapy (May 1961; May, Angel, & Ellenberger, 1958; Ruitenbeck, 1962) has its origin in European existential philosophy (Jaspers, 1956 Kierkegaard, 1954; Sartre, 1947), in the phenomenological method (Husserl, 1929; Straus, 1952, 1956), and in integrative efforts to application of both approaches to therapy (Binswanger, 1956; Boss, 1958, 1963; Heidegger, 1962; Minkowski, 1926; Sartre, 1953). Perhaps of greatest significance historically, in attending to the depersonalization and isolation of modern man in his human relationships, existentialism fills a very real treatment void left behind by Freudian, behavioristic, and trait-and-factor approaches to counseling and psychotherapy. It asks basic questions not asked elsewhere concerning the nature of man and develops in response a core of basic human values that are not developed in other therapeutic orientations. In addition, it posits for the first time a unique combination of both the subjective and objective world in man's phenomenological existence.

An overview of five common although not unqualified

dimensions of the existential approach in relation to therapy can be stated and commented upon as follows:

1. Man, whose sense of self is developed through his relatedness to others, does not know himself except in relation to others.

Man is so concerned with "knowing" others, and knowing himself *only* in relation to them, that he does not know himself. He cannot be creative since he does not have his own experience with which to create.

Although we think that man, as the existentialists suggest, is dependent upon others for self-definition, we must qualify this attitude with the suggestion that a healthy environment produces a self-sustaining person (level 3 or above) who, having incorporated in his identity significant persons from his past, has an identity independent of immediate relationships.

2. Man's principal source of anxiety is his fear of losing others and being alone.

With the breakdown of communication with his fellow man, the threat of being alone elicits high levels of anxiety that preclude man's engagement in creative processes. In addition, man experiences guilt in relation to others. He is in debt to everyone around him for his existence. He flays himself for never living up to the possibilities others offer him but he can never expiate this guilt and he is, therefore, never relieved.

3. Man's real guilt is that he cannot act.

Because of his "other-directed" development, man cannot become an autonomous, acting being. Man is entitled by action to creative processes that he is now unable to achieve. But he has lost his ability to act. In not fulfilling himself as a constantly changing, creative creature, man has let himself, not others, down.

4. Man must face the fact that he is alone, for only he has the responsibilities for acting upon his choices.

This is, perhaps, the key existential proposition with implications for therapy. Since man has an awareness, he can question his existence. By bringing the unconscious into awareness, he is more conscious of his choices and their implications for himself and others. Thus he has a mastery that he has been denied. Because man can choose and because he alone is ultimately responsible for his choice, he is ultimately alone.

5. The task of therapy is to enable man to act and to accept
    the freedom and responsibility for acting.

Although man's life in its very nature has intrinsic meaning, man's
tragic burden is his compulsive search for meaning in a meaning-
less world. In the context of an intimate therapist-to-client relationship, man's experience of freedom will emerge with his
recognition of the meaninglessness of his existence. Only in a full
confrontation with the ultimate in "aloneness" or death can man
choose life.

The therapeutic process begins with the formation of a significant one-to-one relationship in which both therapist and client
"act" as if they were the only persons existing at this point in
time. Through his fulfilled need for intimacy, the patient experiences his own existence as "real"; his false sense of guilt is
relieved and he achieves a continuity within himself, finally
assuming responsibility for his behavior with active decision-
making. A further goal, that of preventing a split between the
helpee's artificial world and his or her real life, is not consistent
with the other aims and appears superfluous since man must, of
necessity, stand independent (in a statistical sense) of the artificial
world, sometimes functioning without regard to it. Sometimes
a split between the real and the artificial is necessary.

Consistent with our descriptions of the core dimensions,
the therapist, in the context of an assumedly genuine relationship, communicates his or her understanding and full regard for
the human dignity of the patient. Most often, the communication
process involves analyzing the existential meaning of human
experience rather than the direct expression of experience. Infrequently, the therapist shares his experience of the patient with
the patient. Nowhere to be found, however, is the ultimate in
regard for a fellow human, acting upon his experience of another.
Thus the process is, as in client-centered therapy, a highly verbal
translation emphasizing words about feelings. *It is as if the thera-*
pist analyzes as the client acts. Yet, only in acting does the
therapist expose his own "being." Instead, regard for human
dignity is communicated in verbiage. It is not that we can act
upon our experience with everyone. Rather, it is the naive way
in which most existentialists treat the notion of respect for the
dignity of another. With those for whom we have the most
respect, we act in terms of another. With those for whom we

have the most respect, we act in terms of our experience of them. With those for whom we have the least respect, we concentrate upon the communication, especially verbal, of respect. Thus we must, on the one hand, recognize fully the necessity for the low-level functioning person's experiencing and his therapist's communicating respect for his dignity and worth and, on the other hand, accept the implicit superiority of the therapist's power role in communicating this respect. The existentialists must acknowledge fully the highly cognitive therapeutic process that moves from experience to awareness to technique, particularly with lower-level functioning patients. Again, however, *the ultimate goal of any successful therapeutic process must be action on the part of both therapist and patient.*

Constructive action for both therapist and client involves each ultimately acting to (1) find himself, and (2) find others in relation or in reaction to him. It is precisely a continuation of the destructive experiences in the artificial world for either party simply to react to (1) find others, and (2) find himself in relation or reaction to others. Most often we are talking about the latter process in existential therapy, *a process of inter-reaction rather than interaction.* Only two actors can interact. The system most often described, heard, or experienced involves reactors, not actors. It is as if the therapist is saying, "Do something I can be spontaneous with." In essence, they imply, "We validate each other by reacting to each other."

THE CONTRIBUTIONS AND LIMITATIONS FOR THERAPIST AND CLIENT

Since the existential stance deals primarily with the dimensions related to our development of the core conditions, it is difficult to discern the unique contributions; that is, those over and above the ones accounted for by the central core of facilitative conditions. Nevertheless, we can benefit from some specificity of description of the contributions and limitations. In doing so, however, we often find it difficult to separate the contributions to the client from those to the therapist. In addition, sometimes potential contributions may constitute limitations under different circumstances.

1. The existential approach offers both client and therapist an opportunity for an honest human encounter.

The existential approach, in spite of its highly intellectual orientation, offers at least the potential for a fully honest communication process. Indeed, of all the major therapeutic orientations, the existential approach offers the greatest possibility for both therapist and client to employ themselves fully.

Again, this potential contribution is not without qualification and, under some circumstances, the honesty of communication may actually constitute a limitation for the progress of therapy. Thus with patients functioning at significantly lower levels than the therapist, the therapist must attend cautiously to the client's condition. He will not share with the client that which would make the client's condition the more desperate. Cognitive processes do provide the transition between the therapist's experience and his communication techniques.

Ultimately, however, *all therapy must offer the prospect of an open and honest exchange.*

2. The existential approach offers both client and therapist a developed cosmology for existence.

The client who has no direction or meaning in his life may accept and incorporate an existential philosophy. However ready-made the cosmology, it may be a more constructive one than that with which the client was previously functioning or than no direction at all. The same holds for the helper, although he or she has the additional benefit of confidence in his or her therapeutic endeavors. Nevertheless, the existential orientation is limited by its own thinking and by what its own thinking excludes.

The existential approach emphasizes a cosmology that might ultimately limit the development of both client and therapist. Any well-developed cosmology can be, at best, transitory: that is, useful until more fundamental and more functional approaches are available. A system of basic "truths" can limit as well as enrich the growth of its adherent, whether client or therapist, and deprive him or her of other enriching possibilities.

3. The existential approach makes explicit values that are left implicit in other approaches while disregarding potentially useful techniques dictated by other approaches.

The therapist is aware of, and the client becomes aware of, an explicit value system. Most systems do not define the value systems that underly them and thus, in a very real sense, do not define the implicit goals of the therapy. [One of the very critical values of existentialism, for example, is the emphasis upon the ultimate responsibility of the client for active decision-making.] While the therapist takes responsibility for making the therapy process happen, the client takes the responsibility in action for giving his life direction.

On the other hand, *many of the explicit values of existentialism deny the possibility of the effective employment of many potentially useful techniques.* Although it may be argued that techniques are most useful when more human and natural processes have broken down, nevertheless it is evident that they are useful under just those circumstances. Thus, techniques such as the counterconditioning of isolated symptomatology and the vocational counseling involved in realistic decision-making, both dictated from a deterministic base, are excluded by the value system of existentialism. A fearful thought strikes us that the therapist is both restrained from intervention and freed to intervene out of his deep awareness that life, as he and the client both live it, is ridiculous: his intervention does not, after all, matter.

4. The existential approach minimizes the definition of roles for both therapist and client.

The existential approach allows for a more free and spontaneous interaction. Role definitions exclude many important functional characteristics of each party to the relationship, and insofar as this constitutes a limiting factor, the lack of role definition is a contribution. However, the necessity for going beyond the absence of roles is clear. In a logical extension of existential thinking, the helper, and ultimately each party to the relationship, can be guided by what is effective for the other. Thus if the absence of role definition can be extended to *the free selection of any appropriate role definition,* an existential therapeutic encounter might incorporate any of a number of potentially useful contributions from any of a number of potentially useful orientations.

5. The existential approach assumes a most healthy therapist—something that it cannot always do.

As in all psychotherapy, the process is as effective as the therapist is whole. However, in existential therapy the therapist is the living embodiment of the values the system makes so explicit. It must be underscored that insufficient attention is given this logical extension of existential thinking: *the therapist must teach by the example of his person, not his analysis. In acting, the therapist exposes his existence—and it had better be a good one!*

THE CONDITIONS OF SUCCESS
AND FAILURE

The conditions under which the existential approach would appear to be most efficacious are those involving (1) a creative therapist who communicates in his "being" the secret of health, (2) an intelligent but lost and confused client seeking the meaning he has lost in his "lonely crowd," and (3) a free environment, in which a process which is open in the sense that experiences which are not defined can take place in the context of explicit abstract values that have been defined. Of all the major therapeutic systems, the existential approach defines most clearly the second half of the necessary movement in therapy from technique to person. At the same time it inadvertently allows for the necessary utilization of technique with the lower-level functioning patient.

Thus the existential approach is most effective with the level 3 client where the therapist may employ his experience, awareness, and technique simultaneously in an open-ended interaction with a person who is capable of choosing but has not yet acted upon any of his choices. Indeed, the existential approach is the only approach, aside from the trait-and-factor orientation, that seeks primarily to clear away the obstacles to decision-making with higher-level functioning clients and that offers high-level functioning clients the opportunity for moving to higher levels of creative processes.

On the other hand, the existential approach could be effective with level 1 patients where the healthy therapist's conscious awareness of his experience of the patient dictates the utilization of one set of techniques or another in restoring the integrity of the communication process for this individual. Unfortunately, the existential therapist's techniques are confined mostly to the communication of attitudinal conditions related to the dignity and worth of the patient as a human being. Valuable techniques, such as the operant conditioning of patients to interact meaningfully with other patients, are precluded.

The existential approach is, however, least likely to be effective with patients functioning at the lower levels, simply because they will be unable to employ the cosmology and the value system in other than a rigid, dogmatic way. Most therapies fail because they are insight therapies geared to clear the distortions of the level 2 neurotics. They fail because neurotics—simply because they are neurotic—cannot constructively utilize insights. Neurotics cannot effectively employ a useful cosmology because they must distort even the most effective one.

The existential approach is most subtly dangerous for the high-level functioning person who is closest to autonomy in choice and action. It provides him with a most lucid rationalization for lingering at level 3 rather than proceeding to higher levels of relating to himself and others. The consequence is a desperate juggling act by the person who sees the artificial world clearly but cannot act to choose life for himself—or for another. In the client's crisis, the existential therapist observes but does not intervene.

6. The existential helper suggests that he or she hopes to experience less fear by producing fearful people who no longer care about anything or anyone.

The strange need to seduce others to share only their isolation and fear of isolation and then to turn away recommends the existentialist as a twisted person.

7. There are limits referring to where humanity should be but no clues about how to get there other than by allowing depression to feed upon personal and social isolation.

There are no effective helping approaches based upon concepts alone, no matter how universal those concepts may appear to be.

8. The existential helper must, in the last analysis, deny the client what the client wanted most: interpersonal skills. Equipped with effective interpersonal skills, the client could experience all those things the helper cannot experience, the fullness of life and other people.

Like others who have stopped growing, the isolated helper cannot allow the client to have more than he, the helper has.

9. Directionless people can only provide others with directionless and empty experiences.

There are few value judgments in the existential approach because all roles and behavior may be good or bad with reference to the individual's private experience rather than to the individual's observable growth and productivity.

10. The helper does not need to personalize understanding because the problems people have are common to all and are also limited.

Personalizing is in reality impossible. The existential helper offers only general concepts and a few general principles, because the helper does not need to attend or observe even the simplest aspect of the helpee that is unique. All experience is the same for everyone.

11. The existential helper tolerates and even encourages a level of honesty and openness as long as there is no possibility of being held accountable for the outcome.

There can be "open" communication between the helper and the helpee only when all possibility of active intervention is eliminated.

12. The existential position creates its own kind of insanity and gives license to venting impulses because it denies social responsibility.

It is strange, indeed frightening, to contemplate the implications of "being together (socially) in mutual aloneness." At best, others and self become objects; at worst, targets for use, abuse, and ignoring.

13. Not making a difference in the lives of others is a necessary condition of existential interactions.

It is not only acceptable but preferable for the helper not to measurably impact the client.

14. The existential helper depersonalizes life while claiming to personalize experience.

The existential helper fabricates an approach to helping from the obvious and superficial because effective helping requires work and learning.

15. The existential helper is seductive because such a

helper has few skills and is closed to learning others because learning requires work.

Those without effective skills must rely upon personality and charm because they have no programs that can make an effective delivery. The psychopath knows that it is not enough to share a moment in time with one who can respond negatively to what it means to be alone, but that is all they can do and will ever do because they choose to.

✓SUMMARY AND CONCLUSIONS

The existential approach is not merely an adjective but rather a position of relatively well defined propositions. However, its assumptions concerning the nature of man address themselves primarily to the existence and effect of the core conditions to which we have attended and, thus, it makes few unique contributions over and above those accounted for by the core conditions. Concerning the core conditions, many of the existential assumptions must be modified and extended. The core conditions are most compatible with (1) the existential spelling out of the goals of therapy, and (2) the existential emphasis upon the necessary movement within therapy toward the full persons of both therapist and client.

The existential approach would appear to be the highest form of psychotherapy within the artificial world. Its adherents see the artificial world most clearly while at the same time being within the tolerance limits of that world. The existential approach comes closest to the point of defining free man. It is handicapped only by its need for a system as well as a consistent value. *Free man*, whether therapist or client, *needs no one system;* rather if he is to live effectively, he draws upon many systems, utilizing those, or the aspects of those, that are most effective in a given instance.

In general, we could summarize our experience in listening to tapes of existential therapy by saying that the existentialists write at level 4 but live at level 3 or less: they formulate precise definitions of man's condition and necessary direction without acting in therapy upon this knowledge. The existentialists write, they do not act. To define yourself is not to live; to act to define yourself is to live. In a sense, then, in its clarity of perception, existentialism is most painful for those who cannot act upon what they see and fear most clearly.

The existential approach, ironically enough, in some ways offers the most potential for an open-ended stance. In its extension, existentialism need not be incompatible with a free eclectic position where the therapist is shaped by what is effective for both parties to the relationship. Because of its loose role definitions, both therapist and client could be open to a variety of meaningful and effective experiences and techniques that would allow each, in turn, to move to higher levels of functioning. *The dogmatic stance of precluding the techniques of more deterministic positions is unnecessary.*

Man's ultimate fear is not, as the existentialists suggest, to be alone. Man's ultimate fear is to be alone with himself. In their thinking the existentialists have developed man from an empty, dependent person through an awareness of his alienation to a stage of effective interaction with others. They have not gone far enough. They have moved from "man for himself" to "man for each other." They must move to where man can live alone with himself—to where he is not, as in therapy, accompanied by others in his voyage into the unknown—for the unknown is in him. He must come to love what is in him before he can return to the world to love and care for what is in others. Initial interactions with a fellow man is only a phase along the way, to be left to return to oneself. At best, the existential position is a transitory phase; at worst, a tomb.

In its focus upon the necessity of man's facing death before choosing life, the existential stance does not attend to the man who has moved to the phase beyond. It suggests, further, that man must face the fact that there is nothing before and nothing after life before he can choose life. It leaves no room for the healthy product of the healthy environment. It leaves no room for the healthy man who alone can implement this stance. Those who fear death must face death before they can live life; those who do not fear death, live life.

When the world is artificial as well as the people in it, it is because humanity cannot act upon the world or themselves, to learn or work.

In summary, the existential approach is an empty and desperate search for profound meaning that will not make a difference.

REFERENCES

BINSWANGER, L. Existential analysis and psychotherapy. In F. Fromm-Reichmann & J. L. Moreno (Eds.), *Progress in psychotherapy.* New York: Grune & Stratton, 1956.

BOSS, M. *The analysis of dreams.* New York: Philosophical Library, 1958.

BOSS, M. *Daseinanalyse and psychoanalysis.* New York: Basic Books, 1963.

HEIDEGGER, M. *Being and time.* London: SCM Press, 1962.

HUSSERL, E. Phenomenology. In *Encyclopaedia Britannica* (14th ed.), 1929, *17,* 699–702.

JASPERS, K. On my philosophy. In W. A. Kaufmann (Ed.), *Existentialism from Dostoevsky to Sartre.* New York: Meridian, 1956, pp. 131–158.

KIERKEGAARD, S. *The sickness unto death.* New York: Doubleday, 1954.

MAY, R. (Ed.) *Existential psychology.* New York: Random House, 1961.

MAY, R., ANGEL, E., & ELLENBERGER, H. F. (Eds.). *Existence: A new dimension in psychiatry and psychology.* New York: Basic Books, 1958.

MINKOWSKI, E. Bergson's conceptions as applied to psychopathology. *Journal of Nervous and Mental Disorders,* 1926, *63,* 553–568.

RUITENBECK, H. M. *Psychoanalysis and existential philosophy.* New York: Dutton, 1962.

SARTRE, J. P. *Existentialism.* New York: Philosophical Library, 1947.

SARTRE, J. P. *Existential psychoanalysis.* New York: Philosophical Library, 1953.

STRAUS, E. The upright posture. *Psychiatric Quarterly,* 1952, *26,* 529–561.

STRAUS, E. *Von sinn der sinne* (On the meaning of the senses) (2d ed.), Berlin: Springer, 1956.

6

. . . a passive acceptance of life as a series
of painful episodes with infrequent periods
of balance and no real joy.

The Illusive Suicide

The Unique Contributions of the Psychoanalytic Approach

Freud was keenly aware of the tragedy in human history and its compulsion to record crimes on larger and grander scales. Freud understood that the average man is truly an impotent victim who can only hope to tolerate the pain of living (Brill, 1938; Freud, 1924b, 1927, 1933, 1943; Jones, 1953). The raw data for any theory of personality and therapy arises out of stressful situations (Freud, 1924a, 1935, 1936, 1943). It is precisely these crisis periods that are focused upon in life and therapy; the rest of the patient's life receives summary dismissal. From the psychoanalytic point of view, crises involve periods of acute pain only, without the possibility of high levels of pleasure, joy, or creativity upon "breaking through" the crisis experience. Perhaps this, in part, explains why psychoanalytic theory and practice has been unable to cope fully with the free man while, at the same time, it has offered the most comprehensive insights into the psychodynamics of the sick man. *To understand and accept fully the validity of the psychoanalytic stance promotes a passive acceptance of life as a series of painful episodes with infrequent periods of balance and no real joy.*

The dismal state of man is depicted vividly in the psycho-analytic postulate stating that pleasure is sought only to reduce tension (Freud, 1936). Furthermore, tension is likely to become pain, for there are few if any opportunities for direct discharge. When discharge of tension is accomplished, it is done through a highly complex system of energy changes and compromises that, once again, leave the individual prey to the conflict between internal and external pressures.

The implications of facing this cycle again and again with-out the gain of *constructive* learnings can only lead to the develop-ment of a defeated and empty man. Freud's insight into the vic-tim's subjugation to these destructive forces in society was profound. His stance, woven out of this neurotic fabric, filled a need at a time when there was an accelerated growth in the great middle class. It supplied the empty man with some considerable substance and conceptually emptied the whole man.

The major contributions of psychoanalytic theory are his-torical and center largely around man's effort to maintain some minimal or tolerable level of survival (Freud, 1920, 1933, 1936). In addition, from our view, Freud identified and described what persons functioning above level 3 must escape from. *In its es-*

sence, psychoanalytic theory supplies a highly complex and all-encompassing intellectual justification for a substantive but essentially impotent stance toward life.

THE PSYCHOANALYTIC STANCE

It is our purpose here only to present the briefest of outlines of essential psychoanalytic constructs or assumptions. The focus will center on Freud's view of psychodynamics and their implications for therapy. With the notable exception of Adler (1917, 1927), we view all neo-Freudians (Fromm, 1941, 1947; Horney, 1939, 1942, 1945; Jung, 1927, 1928, 1939; Rank, 1929; Sullivan, 1938, 1948) as having lived largely in qualification of Freud rather than emerging as vitally new and original contributors. The credits are due Freud, the limitations may be charged to his socially acceptable followers.

Some Basic Assumptions

1. Man is basically evil and is governed by rudimentary instincts; he is destined to become a victim of the interaction and conflict between these instincts and social forces.

2. Man's only real hope is to achieve and then diligently maintain a tolerable balance between internal impulses and external demands and restrictions. In this way he may be able to tolerate life and living.

3. Man can accomplish this delicate balance through a deep understanding of what makes him weak. He achieves this understanding, and learns to employ it in an effort to live more rationally, by analysis.

4. A basically evil person who has achieved some reasonable level of balance between inner and outer forces can help another basically evil person.

Psychoanalysis is firmly based on a theory of instincts. In addition to a reflex reaction to external stimuli, the organism is subject to the forces of powerful and incessant inner stimuli. The internal stimuli are said to be instinctual. For Freud, the energy expended to relieve the tension brought on by an instinct is directly related to the strength of the inner stimuli (Mullahy, 1948). The major objective for the individual is to overcome or control the stimuli. Thus he lives in continual fear of being overwhelmed by internal and external forces. The basic organism, however, seeks some kind of equilibrium, an equilibrium that is difficult to achieve because of the limited opportunities in society for direct discharge of tension. The individual is often caught between the possibility of being severely punished from the outside and of being overcome by the intensity of his instinctual tensions and impulses. In order to maintain some minimal level of ego integrity and tolerable survival, he is forced to create and employ mechanisms that serve to mediate and compromise these demands.

The defense mechanisms are a "mixed blessing." On the one hand they allow the person to come to some adjustment with the outside world, yet on the other hand they can come to dominate the psychic life to such an extent that the basic energies which have to be diverted, changed, or repressed can build up to a point where the individual is living a basically sick life. When stored-up or repressed energies govern behavior without the awareness of the individual, that individual must understand how the defense mechanisms work and what they are keeping from consciousness. To the fully acculturated person, the internal impulses are mainly acceptable wishes. The aim in therapy is to attempt to make possible an awareness of this core of buried fears and anxieties.

Simply expressed, the aim of the instinct is activity and the aim of the superego (internalized social restrictions on behavior) is to curb behavior directed by instincts (of the id). Activity is then most often moderated or entirely neutralized, moving behavior toward some kind of golden social mean. The discrepancy between what the organism wishes to do and what his or her acquired psychic system allows him or her to do is often immense. The successful resolution of the ensuing frustration may constitute a moment of growth toward a more balanced adjustment. Therapy supplies the patient with painful frustration and resolution of the frustration, such as that involved in the working through of the transference. Since a weakened ego constitutes the conditions for the development of neurosis, the therapist is committed to ally himself with the ego against the id and superego.

The role of the therapist is largely a didactic one in which he or she uncovers and integrates unconscious material. He is also involved in making judgments as to whether or not a defense is appropriate or inappropriate. The question here rests on the influence of the defense. If it weakens the ego, denies reality, or threatens to change the structure of the entire psychic system, it is maladaptive. In a real sense, the therapist judges a defense helpful or not in accordance with the difficulty or ease in making psychoanalytic interpretations. The patient most difficult to analyze is the most sick. Although Freud did not extend his explicit thinking this far, the implications are clear: *The free man or the artist would be seen as the most acutely ill individual in society because he cannot be readily analyzed.*

The therapist is a somewhat distant but all-knowing and understanding authority. His theory and manner communicate to the patient that he (the therapist) is truly a superior person. The therapist not only understands the patient's unconscious processes but also is able to render irrational material rational. There is an implicit assumption that therapy cannot work if the patient insists on questioning the therapist's knowledge and authority. In such cases the patient may be judged to be too resistant to be amenable to treatment. The level of intensity of any denial is a reflection of the validity of the interpretation.

The entire course of therapy is enhanced by the skillful handling of the transference; that is, the patient grows to view the therapist as a reincarnation of important figures of the patient's past. In the case of a positive transference, the patient gets well out of a love for the therapist. Negative transference encourages high levels of resistance as well as the operation of a cruel superego and the blockage of the affect associated with the original trauma.

It is obvious that the patient who has a great deal of intellectual curiosity about himself enjoys a distinct advantage in psychoanalytic therapy.

The patient is considered well to the extent that he or she is aware of the workings of his or her psychic life in psychoanalytic terminology, free of the intensity of original affect as well as intense direct discharge of impulses and feelings.

HISTORICAL AND OTHER CONTRIBUTIONS

The major historical contributions of psychoanalytic theory and practice center around several broad and major theses: (1) the real possibility that mental life and the nature of man can not only be understood but that these insights can be applied to alleviate, to some degree, human suffering (Freud, 1943); (2) the greatest part of man's behavior is irrational, and is governed by unconscious forces and processes (Freud, 1920, 1935); (3) the findings of the therapist can be applied to areas of life beyond therapy (Sullivan, 1938); (4) that it is possible to depict the development and maintenance of destructive forces in man and society (Fromm, 1941, 1947; Sullivan, 1948).

From our viewpoint, there are no major contributions of psychoanalytic theory (above and beyond the limited concentration upon the central core of facilitative therapeutic conditions) that can be applied to therapy and counseling.

If there are contributions beyond the historical, they are infrequent and limited to the rather unique experiences of a small number of people amenable to this kind of therapy: (1) persons functioning at level 2; (2) psychologically attuned, affluent, intelligent, sophisticated, and intellectually curious persons who are functioning adequately at a concrete level; and (3) future analysts.

    1. Psychoanalytic theory has provided a base for the interpretation of fields of study beyond the helping professions.

Psychoanalytic theory has been directly applied in anthropology, sociology, literature, economics, politics, the arts, history, and religion.

    2. Psychoanalytic theory has provided a systematic focus for interpreting the symbolism in behavior and interpersonal relationships.

By going beyond the myths and the obvious, psychoanalytic theory rendered the more subtle aspects of behavior and the therapist–patient relationship not only comprehensible but therapeutically useful.

    3. Psychoanalytic theory has offered the most compre-

hensive view of the interpersonal relationships in the family and their implications for psychological development.

In essence, the child learns to be acted upon and not to become an actor. He then carries into life a mental set that allows him to relate to others as a sibling or parental surrogate. The sequence and nature of psychosexual stages and development has its roots in the family complex.

4. Psychoanalytic theory has provided a stance emphasizing the common attributes of the sexes.

Freud's concept of bisexuality has led to a deeper understanding of the overlap between the sexes along a number of critical dimensions, with particular focus on active–passive impulses and behavior. This has allowed others as well as Freud to devote their energies to the basic human situation.

5. Psychoanalytic theory was the first system to deal with and begin to comprehend the importance of affect.

The central role of catharsis in successful therapy is now almost universally accepted: emotional discharge is a prerequisite to understanding.

6. The psychoanalytic stance was the first to set up and implement standards for training and practice.

The trainee and novice practitioner is not only provided with intense and ongoing supervision but, in addition, the supervisor is charged with making judgments about the trainee's level of functioning and personal adjustment. This brings into full view the notion that a therapist must be in touch with the nature of his or her own motives before claiming the right and ability to help others.

7. Psychoanalytic theory and practice has given focus and meaning to the polarities of feeling and behavior.

Such constructs as ambivalence, pleasure–pain, subject–object, and active–passive came into full maturity within the psychoanalytic system (Mullahy, 1948).

8. Psychoanalytic theory has provided a meaningful framework from which to understand the means by which the individual attempts to maintain a sense of uniqueness and ward off annihilation.

The postulation of defense mechanisms and the growth of the ego through psychosexual development provides the possibility and the means by which the individual avoids drowning in a flood of anxiety.

> 9. Psychoanalytic theory has provided an explanation of the implications and durable effects of trauma.

While repetitious retarding experiences are essential for severe deterioration, both clinical experience and research attest to the validity of the lasting impact of some kinds of one-trial learning situations.

> 10. Psychoanalytic theory has provided an explanation of the durable influence of early childhood experiences for those functioning below level 3.

The nature and function of the entire symptom process, as well as of the structure of personality, may well have its roots in the early years of childhood.

Most of what has followed Freud as positive contributions to personality theory and psychotherapeutic practice can be credited to these major historical contributions. His attempts at theoretical breakthroughs made possible the development of other systems.

THERAPIST AND PATIENT PROCESS
LIMITATIONS

Most of the limitations are tied to the observation that psychoanalytic theory and practice is applied only to those functioning below level 3. In addition, patients functioning below level 3 are the least able to use constructively the insights and interpretations offered by their therapists. If there is any gain for these patients at all, it is most likely to be due to the extent to which the therapist communicates relatively high levels of facilitative conditions and confidence in interaction with the client's neurotic dependency on authority.

> 1. Psychoanalytic theory explains away everything but the negative and destructive aspects of the human situation.

Freedom from one's own history and creative acts that are not merely sublimations but full expressions of a whole person, are beyond the scope of psychoanalytic theory. The person functioning below level 3 *is* dominated by destructive forces, and only psychoanalytic theory interprets his psychic life comprehensively: *the overall impression is that life is hardly worth living or ending.*

2. Neither the patient nor the therapist can win anything of value.

The patient or the critic who persists in questioning the authority of the theory is seen as operating to defend against the exposure of his deeper motives. Psychoanalytic theory is too often used as a weapon to fend off its critics and explain away its own failures.

3. Psychoanalytic practice often defines success in terms of the patient's degree of acceptance of the therapist's view of life.

This is not only a limitation for the patient but also closes the therapist off from significant new learnings from the patient.

4. Psychoanalytic theory assumes that man is basically evil and he must learn to live with his irrational impulses.

It seems to us that more of man's behavior, history, and society can be better understood by assuming that man is born with the potential for both good and evil. He is largely shaped by what society rewards. Those functioning below level 3 cannot or have not been able to break free of such schedules of reinforcement. In another sense, there seems to be an implicit assumption that if there is any hope for gaining strength, it comes from knowing how really weak one is.

5. Psychoanalytic theory and practice leave room for creative interpretations and synthesis on the part of both the therapist and patient only within the limits of the theory.

Any suggestion that the person can view the world in some way other than through the theory is unacceptable. A personalized interpretation of experience is less likely and most often filtered through a highly intellectual process. The persons of the therapist and patient become encapsulated in the theory. This relegates the therapist to the role of an intellectual "Peeping Tom," peering at life but never participating fully. The patient who adopts this stance must come to the same fate.

6. Psychoanalytic theory and practice do not leave room for environmental manipulations in any systematic way.

Behavioral approaches have demonstrated the efficacy of environmental manipulations for those functioning at low levels. The analyst is likely to interpret a crisis situation, leaving the patient with an intellectual understanding but without the energy to face it fully, or to act and grow. Instead of selectively altering the patient's world, the therapist again offers insights to the person functioning below level 3, the patient least able to use them.

7. Psychoanalytic theory and practice tend to explain away affect before destroying it completely.

Affect (catharsis), when it is encouraged therapeutically, is seen as something the patient must get out of his system. Genuine or strong affect from the therapist is rare and inappropriate, reflecting the incomplete nature of his own analysis. At a deeper level, psychoanalytic theory seems to be saying that its goal is to break the meaningful tie to life: the life one can only tolerate and the life one must eventually lose. An intellectual framework replaces direct expression of affect. Like the client-centered process the perfect product of psychoanalytic therapy only *talks* about feelings; he does not act on them.

8. Psychoanalytic theory and practice offer little or no outlet for direct discharge.

Any direct or full discharge of affect is seen as potentially self-destructive and/or destructive to society. This assumption, like so many others in psychoanalytic theory, does apply to those functioning below level 3. Again, the theory's inability to bring the individual to level 3 and above constitutes its major limitation. Along with the understanding psychoanalytic theory offers of the artificial world, its comprehensive description of the psychic experience and behavior of those functioning below level 3 constitutes its major contribution.

9. Psychoanalytic theory promotes a basic distrust in one's self and others.

There is no room for a direct, honest, and accepting experiencing of one's self or others. Relationships can only develop through a screen of multiple interpretations and, hence, at a great distance.

This point, however, is also appropriate for those functioning below level 3.

> 10. Psychoanalytic theory and practice encourage the belief that the ritualistic aspects of therapy contribute significantly to positive outcome.

Again, this holds only for those functioning at lower levels. Beyond this, the compulsive following of stages of therapy by the therapist dissipates much of his potentially creative energy into a kind of masturbatory behavior. Psychoanalytic therapy leaves no room for the patient or the therapist to enter openly any significant life experience. Psychoanalytic theory and practice tend to destroy spontaneity and creativity.

> 11. Psychoanalytic therapy offers nothing but a retarding experience to the patient functioning above level 3.

A psychoanalytic stance toward life is largely unacceptable for a healthy and whole person. He needs no such complex apology for his motives, impulses, and behavior. The whole person trusts his impulses and acts on them with responsibility. He does not experience an inner evil and the analyst cannot therefore confirm it. He may, as mentioned earlier in this chapter, experience the psychoanalytic interpretations as something he has gone through. To be fully conscious of weaknesses allows one to choose tragedy, a notion alien to the whole person.

> 12. Psychoanalytic theory does not deal fully or reasonably with the area of female sexuality.

Although psychoanalytic theory exposes much of what a Victorian society has done to shape the superficial aspects of female sexual behavior and response, it still describes the average woman as either something more or less than human: more than human in that she allegedly is not distracted by a strong libido; less than human because her identity revolves around not possessing a penis.

SUCCESS AND FAILURE

Psychoanalytic theory had its most significant insights during the period of its initial, marginal struggle; since then it has striven to make its most significant contributions acceptable. Society has

now moved to incorporate the stance in such a way that psychoanalytic theorists now function well within the limits of social
acceptability and, in many quarters, constitute the mainstream of
thinking. Contributions in the form of additions and reinterpre-
tations can now take the form of modifications of and reactions
to earlier writings. Operating within tolerable social limits denies
the very possibility of the emergence of a truly creative contribution. Yet most theorists strive for social acceptance, which,
once achieved, assures their own impotence. Freud's followers
and critics offered innovations to his theory that led to its
stagnation and limited its therapeutic potential largely to those
who aspire to be psychoanalysts. History moves slowly but in-
sidiously to engulf the giant talent and by so doing neutralizes
any potentially creative impact. To seek society's support and
approval places the most powerful limitations on creativity. *Only
sustained and creative existence, responsibility independent of
society, can endure.* Acting to accept society's rewards, as did the
adherents of psychoanalytic theory, leaves no room for further
breakthroughs. In this way, we can account for psychoanalytic
success and failure in the short span of something over fifty
years.

Furthermore, Freud's inability to account for or to accept
the possibility of those functioning at levels above 3 explains why
his insights are only half true. To apply his notions to the person
functioning at level 4 or 5 is to render beauty ugly.

Psychoanalysis fails for many social, sane, and insane
reasons. Among these reasons is the fact that the analytic therapist is oriented toward identifying universal deficits within the
individual patient and then leaves the patient with a belly full of
worms the patient can only analyze. The system is another instance where insight without behavioral objectives and skills
does not make a constructive difference. The approach only
confirms the therapist's narrow bias or, rather, ignorance.

Mostly, it may be absurd to consider psychoanalysis as an
approach to helping because it only deals with how losers lose
and how one may discover over and over and over again that
the depressed loser has an infinite variety of strategies to lose
and invites others to do the same.

In addition, psychoanalysis fails because it actually promotes irrational behavior while promising rational understanding. It does so by teaching those few who can financially afford

it limited intellectual responses to limited emotional stimuli. These limited intellectual responses become rigidly stereotyped and hence closed to changes within the social and/or personal systems of the patient. Instead of systematically increasing the quality and quantity of the physical, emotional, *and* intellectual responses to the emotional *and* intellectual stimuli, the approach encourages intellectual rigidity, emotional blunting, and even an ignorance of the physical aspects of life.

The perfect product of psychoanalytic therapy can, at most, be an empty person functioning at level 3—the full embodiment of the aspirations of middle-class society. Psychoanalytic treatment is doomed to failure because it provides the middle-class patient with what he or she experiences in everyday life— the treatment can only confirm his or her emptiness. Psychoanalytic treatment serves as a model of interpersonal relationships in which each person can experience only human deprivation.

SUMMARY AND CONCLUSIONS

Although the psychoanalytic movement began with efforts to borrow from biological and physiological systems, it now appears to deny that life has a physical base in several important ways: first, in the assumption that psychoanalytic insights and the proper use of intellect can dominate affect; second, in the *implication* that all intense feelings, impulses, and behavior are pathological. It has been our experience that often the success or failure of therapy depends largely on the therapist's and the client's energy level, in addition to the therapist's and client's direct and intense expression of feeling, in such a way that the experience is primarily a physical one. *If, at the most intense moments of therapy, the therapist acts to render the moment anything less than fully honest, he acts to abuse the physical base of life.*

The final summary points can be listed without additional comment:

1. *Psychoanalytic theory has become a widespread game rarely applied effectively to therapy.*

2. *The perfect product is at best a person functioning at level 3.*

3. In its essence, life from a psychoanalytic point of view may not even be worth ending; on the other hand, the fully analyzed person is too impotent to undertake a perfectly reasonable suicide.

4. The psychoanalytic therapist can really hope to treat patients successfully only if he breaks free of his role.

5. Some of the therapy outcomes judged to be poor by the psychoanalytic therapist may, in fact, be among his success cases, in that the patient escaped.

6. The fact is that a great deal of human behavior is irrational and inefficient as well as rigid because people in difficulty are not taught much of anything else by professional helpers. The analyst perpetuates this nonsense.

7. Society has moved to accept psychoanalysis because at some level society understands the analyst's inability to make a difference with insights alone.

8. Over the decades, psychoanalysis has merely developed a rationale to justify psychopathy.

9. The psychological cripple contributes nothing to human resource development and psychoanalysis does not understand even the cripple.

10. Psychoanalysis demonstrates its impotence when it stresses exploration and understanding with no system or reason to develop action strategies.

11. Psychoanalysts and their patients are trapped by the brilliant insights about unhealthy families and pathology in limited experiences.

12. The unconscious is the major psychological component for those who cheat and abuse their resources and ask others to do the same.

13. Psychoanalysis is an effort to be intelligent about the use of insights while the promolgators of psychoanalysis can never hope to escape the tragedy of their inability to learn.

The future of theory and practice in counseling and psychotherapy, whatever shape it assumes, rests on Freud's shoulders. Psychoanalytic theory and practice spent its creative energies because those who followed Freud did not seek their own direction, a fate perhaps inevitable for every school or system, but one that is most dramatically illustrated by the rise and fall of psychoanalytic theory.

The implications of a society's acceptance of psychoanalytic theory are chilling. The world and the people in it are doomed to be victims of the neurotic and destructive motives of those functioning below level 3. It offers no hope either for realizing or for using the potential of those functioning at higher levels or for bringing those at lower levels to higher levels. Psychoanalytic treatment at best appears to fix acceptable growth, satisfaction, and tolerable creativity at level 3.

Life below level 3 becomes a battle to fend off tragedy and pain with frequent periods of acute fear, anxiety, and even panic. The rare moments of balance only prepare the individual for the series of tragedies and complete loss of love of life that will enable him to accept death. The person below level 3 strives to cope with and measure out his energies with earnest effort, knowing he must in the end capitulate to overwhelming forces. Even his apparent success is a hollow experience; deep inside himself he is aware that he has not stood for anything real, attested to by the fact that his former critics now give him his due. *He has lived life as if it were real.*

In the end there is a complete submission of both the therapist and the patient to the theory. This degree of depersonalization of both parties must culminate in an immense mutual disgust or hate, but each is now too impotent and resigned to act on that hate. They have come to view one another in the same way the therapist has viewed the rest of humanity—with a mixture of pity and contempt. Each now can justify how the other has lived.

What follows in life must, however subtle, include the full experiencing of not only impotence but also the growth of cruelty. It is a blessing that reviewers dealing with the efficacy of psychoanalytic therapy report a low percentage of success. In the light of those who followed Freud and now of society's eager effort to include their theories, psychoanalysis has become a gross perversion for the empty man. By withholding affect, the therapist allows this man to seek a personage with only the outer attributes of humanity.

In summary, while Freud's unique contribution may have been his accurate perception of the world in all of its destructiveness, it is destructive for any individual to accept the implications that Freud uncovered. After peeling back the trappings and exposing the undergarments of an ugly world, Freud found no alternatives. The irony is that in spite of his own creative output, he himself did not understand creativity without agony. The irony is that in spite of his comprehensive description of the world and its victims, he became one of the victims. Even allowing for his deep understanding of the arbitrariness of institutional structures, he did not understand the possibility for a man to live freely and creatively within the world—or, perhaps, independently of it. The final irony is that only the free man, the person whom psychoanalysis does not comprehend, can make the discriminations necessary to put psychoanalysis in perspective and to make appropriate application of the stance.

In summary, the psychoanalytic approach reduces to an effort to create a lasting and secure place for the inevitable triumph of psychopathy and tragedy.

REFERENCES

ADLER, A.   The neurotic constitution (Glueck and Lind, trans.). New York: Moffat, Yard and Company, 1917.

ADLER, A.   Understanding human nature (Beran, trans.). New York: Wolfe & Greenberg Publishers, 1927.

BRILL, A. A.   The basic writings of Sigmund Freud (A. A. Brill, Ed.). New York: Random House, 1938.

FREUD, S.   Selected papers on hysteria and other psychoneuroses (A. A. Brill, trans.). Nervous and Mental Disease Monograph Series, No. 4, 1920.

FREUD, S.   Beyond the pleasure principle. London: Hogarth and The Institute of Psycho-analysis, 1924.(a)

FREUD, S.   Collected papers. London: Hogarth and The Institute of Psycho-analysis, 1924.(b)

FREUD, S.   Totem and taboo (A. A. Brill, trans.). New York: New Republic, Inc., 1927.

FREUD, S.   New introductory lectures (H. Spott, trans.). New York: Norton, 1933.

FREUD, S.   The ego and the id. London: Hogarth and the Institute of Psycho-analysis, 1935.

FREUD, S. *The problem of anxiety*. New York: The Psycho-analytic Quarterly Press and Norton, 1936.

FREUD, S. *The future of an illusion*. New York: The International Psycho-analytic Library, No. 15, 1943.

FROMM, E. *Escape from freedom*. New York: Holt, Rinehart and Winston, 1941.

FROMM, E. *Man and himself*. New York: Holt, Rinehart and Winston, 1947.

HORNEY, K. *New ways in psychoanalysis*. New York: Norton, 1939.

HORNEY, K. *Self-analysis*. New York: Norton, 1942.

HORNEY, K. *Our inner conflicts*. New York: Norton, 1945.

JONES, E. *The life and work of Sigmund Freud*. New York: Basic Books, 1953.

JUNG, C. G. *The psychology of the unconscious* (trans. and intro. by Beatrice M. Hinkle). New York: Dodd, Mead, 1927.

JUNG, C. G. *Contributions to analytical psychology* (H. G. and C. F. Baynes, trans.). New York: Harcourt, 1928.

JUNG, C. G. *The integration of the personality* (Stanley M. Dell, trans.). New York: Holt, Rinehart and Winston, 1939.

MULLAHY, P. *Oedipus: Myth and complex, a review of psychoanalytic theory*. New York: Grove, 1948.

RANK, O. *The trauma of birth*. New York: Harcourt, 1929.

SULLIVAN, H. S. Introduction to the study of interpersonal relations. *Psychiatry*, 1938, Vol. 1.

SULLIVAN, H. S. The meaning of anxiety in psychiatry and life. *Psychiatry*, 1948, *11*, No. 1.

7

... an effort to systematize man's
efforts to systematize man's life ...

Chance, Not Choice
or Change

The Unique Contributions of the
Trait-and-Factor Counseling Approach

Man spends the greater part of his life attempting to bring order and reason into the major decisions of his life. The trait-and-factor approach addresses itself to this end. It is neither stance nor theory but rather an immense effort to bring order and reason into the major decisions of life. Although its efforts to reduce the contributions of chance factors confounding vocational and educational choice have created a large and useful pool of information about man's attributes, the socio-economic world, and their complex interactions, the utility of these findings has been limited, largely because trait-and-factor adherents have not gone beyond the early concept of matching men and jobs (Parsons, 1909). When, for example, a client is determined to make a choice in opposition to the predictions of tests, the trait-and-factor counselor then helps the client to upset the unfavorable prediction. The implication here is simple: *there is more hope for the client than there is for the counselor.*

THE TRAIT-AND-FACTOR APPROACH AND ITS HISTORICAL CONTRIBUTIONS

As its core the trait-and-factor approach to counseling focuses on an effort to match men to their occupational environments (Parsons, 1909). The assumptions posited to justify this effort are simple and direct: (1) *men differ along measurable and relatively stable dimensions;* (2) *jobs differ along measurable and relatively stable dimensions.*

The task has been to identify important variables upon which people and jobs vary, to develop reliable and valid measuring instruments, and to apply these tools along with occupational information to the problem of matching. Ideally, the resolution is accompanied by a statement reflecting the probability that a good or bad choice has been made, within the limits of available data. The counselor is aware of the fact that he and his client will never have all the data. They attempt only to reach an apparently reasonable choice.

What begins with two simple assumptions becomes very tenuous and arbitrary along the route. The very determination of what constitutes an important variable is often influenced by theories of vocational choice, if indeed there are such "theories."

Methods used to study occupational choice have varied from pure speculation to attempts at rigorous experimentation. Even though the trait-and-factor counselor lays claim to an empirical base, the tools of his research vary and are often found to be unreliable and/or interdependent. Questions which center around fitting men to jobs (Hoppock, 1957; Shartle, 1946), appropriateness of choice (Strong, 1943, 1955; Super, 1949, 1957), interest development (Ginzberg, Ginsberg, Axelrad, & Herma, 1951; Holland, 1962; Roe, 1956; Super, 1949, 1957; Tiedeman, O'Hara, & Baruch, 1963), personality (Darley & Hagenah, 1955; Roe, 1956; Tyler, 1953), hereditary, environmental, and other socioeconomic factors (Caplow, 1954), and basic learning processes in general, include an overwhelming number of considerations and likely variables for investigation. The most pressing task to be met is an integrative one. Yet the complexity of the material cannot be rendered more coherent without a stance capable of going beyond the use and abuse of empirical methodology and philosophy.

With the goal that the trait-and-factor adherents have set for themselves, helping clients to make appropriate choices, empiricism is not enough. The tenacious clinging to objectivity has led to a rigidity culminating in a collector's role for the counselor based on self-neutralizing research and practice. For example, there is a strong deterministic base to the trait-and-factor approach, yet it searches for ways and means to supply clients with data relevant to critical choices. This is something of a paradox! *Perhaps underlying this effort is the implicit awareness or assumption that with adequate data the client will make his inevitable choice more quickly and with less trial and error groping.* The implication is that most men and women are suited for rather specific work roles, and discordance in life can be greatly reduced by matching men and women to appropriate work situations.

Perhaps the trait-and-factor approach is the most heroic of all the major systems. Its adherents have unfortunately been seduced by the apparent logic of the basic assumptions, the conceptual simplicity of the tools, and a reverence for objective data that is not itself objective. A close examination of the large volume of literature and consequent impact of trait-and-factor efforts strongly suggests that *the system has either attempted to stabilize modern social-vocational movements or, at another level, to render reasonable a great portion of man's behavior which has been historically unreasonable.* Even the historians, by using creatively artistic methods, have managed to weave only some semblance of reason into human history.

If the trait-and-factor theorist is making an effort to systematize man's effort to systematize man's life, in essence he is fighting two formidable and basic sets of events that he needs to recognize: (1) man was and continues to be a biological accident, and (2) man's history reads like a chronology of interactions of social, economic, and political accidents, complicated and contaminated by periodic and violent physical accidents. On rare occasions violent change was brought about by some atypical and unpredictable personality functioning independently of the conditions around him, further upsetting the web of assumed predictions about the interaction among the basic components of society, culture, and the individual's situation.

Nevertheless, there are a number of rather specific historical contributions that the trait-and-factor approach makes to counseling and psychotherapy.

1. The trait-and-factor counselor attempts to move the client within the environment, with a minimum change or no change in either the client or the environment.

Most therapies attempt to change the person to fit the environment or adjust to it. The behavior therapist may change the environment to fit the client. Environmental manipulation may be considered by the trait-and-factor counselor only when human limits are reached. In general, there is minimum upheaval of what exists.

2. The trait-and-factor approach emphasizes information assumed to be useful to the client in his or her effort to make a choice.

An effective counselor does not need a trait-and-factor orientation to justify providing the client with selected and useful information; however, the trait-and-factor adherents build the counseling sessions around information-giving and receiving.

3. The trait-and-factor approach provides descriptive information about a variety of relevant aspects of life as it is.

From this base of descriptive data, large numbers of people can be placed with a success rate better than chance. These data have served to identify levels of available human and environmental resources.

4. The trait-and-factor approach offers a reason for believing that, for most people, life is predictable.

The level of satisfaction for the great majority can be anticipated and influenced by appropriate and inappropriate choices. Accident theories of occupational choice offer more excitement and surprise for those who are not predictable.

5. The trait-and-factor approach provides the client a base from which he or she can act.

Once a choice is made, the client is encouraged to act on it, thus providing him with the most important sources of learning about himself in relation to his world.

6. The trait-and-factor approach has provided a large number of useful comparisons.

The search for basic dimensions via factor analysis and comparisons among a wide variety of human attributes has led to the development of occupational ability patterns, occupational reinforcement patterns, expectancy tables, and social-educational characteristics scales.

The total impression of the trait-and-factor approach is one of a shotgun effort, using overlapping data to fit a set of overlapping assumptions. The integration needed for a dynamic theory is lacking; the inability to go beyond the basic tenet of its founder is obvious; the adherents' devaluation of its essential contributions dominates their presentation and use of the position. The emphasis in all cases is upon "choice, not change."

COUNSELOR AND CLIENT CONTRIBUTIONS

It is very difficult to separate the unique contributions and limitations of the trait-and-factor approach because the system neutralizes itself for the following reasons: (1) it attempts to deal reasonably with what is often an unreasonable life situation; (2) it is not able to incorporate or to interpret extremes meaningfully; (3) it cannot deal with affect; (4) it relies on summary information about the world and on modal or normative data; (5) its values are rooted firmly in the middle class.

The effort to take the extremes out of life, ignore affect, and make decisions on the basis of objective data shapes the whole system as a product of middle-class values. *Life is rendered perfectly reasonable on the surface.*

1. The trait-and-factor approach focuses upon one of the two most important choices in life.

Vocational choice and marital choice are two of the most important and basic choices influencing the life of the individual in our society. Information about the foundations for such choices, alternative choices, and the implications of each, provides a considerable mass of useful data.

2. The trait-and-factor counselor can reduce anxiety significantly for the client by focusing on information, and making concrete the decision-making process.

The specific reliance on test data and occupational information reduces ambiguity not only for the client but also for the counselor. There is little if any need for the trait-and-factor counselor to probe or venture into the "unknown" areas such as the many and varied aspects of interpersonal relationships. The counselor does not go beyond his level of confidence in the data he has available to him.

3. The trait-and-factor emphasis upon the reality aspects of choice and upon the maximum use of available data often aids in the consideration of factors not previously considered by the client and counselor.

Discussion of information often points out what is not known and what kinds of additional information or clinical treatment are needed. It may also lead to a feeling that there are too many factors to take into account and that a reasonable choice is not really possible.

4. The trait-and-factor approach is particularly useful in situations where prospects for change are minimal.

When the environment is determined and/or the characteristics of the client offer no hope for change, the trait-and-factor counselor may be in the best position to create an optimum solution or adjustment. This contribution also holds for situations where there is not enough time to change either the person or his life situation. Such conditions often occur when dealing with the geriatric, the handicapped, the culturally deprived, and with people attempting a second career. Of all major systems, the trait-and-factor approach offers the most promise for making such choices with the creative use of computer facilities.

5. The trait-and-factor approach serves a growing, technologically oriented society.

When dealing with large numbers of people, the trait-and-factor counselor can employ an expedient and practical system based upon objective public criteria. The results can be evaluated in terms of change in the rate of productivity and other variables reflecting satisfaction. For the good clinician, however, objective data serve as a contributory appendage. Creative acts at the highest levels are not predictable.

6. The trait-and-factor counselor often leads the client to a better definition of the client's values.

The determination of a choice point, accompanied by useful information, is greatly influenced by the degree to which the client is aware of what is important to him as a human being living in a complex society; that is, a good decision, from the trait-and-factor point of view, is a consequence of what the client is willing to accept. The client is not seen as a "black box." Values come from the client. But to respond and to realize fully the constructive potential of what is in the client, the counselor himself or herself must be something more than a "black box" filled with information.

7. The trait-and-factor practitioner-counselor requires the least amount of training.

From this stance, a modestly endowed lay person can be trained to use and dispense information in a very short period of time and, indeed, many guidance counselors who employ this orientation are untrained or minimally trained.

8. The trait-and-factor approach provides a didactic role for the counselor.

The trait-and-factor counselor is allowed, even encouraged, to become involved in the life of his clients to the extent that he can teach them something useful; that is, to bring the client directly to the level where he, the client, can improve the quality of his experiences.

9. The trait-and-factor approach is often most useful in short-term consulting roles.

The clinical versus statistical approaches to prediction have been resolved: *The actuarial approach is a more successful base from which to operate than can be provided by the average counselor.* The alive issue before the field involves, however, the discrimination and development of the potent counselor.

COUNSELOR AND CLIENT LIMITATIONS

The limitations of the trait-and-factor approach reflect, for the most part, the problems inherent in attempts to apply normative data to the individual and to his unique and often extreme situations. In addition, the role of the counselor, when structured primarily as a source of information, does not fully attend to the subtle and complex aspects of a one-to-one interaction.

1. The trait-and-factor literature has not as yet reported the critical test of the approach.

Clients could be randomly assigned to one of two groups, one group counseled on the basis of test data to enter certain fields of work and the other group counseled to enter the "wrong" field. A follow-up study employing a variety of appropriate indexes could serve as a useful test. Choices of a less critical nature may be employed for experimental purposes.

2. The trait-and-factor approach has been largely limited to initial choice and career patterns to maturity.

Early developmental trends offer conflicting impressions. Extensive study of vocational patterns of late maturity, the relationship between the major work role and the movement to other jobs, has not been carried out. The use of data reflecting the decision-making process at crisis points in life may yield a pool of variables more critical than those traditionally employed.

3. The trait-and-factor approach has emphasized the analysis of worker attributes with a tendency to exclude systematic patterns of job changes over time.

Little is offered in the way of systematic patterns of job changes over time. If there is any hope for relatively lasting and satisfying matching, such data is essential. This is especially true in a time when entire industries are in the process of radical change in production systems. At a more simple level, more information is needed in any specific case, reflecting situational factors such as the personality of the supervisor, the status of the job on the local scene, and whether it is a family business, corporation, or governmental agency.

4. The trait-and-factor approach does not give sufficient attention to the counseling relationship and related attitudes and motives.

The ability of the client to accept and use information maximally may be directly related to how the client perceives the counselor. The willingness of the client to share aspects of his or her life that interfere with his or her optimum functioning is related to the level of therapeutic conditions offered by the counselor. It is absurd to treat personal choices in an objective, impersonal manner. Clients may be more in tune with this absurdity than the average trait-and-factor counselor. The counselor trained to deal directly with counselor–client differences is at a distinct advantage.

5. The trait-and-factor approach appears to be limited in effectiveness to the upwardly mobile.

The nature of the normative data employed renders it minimally useful to those clients representing the extremes of socioeconomic status.

6. The trait-and-factor approach gives little recognition to the fact that decisions vary in significance.

The implications of major and minor decisions are not systematically and differentially weighted. There is an implicit set that the goal in counseling is to help the client to become settled in life, thus discouraging further explorations. A decision at age 15 to study engineering is—or should be—more reversible than the same decision at age 24. Some decisions require more data, reflecting higher levels of reliability and validity, than do other decisions.

7. The trait-and-factor approach is basically dependent upon only three main sources of information and often the major determinants of choice are never uncovered.

The counselor attempts to integrate information gleaned from tests, occupational information, and the client. Some test results are of questionable reliability and validity, and occupational information is often scant and out of date. Information offered by the client is often reduced to efforts on the part of the client to be objective about his or her history and future. The deeper feelings of the client are often the major determinants of choices but may never come to light. Too little attention has been given to building by way of discriminating useful from useless sources of information.

8. The trait-and-factor approach emphasizes a reasonable consideration of choice to the exclusion of the crises that constitute the fabric of life.

The most compelling moments in life are made up of crisis points. These moments of stress or heightened activity constitute the fabric of the life style of the client and her or his spurts of growth. Crises rarely occur in trait-and-factor counseling. A calm, careful, and reasoned consideration of a personal choice offers little that constitutes significant learning or growth.

9. The trait-and-factor approach implies that choice = information + client values + probability of success.

This raises the question about the efficacy of training counselors (1) to compartmentalize life experiences, and (2) to render all subjective experiences objective.

10. The trait-and-factor reliance on data seemingly excuses the counselor from functioning at high levels of interpersonal skills.

The utility of the information is likely to be directly related to the level of functioning of both the counselor and the client. A counselor functioning at low levels might not communicate the full value of the data. A level 4 counselor contributes over and above the value of the information alone.

11. In a trait-and-factor counseling situation there is often not enough information to act on.

This system frequently forces choices in the name of norms. When action is taken, it is done only on the basis of the available information. This somehow makes critical life choices analogous to a bridge game.

12. The trait-and-factor approach gives little attention to client energy levels, motivation, and neuroticism.

The ability to act is directly dependent upon the energy level of the individual. High energy levels, coupled with the motivation to break free of one's own history and measured limitations, are the behavioral components necessary to upset actuarial predictions. However, if these components are subject to a high level of neurotic drainage, inaction or inappropriate action is the rule.

THE CONDITIONS OF SUCCESS
AND FAILURE

The trait-and-factor approach appears to have the greatest contribution to make in the counseling and/or assigning of those who could not otherwise make necessary choices. *Thus with mentally or emotionally disabled (level 1) or with physically disabled persons, vocational assessment and assignment would appear to be most efficacious.* The relevant dimensions of the person and the job may be assessed and the man may be matched to the job or the job to the man. Assignments making maximum use of human and vocational resources can be made accordingly.

Similarly, *vocational and educational counseling, in turn, would appear to be most effective with the level 2 individual who is hampered by obstacles and is unable to make necessary life choices.* Counseling can clear away the obstacles or, at a minimum, give the client a clear perspective on the obstacles involved and a probability statement on his or her success or failure in action. Hopefully, appropriate choices will free the individual to function at higher levels.

However, although it may free the individual to function at higher levels, *the trait-and-factor approach appears to be least effective in the assigning or counseling of higher-level functioning persons.* Thus, persons functioning above level 3 are already self-sustaining and facilitative of the efforts of others as well as their own. They are capable of making their own choices, vocational as well as marital. The choices they make are appropriate for them and independent of actuarial tables. Often their choices can be made and directionality can be found only by denying most of their previous experiences in life.

There are more broad implications of the use of the trait-and-factor approach:

1. The reliance on normative data encourages passivity on the part of the client and the counselor.

There is an implicit and often explicit distrust of impulses and feelings. Decisions based on the best available facts, without a deep level of personal involvement, absolve both the client and counselor of some vital level of responsibility. Both learn to trust outside sources of information more than they trust their own experiencing of the world. With this set, only minimum personal change is possible.

2. The trait-and-factor approach reinforces the client's identity as an object or commodity.

The client is related to as a potential source of productivity valued by society, and his worth weighted in terms of occupational, economic, and educational levels. In order to depersonalize counseling to this degree, the counselor must see himself or herself as a commodity.

3. Measuring job satisfaction in terms of norms is absurd.

This leaves little or no room for the possibility that the average is miserable; the extremes often serve as the impetus for change. But to rely on a norm table to determine something as personal and unique as satisfaction is even more absurd.

4. The extended hope is a regulated world with data on everyone and every job.

Where does new data come from? One often does not creatively understand the game while playing it.

5. The trait-and-factor approach has done little to understand the individual's frame of reference, and as a consequence, has failed to operationalize subjective experience for the individual.

Because the trait-and-factor counselor lacks responsive skills, the main source of the input he receives is "objective" tests. The counselor lacks the input contributed directly from the client to the counselor; as a consequence, the counselor's behavior is minimally shaped by the feedback the counselor receives from the client.

6. The trait-and-factor approach is most often geared toward attempting to systematically narrow choices before systematically expanding choices.

Within this framework, the client is often denied experiences and alternatives as well as information he or she needs in order to define goals and develop steps to achieve those goals.

7. Once goals are selected, the trait-and-factor counselor does little to develop career-preparation programs that

give the client the skills necessary to attain, and retain, employment.

In addition, the counselor does not help the client to learn the skills necessary for the client to be promoted within the client's chosen areas of work. The lack of such preparation should be, but never is, considered when interpreting the trait-and-factor counselor's probability statements about the success or failure of various alternative career choices. The irony is that this approach may be best equipped to develop such programs, but has not done so.

8. The trait-and-factor counselor does little or nothing to help the client develop transferable strategies.

How to obtain, select, interpret, and use information for decision-making can translate to methods that are useful in all areas of life, including the emotional and intellectual in addition to career development.

9. The strategies employed by the trait-and-factor system to organize large volumes of data so that the data can be rendered useful for hypothesis testing as well as helping provide the first steps toward model building.

The identification of fundamental and essential ingredients of complex behaviors, such as decision-making, often provides the basic dimensions of models employed to understand and predict such complex behavior.

10. The methods and logic of trait-and-factor strategies has provided the roots of modern computer-based management information systems in human services.

In addition, such strategies could be expanded to provide the necessary ingredients for answering questions about cost effectiveness in the helping professions, as demonstrated by the human- and computer-based guidance systems developed by Carkhuff and Friel (1974).

SUMMARY AND CONCLUSIONS

Any system geared to operating in terms of norms tends, over time, to neutralize itself to such an extent that real change is extremely difficult. Creating within these limits is not possible. Such a system does, however, lead to results that are socially acceptable at the moment simply because they upset nothing.

The fact that the system restricts certain behaviors (affective and physical) is perfectly consistent with the dominant middle-class values.

In addition to assuming a deterministic-empirical base, the trait-and-factor approach to counseling places great emphasis on factors of heredity. This further reduces the possibility for change and justifies ignoring motivation, energy levels, and dominating neurotic needs. *If nothing else changes, man does change, not only within his life span but over the span of modern history.* Man's day-to-day behaviors have become increasingly more moderate, or at least more subtle. In times of crises his behaviors are more indirectly violent (war, nuclear arms). The polite, quiet, conforming child is often the one who shocks his community with some violent act.

The assumed causes of behavior naturally lead to the question of what is to be done to change behavior. Thus we find the trait-and-factor counselor creating and collecting more and more descriptive knowledge. He shares his knowledge and can do so at a great personal distance from his clients. His clients, like himself, can change only very little beyond the natural influences of hereditary factors in their life span.

In summary, there are many general points to be made about the contribution and potential of the logical and reasoned methods of this approach:

1. The trait-and-factor approach deals with the larger issues and goals of life related to learning and working; the issues most other approaches avoid.

2. The trait-and-factor approach develops strategies to obtain information about achieving substantive goals that can make a real difference for the individual.

3. Although the approach leaves out important sources of information, it is the only traditional approach that has tested, over long periods of time with very large numbers, the reliability and validity of its techniques and tools.

4. Although the trait-and-factor approach leaves little room for a truly impactful environment, its contributors have done much to identify a broad spectrum of environmental factors that influence or should influence rational decision-making.

5. Although the trait-and-factor approach has had difficulty with its efforts to operationalize human values, it has come closer to doing so than any other traditional approach to helping.

6. From a technical point of view, the trait-and-factor approach may require the greatest amount of training and education.

The organization, understanding, and use of relevant human–resource-development data requires training in the social, economic, mathematical, and computer sciences.

7. The trait-and-factor approach was the first organized and selectively effective attempt to integrate the physical, emotional, intellectual, and contextual ingredients of career achievement.

The approach directly and indirectly raised these basic considerations of interacting physical, emotional, and intellectual factors for human and educational achievement as well. The effective trait-and-factor counselor most usually equips his or her clients with at least crude programs for using information to achieve individual goals.

8. Perhaps most important, the trait-and-factor approach contains many of the roots of rational and just human resource development if it expands to include skills to obtain more input from the client's frame of reference (Carkhuff, 1972, 1973, 1974).

9. The built-in questions of accountability in making predictions perhaps qualify the trait-and-factor approach as the most ethical of all traditional helping approaches.

If employed with great success on a large scale, trait-and-factor counseling would produce, in each generation, an army of determined people who follow or live in reaction to free people. The free person, in turn, is able to disregard his or her total life history and live life independently of norms.

Confirmation of existence can be obtained only from a physical and affective base, not at a distance through a complex web of logic alone.

In summary, the trait-and-factor approach is a systematic effort to make an observable difference for purely logical reasons.

REFERENCES

CAPLOW, T. *The sociology of work.* Minneapolis: University of Minnesota Press, 1954.

CARKHUFF, R. R. *The art of helping.* Amherst, Massachusetts: Human Resource Development Press, 1972.

CARKHUFF, R. R. *The art of problem solving.* Amherst, Massachusetts: Human Resource Development Press, 1973.

CARKHUFF, R. R. *How to help yourself: The art of program development.* Amherst, Massachusetts: Human Resource Development Press, 1974.

CARKHUFF, R. R., & FRIEL, T. W. *The art of developing a career: Helper's guide.* Amherst, Massachusetts: Human Resource Development Press, 1974.

DARLEY, J. G., & HAGENAH, T. *Vocational interest measurement: Theory and practice,* Minneapolis: University of Minnesota Press, 1955.

GINZBERG, E., GINSBURG, S. W., AXELRAD, S., & HERMA, J. L. *Occupational choice.* New York: Columbia University Press, 1951.

HOLLAND, J. L. Some explorations of a theory of vocational choice: I. One- and two-year longitudinal studies. *Psychological Monographs,* 1962, *76,* No. 26 (whole No. 545).

HOPPOCK, R. *Occupational information.* New York: McGraw-Hill, 1957.

PARSONS, F. *Choosing a vocation.* Boston: Houghton Mifflin, 1909.

ROE, A. *The psychology of occupations.* New York: Wiley, 1956.

SHARTLE, C. L. *Occupational information.* New York: Prentice-Hall, 1946.

STRONG, E. K., JR. *Vocational interests 18 years after college.* Minneapolis: University of Minnesota Press, 1955.

STRONG, E. K., JR. *Vocational interests of men and women.* Stanford, California: Stanford University Press, 1943.

SUPER, D. E. *Appraising vocational fitness.* New York: Harper & Row, 1949.

SUPER, D. E. *The psychology of careers.* New York: Harper & Row, 1957.

TIEDEMAN, D. V., O'HARA, R. P., & BARUCH, R. W. *Career development: Choice and adjustment.* Princeton, New Jersey: College Entrance Examination Board, 1963.

TYLER, L. *The work of the counselor.* New York: Appleton, 1953.

8

... there is no significant
learning without action.

To Act or Not to Act

The Unique Contributions of
Behavior Modification Approaches

To the extent that therapy does not translate itself into action in life, it is not therapeutic. All counselors and therapists should serve to alter the overt real-life behavior of their client. However, most counselors do not, in fact, focus upon manifest behavior.

Counselors and clinicians have, for too long, settled for apparent insight as the criterion for success, with little or no concern for the behavior of the patient outside of or following therapy. Perhaps most significant, the complexity of our abtsractions and their vague implications for therapeutic treatment are so far removed from behavior and life that assessing efficacy takes the form of crude judgments based upon modification of hypothetical dynamics. The dynamic, living, behaving person is lost in the labels.

It is ironic that the behaviorists, those who lay no direct claim to a cohesive therapy or complete therapy program, focus our attention upon the patient's real life behavior; and they do so without the need or the concern for the "inner person"! *Behavior modification for the benefit of the patient is the primary goal.*

Since Watson (1916), it has only been a matter of time before learning principles would be applied to helping problems. Learning theory and research has, for some time now, dominated the academic scene in general and psychology in particular. Since World War II the prominence of the applied clinician at the university has been on the decline. The teaching of behavior modification techniques ensures the clinical professor of academic respectability even though he or she may not employ them in his or her work with patients or may not even work with patients at all. Applicants with scientific talent and inclinations are more favored for admission into graduate counseling and clinical programs. *There is no doubt that therapeutic techniques first formulated in the experimental laboratory will become increasingly acceptable to this future generation of therapists.*

BEHAVIOR MODIFICATION

Since the principles of learning and the field of learning theory itself are attempts to account for the acquisition, performance, and extinction of behavior, and since psychotherapy itself is truly a process of inducing behavioral change, it is natural enough that these principles of learning be applied to the explication of the therapeutic process. The behavioristic approach, in general, holds that psychotherapy is a learning process or a complex of learning processes. Stripped to its essentials, this "tough-minded" stance assumes (1) that psychotherapy is a lawful and directive process which can be investigated most economically within a learning-theory framework, and (2) that the variables which effect psychotherapy are essentially the same as those in other interpersonal situations, involving reinforcement, extinction acquisition, and other constructs. In addition, the behaviorists insist upon the application of empirical procedures to theory building.

The behaviorists have split into two schools of thought on the issue of behavior control. There are those who advocate certain techniques "derived" from learning theory and emphasizing conditioning procedures based upon classical (Eysenck, 1960; Salter, 1961; Wolpe, 1958) or instrumental (Bandura, 1961; Frank, 1961; Krasner & Ullmann, 1965; Salzinger, 1959; Shaw, 1961; Ullmann & Krasner, 1965) learning. These theorists, as well as others employing directive forms of control and impersonal manipulations of primary drives, have put the therapist back in therapy but have focused upon the therapist as the manipulator and controller of the therapy situation. The therapist is thus seen as a programmed therapy machine or computer that administers specified reinforcement schedules to the response system of a machinelike patient.

Murray's (1963) "biotropic" designation (as contrasted with his "sociotropic" stance) has been appropriately applied to this group of theorists who emphasize constitutional and genetic factors as relevant variables in psychotherapeutic personality change. They focus upon considerations such as innate differences in client "conditionability" as ultimate causal factors in psychopathology. Also, there is a tendency for the biotropic group to view pathology with an implicit disease orientation, where symptoms are characterized as "bad" things that, therefore, must be extinguished or eliminated. They reject the more "tender-minded" view of symptoms as motivated responses serving some life function of the client.

At no point are the "biotropes" further apart from their "sociotropic" brethren than in their rejection of the basic views and evolutionary tendencies of dynamic psychology and in their concomitant de-emphasis of the therapeutic relationship itself as the "something more" of the psychotherapy process.

Miller (1959) and Murray (1963), with their historical antecedents in Dollard and Miller (1950), Mowrer (1953), and Shaffer and Lazarus (1952), have attempted to incorporate the more "tender-minded" view of psychotherapy within the framework of learning or social reinforcement theory. Their attempts, however, have been theoretically limited since they tend only to translate therapy as we know it today into learning theory terminology without really offering anything new. They have been accused of simply translating the form without in any way altering the substance. They have attempted to fit the process of psychotherapy into traditional learning theory by liberalizing the stimulus–response (S–R) concepts to include more functional definitions of S and R (Miller, 1959).

Only the behavior therapists, among learning theorists, have been concerned with exactly how the patient learns. Most often, these approaches make operational only a few principles to the exclusion of others. While the "sociotropes" focus upon the translation of the more traditional, psychoanalytically oriented therapy into the terms of (1) the extinction of inappropriate affective responses and (2) discrimination learning due to the distinctive cues of traditional interpretations that label behavior, the other behavior approaches directly emphasize techniques derived from learning theory and focus upon overt or public behavior. Thus the Wolpe-Eysenck school makes extensive use of counterconditioning with the assumption that neurosis consists of systems of maladaptive, learned habits which can be ameliorated only by a reverse learning process involving the active induction of antagonistic responses, usually of an assertive, relaxing, or sexual nature. The instrumental school is oriented toward the acquisition of new behavior and emphasizes systematic, simple, primary and secondary reinforcement in a variety of forms to teach or "share" new responses to situations and cues.

Krasner and Ullmann (1965) spell out three major initial questions for the behavior therapist: (1) "What behavior is maladaptive and with what frequency does it occur?" (a question that enables the therapist to distinguish between behaviors that need to be enhanced and those that need to be extinguished); (2) "What aspects of the situation or environment are supporting and maintaining the symptom?" (that is, what events in the life of the client may reduce the chance that normal or healthy responses can be elicited by the client?); and (3) "What situational or environmental events are amenable to manipulation?" Again, it is important to note that there is no assumption concerning pathological processes in the client and no employment of the usual diagnostic categories and techniques. Indeed, and to the consternation of the psychoanalysts, the ignorance of inner dynamics did not lead to symptom substitution (Wolpe, Salter, & Reyna, 1964)!

The means of understanding maladaptive or pathological behavior depart sharply from the more traditional clinical systems. The behavior modification approach classifies abnormal behavior into four major categories (Krasner & Ullmann, 1965): (1) *behavior deficits,* as characterized by the catatonic or autistic child; (2) *surplus or inappropriate behaviors,* such as repetitive behaviors that require no apparent reinforcement and that describe many acute psychotics; (3) *improper stimulus control,* illustrated by psychosomatic illnesses and enuresis; and (4) *inadequate reinforcing systems,* where normal reinforcers are lacking or have been replaced by damaging reinforcers such as drugs.

Obviously, the manner in which the behavior therapist explains behavior dictates the way he or she treats it. Whatever the specific technique employed, the behavior therapist attempts to effect change by manipulating conditions systematically in the therapy hour and/or in the social-physical environment between therapy sessions. Thus Bachrach, Erwin, and Mohr (1963) successfully treated anorexia by "shaping" patient behavior so that appropriate responses were made to food employed as a secondary reinforcer. Using the same basic approach but employing physical rewards, Lovaas (1964) treated autistic children. Ayllon and Haughton (1962) treated a fastidious female by spilling food on the patient whenever she did not eat. The patient could avoid this aversive stimulus only when she ate. Other clinical problems have been handled by the use of negative practice (Yates, 1958) and various other forms of extinction (Williams, 1959) and by counterconditioning procedures (Lazovik & Lang, 1960).

The behavior therapist has at his disposal a wide variety of learning principles. The creative therapist of any stance has, to some degree, employed behavior modification techniques without identifying them as such. More than likely, his use of the procedures is not very systematic, and he may very well miss opportunities for their effective employment.

As a preferred mode of treatment (for clinicians of any system) behavior therapy offers the following sample of modification principles dervied from classical conditioning: (1) counter-conditioning; (2) direct conditioning; (3) reciprocal inhibition; and (4) extinction. Instrumental conditioning yields procedures based upon (1) shaping by the successive reinforcement of small segments of desired behavior; (2) direct manipulation of the social-physical environment; (3) punishment; and (4) omission learning.

The behavior therapist must be willing to dictate the procedures and direction of therapy. The client influences the process only with his or her responses to treatment. Client feedback enables the therapist to assess the efficacy of what he or she is professing to do. The client is not a thinking, feeling, valuing person; he or she is, however, a behaving, acting organism, subject to the influence and impact of any interaction with the present environment. The therapist can act upon the client only from the outside with the use of rewards, punishments, and the various other behavior-modification techniques leading to the possible alleviation of symptoms.

As the research literature related to learning grows, so will the boundaries of behavior therapy. The direct linkage to a basic area of psychology is perhaps the most distinct advantage of the behavior modification stance (Wolpe, Salter, & Reyna, 1965).

HISTORICAL CREDITS

The scientific respectability of the application of learning theory principles to problems of behavior modification dates back to the beginning of the twentieth century and, in this sense, behavior therapy may indeed be considered a traditional approach. Unlike psychoanalytic theory and client-centered counseling, however, the learning approach is not dependent upon other disciplines and does not deal with philosophical issues such as whether or not man is basically good or evil. The turning away from the mysteries of the "inner" man and the focus on overt, public behavior freed the behavior therapist from the necessity for abstract speculation. Thus a concentration of effort bringing together explanations of behavior and the means of changing that behavior became possible. In other systems, it is difficult if not impossible to see the relationship between the theory and the technique. The behaviorists' direct translation from theory to technique has forced other orientations to re-examine their stances, attempt operational definitions of constructs, assess outcomes, and consider giving up the vestigial appendages of assumption and practice. These efforts on both sides may lead to statements of theory and practice that are more direct, simple, and more easily incorporated by the trainee-therapist and better understood by the client. Learning theory translations to the practice of therapy may provide society at long last with a language about adaptive and maladaptive behavior that it can understand, use, and verify.

By bridging the gap between clinical practice and the experimental laboratory, behavior modification techniques have accomplished more than encouraging communication between hitherto separate camps in psychology. This growing alliance has, for the first time, built into therapy checks on the utility of the techniques employed at all critical stages and clearly defined goals and outcomes. The commitment to do what works, to innovate, to assess efficacy, and to re-examine assumptions directly are indeed major contributions. There is less chance of explaining away failures in terms of client resistance or a lack of readiness for treatment. When the data do not fit the theory, the behavior therapist is more apt to re-examine his or her assumptions while others summarily dismiss or broaden their theory to explain away the phenomena.

The observation that the role and responsibilities of the therapist are well defined, at least within the limits of the theory and data, is compelling. In addition, for the first time the role of the client is well defined. Although often a passive recipient of the techniques, he or she is well informed about the procedures and goals. There is no burden of introspections, free associations, or learning an obtuse and abstract language. He or she need only share with his or her therapist that material which allows for an understanding of symptoms and the formulation of manipulative techniques. Although the therapist has principal responsibility, the client is the major focus of attention, with little regard for social values, parental influence, and unconscious processes. To their credit, *the behavior modification therapists are the first to share with their patients a detailed explanation of what is being done and what will be done at each stage of the treatment process.*

The apparent simplicity and directness of the behaviorists challenged therapists of other orientations to focus on the measurable and observable. In other systems, it is really quite impossible for the client to "win," in that all or any aspect of his or her behavior can be explained or explained away in terms of his or her dynamics. *With behavior modification techniques, either the symptom dissipates or it does not.*

The supporters of the behavior approach, quite unlike their clinical counterparts, make no broad claim to being able to manipulate or change all maladaptive behavior. However, they accept the challenge to extend their treatment boundaries—often with clinical problems others would not and have not touched.

The specificity of procedures and the direct statement of the rationale lend a strong base, hitherto unknown, for therapist confidence. The therapist is not "on the line" as a person and needs no personal treatment prior to implementing these techniques. He is, during the course of treatment, a technician. Although there is recognition of the fact that the behavior therapist must become in some way a potent reinforcer, it is believed that he need not be functioning at high levels himself nor must he necessarily be deeply involved personally with the client. However, there is a growing recognition by some that the therapist's emergence as a potent reinforcer is a function of his interacting at high levels of interpersonal dimensions.

In most systems of counseling and psychotherapy, understanding and communication among clinicians and modifications of theory rely heavily upon constructs used to describe the psychodynamic life of the patient. In turn, psychodynamic structure depends upon or relates to the uncoverings of psychodiagnostics. The behavior modification approach has no need for either and has demonstrated effective behavior change without deep or detailed knowledge of or interest in psychodynamics or diagnostic categories. Related to this are the relatively large number of apparently dramatic cures within a short time span of treatment; demonstrations that are lacking in other systems.

From another vantage point, this approach has opened a

rather basic and usable means for exploring and implementing social engineering by the use of systematic alteration and manipulation of the physical and social environment.

The most unique historical credits, however, center around the promise of a timely, systematic approach to behavior change and the use of a minimum number of constructs to describe behavior change.

In summary, the historical contributions of behavior modification techniques are many. In addition to tapping the roots and contributions of learning theory, the explicit search for translations to life, freeing helpers of excess theoretical and mystical baggage, are among the most valued. The commitment to implementing and incorporating what works puts the system "on the line" without employing client defenses as an explanation for failure.

Finally, perhaps the most vital message is that *there is no significant learning without action.*

THE UNIQUE CONTRIBUTIONS

The unique contributions of the behavior modification approach center around (1) the clear and relatively systematic direction it gives to treatment, (2) the well-defined criteria for outcome, and (3) the capacity for offering real hope for some of the most neglected patient populations.

When the behavior therapist provides appropriate levels of facilitative conditions, this approach appears to make the following unique contributions above and beyond contributions accounted for by high levels of those conditions.

PROCESS CONTRIBUTIONS TO THE CLIENT

1. The behavior modification approach provides the client with an understanding of the treatment process and his or her role.

The direction and implementation of techniques and roles are shared with the patient and, to that extent, the patient is a part of the process.

2. The behavior modification approach provides the client with concrete information about his or her level of progress in therapy.

The client is aware at every stage of the extent to which his or her symptoms have been extinguished. It is therefore possible that the client is also aware of the duration of treatment, which most often is relatively short.

3. The behavior modification approach provides the client with a useful knowledge of the history of the reinforcements that have created and sustained his or her symptoms.

The use of learning theory constructs to explain the development of a symptom is likely to be more easily understood and accepted by the patient than are explanations rooted in dynamic theory. Most people have some rudimentary knowledge or intuitive understanding of learning principles, which simplifies the complexity of mental illness.

4. The behavior modification approach provides the client with knowledge that the therapist is guided by client feedback insofar as it fits the therapist's system.

The client in this sense has an awareness that his or her response to treatment does have an influence on the process and the use of techniques. That is, he or she can influence the therapeutic process.

5. The behavior modification approach provides the client with an opportunity to actively accelerate the treatment process.

By translating therapy gains into life between sessions and practicing (relaxation, assertion, and so on), the client may materially contribute to the symptom amelioration. In addition, the client is forced to try out new modes of functioning with some minimal level of confidence.

6. The behavior modification approach provides the client with an opportunity to deal with maladaptive autonomic functions.

Behavior therapy is the only psychotherapeutic system other than hypnosis that deals directly with autonomic dysfunction.

7. The behavior modification approach provides the client

with the assurance that the treatment process is geared to "curing" what it sets out to "cure."
In expressing the goals of therapy clearly, the client is assured that the procedures will not get sidetracked or uncover some conditions the client deems private or adaptive.

PROCESS CONTRIBUTIONS TO THE THERAPIST

1. The behavior modification approach provides the therapist with a system of well-defined procedures.

Well-defined procedures enable the therapist to spend less energy and time in trial-and-error behavior.

2. The behavior modification approach provides the therapist with a well-defined role.

The therapist's role is explicit, his goals clear and well understood. Role definition further provides the therapist with a direct relationship between diagnosis and differential treatment and with a full and less ambiguous awareness of his responsibility to the client.

3. The behavior modification approach provides the therapist with a high and extremely useful level of confidence.

The specificity of techniques and the focus on symptoms rather than dynamics provide the therapist with a knowledge of what he or she is doing—a knowledge unmatched in other systems and undoubtedly reflected in client benefits.

4. The behavior modification approach provides the therapist with the opportunity to become meaningfully involved beyond the therapy hour.

The therapist is free and is encouraged to act between sessions. He or she may, for example, manipulate the social and/or physical environment or rework therapeutic techniques and the sequence of treatment.

5. The behavior modification approach provides the therapist with an opportunity to look for translations from therapy to life.

The therapist searches out and explicitly encourages meaningful and direct actions to be taken by the client in his or her real-life situation.

> 6. The behavior modification approach may be implemented by a reasonably well functioning person.

The implementation of many of the techniques does not require a high level of knowledge or talent and, thus, lay practitioners may be trained to employ them effectively.

> 7. The behavior modification approach eliminates the transference/countertransference neurosis.

The therapist not functioning effectively himself need not fear that his neurotic needs will damage the treatment process.

> 8. The behavior modification approach encourages the therapist to attend fully to nonverbal cues.

By focusing on all public and overt behavior, the therapist has a larger and broader base of client behavior to observe, discriminate, and evaluate. He or she is not limited to the complex meanings of client verbal expressions.

> 9. The behavior modification approach provides the therapist with a specific (behavioral) base for understanding behavior after the fact (post hoc), thus increasing his level of confidence for the next encounter with the patient and with other patients with similar symptomatology.

The specificity of learning theory encourages direct modification of techniques toward a higher level of efficacy, thus providing a high level of learning and communication. As such, the orientation taps a ready source of data for the growth and expansion of the therapeutic system.

> 10. The behavior modification approach gives the therapist an opportunity to fill the behavior vacuum with adaptive behavior.

The therapist can, if creative enough and willing to assume the responsibility, enhance the client's chances to realize a more full life by conditioning or suggesting behaviors to take the place of extinguished symptoms.

THE LIMITATIONS OF THE BEHAVIOR MODIFICATION APPROACH

Any broad statement about the limitations of the behavior modification approach surprisingly resembles that made about the client-centered approach; that is, most of the limitations center around the therapist's inability to employ himself or herself fully and the inability of the client to do the same.

PROCESS LIMITATIONS FOR THE CLIENT

1. The behavior modification approach cannot work effectively with clients who are unable to emit public cues.

With the absence of the overt behaviors necessary to identify treatable symptoms, an appropriate and economical set of procedures and the frequent evaluations of their efficacy that typify the behavioral approach will be difficult.

2. The behavior modification approach limits the extent of client gain whenever the client's feedback goes beyond the scope of the rigorous system.

The therapist in reality is not influenced by the client's responses that carry the therapist away from his or her specific orientation and techniques.

3. The behavior modification approach is geared to a minimal coping with the world.

The approach is not geared to go beyond the fundamental relief of symptomatology. In many instances it brings the client only to the point where he or she can maintain a marginal tolerance for life.

4. The behavior modification approach drains the therapy experience of all creativity for the client.

The experience of *creatively* participating in opening new experiential frontiers is denied so that the probability of the client meeting the demands of living more creatively is likely to be very little greater than it was before therapy.

5. The behavior modification approach can set the stage for aversive conditioning.

The danger of aversive conditioning is always present. Without adequate client feedback the danger is very likely to become a reality.

6. The behavior modification approach does not provide the client with the experience and conditions for self-fulfillment or self-actualization.

The basic and only aim is rehabilitative. The basic conditioning techniques alleviate some degree of suffering; but a rich awareness, discriminations, and a full life are not products of these techniques. If a cosmology is developed, it has its roots in a deterministic stance and a predictable future. There is reason to believe that those functioning at levels 3 and 4 would not be subject to the same rewards and punishments and are likely not to be predictable. Left with only the devices of conditioning procedures, the client can reach only level 2 or 2.5.

7. The behavior modification approach may promote client complacency with problems once symptoms have been successfully controlled or extinguished.

The voluntary control of anxious feelings or the capacity to relax selected parts of the body, when inappropriately employed by the client, may be more maladaptive than the effect of the treated symptom.

8. The behavior modification approach encourages the client to externalize or depersonalize his or her psychopathology.

Rather than reaching some level of functioning when he can assume some responsibility for his actions, the client is free to live life passively, ready to be conditioned to a new fear or to take on psychopathic and manipulative modes of social interaction. With treatment, the client's concomitant learning leads him, in his crisis moments, to be repetitiously dependent upon men and means that are often highly impersonal and mechanistic.

PROCESS LIMITATIONS FOR THE THERAPIST

1. The behavior modification approach rests its success on the assumption that the therapist can become a potent reinforcer for the client.

The individual therapist's ability to acquire reinforcing value to clients varies widely. To have maximum impact, this approach must train or select potent reinforcers.

2. The behavior modification approach does not control for the faulty model or faulty schedule that a poor clinician might develop.

In the end, the employment of any system or system of techniques is dependent upon the skill and sensitivity of the clinician. A poor clinician might develop inappropriate goals and schedules for behavior modification.

3. The behavior modification approach sets up the danger of the therapist becoming aversively conditioned to behavior therapy itself.

Once the hierarchy and schedules are worked out, there is little or no challenge and considerable boredom. In its emphasis upon the present and the concrete, it limits the creative process of therapy.

4. The behavior modification approach limits the number of clients with whom the therapist can work.

It is very doubtful that any therapist could for any length of time work with even three or four desensitization cases per day.

5. The behavior modification approach does not allow the therapist to learn more about who he or she is.

With this approach, the theory and techniques, not the therapist, are "on the line." The degree of personal involvement is minimal beyond the initial contacts used to establish the therapist as a potent reinforcer. The system creates distance and exploits closeness only for potency in reinforcement.

6. The behavior modification approach may be destructively employed by a sick society.

A "1984" is possible.

THE CONDITIONS OF SUCCESS
AND FAILURE

The behavior modification approach focuses upon several conditions in which it can be employed most effectively. These conditions or problem areas are largely those avoided or inadequately understood by other systems. The specificity and emphasis on overt behavior and the knowledge that behavior can be modified with disregard for "inner" processes enable the behavior modification therapist to extend the boundaries of treatment efforts.

There is extensive evidence that behavior modification techniques are effective with level 1 patient populations. In order to make a minimal or self-sustaining adjustment, the patient for whom the communication process has broken down must eat, sleep, and attend to fundamental hygienic tasks. Verbal communication is frequently of no avail. Basic schedules designed to shape these behaviors have (1) relieved some custodial burdens and (2) readied the patient to regain contact with his or her body and immediate environment. At this later stage, verbal efforts or more traditional therapies can be employed or attempted.

In addition, there is evidence, both clinical and research, to indicate that behavior modification techniques are effective with level 2 or higher level clients exhibiting relatively isolated anxiety reactions. An acutely neurotic population may have the potential for more adequate levels of adjustment but for some obvious and restricting behavior. These patients, in addition to having distorted perceptions of themselves in relation to their environment, are often led to deeper degrees of deterioration as a function of inappropriate physical or social behavior or behaviors. In addition and with less frequency, behavioral approaches may alleviate the distress of higher-level functioning clients who have vestigial or isolated symptomatology that is no longer functional but that causes the person some degree of distress.

There are three additional conditions with more broad implications: (1) *behavior modification techniques are particularly well suited for use in experimental settings:* The techniques and constructs are easily operationally defined in the laboratory and inter- and intra-therapist variability can be reduced to a minimum; (2) *behavior modification techniques are well-suited for efforts to engineer social and physical environmental manipulations directly:* the system may point to specific aspects of the environment to change, often resulting in social and/or psychological changes in areas such as human engineering, communication, attitude change, social perception, judgments, and beliefs; (3) *the behavior modification approach may be most useful when there is an acute press for time:* we may simply not be able to attend to the therapy as a leisurely effort involving an indefinite long-term period.

In summary, the behavior modification approach appears most effective in shaping behavior essential to basic living in the most severely disabled populations or in less severely disabled populations with relatively isolated anxiety reactions. The behavior modification approach is most effective when the therapist can provide the necessary level of facilitative conditions establishing him or her as a potent reinforcer.

We can now examine the success and failure of behavior modification techniques by pulling together selected points made in other parts of this chapter. Several general statements can be presented.

1. Man is at the beginning a "blank slate" or *tabula rasa.* The behavior technique is not tied to any assumption about the basic nature of man. From this view, man has equal potentials for good and evil; once shaped by society, however, there is no possibility for individual action. Even creative acts are explained in terms of the creator being shaped, with no data to support or fit the learning model.

2. The behavior modification technique applied to therapy is enriching for learning theory.

Although the most dramatic success is obtained with level 1 patients or level 2 clients with isolated symptomatology, there is no evidence or claim from this approach that the client can go on to take his or her own steps toward high levels of self-actualization. This therapy, however, affords the behaviorist a wide field in which to extend his constructs and to reformulate techniques for manipulating behavior and theoretical assumptions.

3. Behavior modification techniques aim at behavior change.

This provides the therapist operating within this system specific and concrete criteria with which to evaluate the progress of therapy. It also frees him of mystical or ambiguous assumptions about the "inner" man typically used by other systems to support their successes or explain away their failures.

4. The behavior modification system puts the therapist back into the therapy process with great emphasis.

The behavior modification therapist assumes considerable apparent responsibility for the success or failure of his therapy. The
theory or techniques, however, are more basically the cause of
success or failure. The therapist as a person is absolved of *total*
responsibility.

       5. There is a behavior vacuum left by the extinguished
          symptom.

True success or long-term success of this system may depend
upon the therapist taking the responsibility to fill this vacuum
with constructive behaviors.

       6. The specificity and systematic base of behavior ther-
          apy reduces ambiguity.

The reduction of anxiety is greatly dependent upon the reduction
of ambiguity, and this may be the major source of variability
accounting for the large number of success cases.

       7. Clients functioning at relatively high levels are left
          wanting.

The very deterministic base of this system allows for only a
narrow view of creative living. The client seeking substantive
meaning to his life, a cosmology, or a deeper experiential base
cannot rely on another "determined" man.

       8. Behavior modification makes the helper aware that
          systematic programs make a difference but does not
          always enable the helper to see his contribution as
          both agent and model.

The helper, acting only as a technician, is unaware of his or her
impact as a model. In addition, there is little to encourage helpers
to do things about their personal growth.

       9. Behavior modification fails to pinpoint the variance
          attributable to the contributions of effective people
          and/or the behavior modification programs.

The failure to pinpoint variance attributable to the contributions
of people, programs, and their interactions limits the potential
contributor of any approach.

      10. Behavior modification attempts to focus only on what
          is relevant for achieving a behavioral goal.

The role of the behavior therapist is a technical one relatively
free of personal values. This lack of full response to personal

values limits the areas of life the helper can respond to, thus limiting input and his or her techniques.

11. Attempts to respond to the helpee's frame of reference by behavior therapists do not make a difference in technique.

The behavior therapists attempt low-level reflections that fail to personalize communication, then go about doing what they would have done had they never attempted to respond to the helpee's frame of reference in the first place.

12. The behavior modification approach does not provide the client or the helper with the responses and skills necessary to develop transferable strategies.

By limiting helping to a specific stimulus complex and to conditioning techniques, the client and the helper may elicit conditioned responses only to those stimuli closely related to the original stimulus.

13. Behavior modification does little or nothing to help the therapist and the client to personalize goals and to initiate behaviors to achieve personal goals.

The limited responsive skills (and the resulting limited input) of the behavior therapist encourage working with generalizations while seeming to attend only to details.

14. The rights and responsibilities of a technical role are very limited.

Without a full set of responsive skills employed throughout the helping process, the helper cannot integrate human values with his or her technology. The focus is technique rather than human benefit.

15. Acting upon personalized goals is impossible.

The fact of conditioning excludes choice and personal direction.

SUMMARY AND CONCLUSIONS

The success or failure of the behavior modification approach to therapy may depend largely upon therapist confidence and the selection of patients functioning as level 1 or level 2 clients with isolated symptomatology. Beyond this we need to raise a number of questions not as yet fully researched or explored.

1. The behavior therapist assumes that he can become a potent reinforcer with the use of some stereotyped procedures which often resemble client-centered techniques.

Basically, this assumption states that the impersonal acting out of a role can be more effective in establishing the therapist as a potent reinforcer than a personal and genuine caring and understanding. We would strongly suggest that a genuinely warm, empathic counselor, not fixed with a calculating, impersonal mask of understanding, would establish himself as a more significantly potent reinforcer.

2. The deterministic position of the behavior modification approach to therapy can be reduced to an existential stance.

As the behavior therapist looks out upon the world, he sees both himself and the client as having been determined. However, *his very act of viewing the world is existential in nature since it describes the viewer's immediate phenomenology.* Just as the existentialist views himself as a free and creative person who chooses "systems," so it is inconceivable to the behaviorist that he could choose. He views himself as having to fit into a system (Carkhuff, 1967).

3. The deterministic stance leaves room for only apparent responsibility on the part of the therapist as well as the client.

The lives of level 1 and 2 clients and the behavior therapist are determined and, within this framework, avoid all real-life responsibility. In behavior therapy the therapist starts with this basic stance: "His life and my life are both determined." It follows that it is difficult to understand who is on who's schedule of reinforcements. Both client and therapist are stimulus-bound. A man who accepts that his life is determined cannot hold himself to be responsible and cannot meet real responsibility. Those functioning at the highest levels live lives that are not predictable. Those people functioning at high levels are both free and responsible.

4. The question remains as to whether or not behavior modification techniques can be employed to widen rather than narrow choices.

Shaping behavior connotes a smaller and smaller number of behavioral choices in the repertoire of the clients. Creative living requires a large pool of responses, not all of which are predictable.

> 5. Does systematic reinforcement lead to symptomatology? Do we need rigorous schedules to eliminate symptoms?

The client may be conditioned so that he or she is cut off from experiencing body tension when it is appropriate. This has far-reaching implications. The therapist, for example, may be aversively conditioned to the therapy situation itself as a function of boredom and the movement of the client's "pinky." Without appropriate bodily feedback, the client, like the therapist, is forced to fake spontaneity, even anger and fear.

> 6. Within this system random schedules allow the person the experience of freedom.

Random schedules at best create apparent freedom. They have nothing to do with the reality of freedom. The experience of freedom can be used to justify the use and abuse of conditioning techniques beyond the therapy setting. It is interesting to contemplate the implications this question has for child-rearing practices.

> 7. How much of the outcome variance can be accounted for by change and attention factors?

The full focus of attention is on the client. The Hawthorne effect or the effect of change or attention is especially likely since each client being seen is an "experimental case."

> 8. Behavior modification makes only a partial delivery to its clients.

Because of the rigid assumptions the behavior therapists make they maintain their ignorance by limiting their own experience to conditioning. The behavior therapist, like the psychoanalyst and existential helper, is a *highly resistent learner.*

> 9. Limited behavior modification is not systematically linked to the larger goals of living, learning, and working.

Limited behavioral goals are only the first steps toward assisting learners to acquire a large repertoire of the living, learning, and working skills needed to create new responses and new skills.

10. Behavior modification, its uses and abuses, renders logic a handicap by limiting its definition and the understanding of learning.

Narrow definitions lead to limited descriptions and manipulations of behavior because there is no built-in vehicle for expanding and improving techniques designed to increase the quality of input from the learner.

11. Systems that do not systematically improve their means to generate input from the learner will reduce personal responsibility.

Attributing all behavior to conditioning makes it impossible to hold any one person or any system responsible for anything. Even those who set the goals and the reinforcement schedules did so as a result of conditioning.

12. The behavior modification helper promises the potential to respond differently to stimuli without the freedom to choose whether to respond or not.

The entire system communicates a hopelessly contemptuous view of human nature as well as its own system when it calls what it does "therapy."

13. The reproduction of any behavior is limited by gradients of generalization based upon the characteristics of the original stimulus-response complex.

The reason most helpees are helpees is that they are products of such experiences rather than of experiences that begin with their experience and systematically equip them with the skills they need to develop transferable strategies for filling their physical, emotional, and intellectual needs and potential.

14. The helper, limited in technique and philosophy to conditioning, may be able to produce specific behaviors but very little learning.

15. Behavior modification as it is presently represented and formulated has nothing to do with learning.

It can readily be seen that not all the data fit the model. But the efficacy of behavior modification techniques has been demonstrated to a level where we are forced to consider social as well as individual goals. The hope for society is, however, in the nurture of creative, free people rather than those so cut off from their bodily experiences. In this regard, the reliance on verbal conditioning reinforcers such as "hmmm" seems now to be absurd.

The behavior modification approach is an outgrowth of our time and of a technical society. *If it is successful to the point of being the "wave of the future" for therapists and social engineers, it will become the next major social problem of our time.* Unless it is geared or coupled with other systems, it cannot hope to become free of low-level obstacles in order to enable the client (or society) to function at higher levels.

We will live in a land where there are only narrow choices and no real choices with regard to interpersonal functioning, creativity, spontaneity, love, and friendship. We will perform our roles and experience only apparent freedom and apparent satisfaction in an apparent world.

The contributions and development of behavior modification is limited by the behaviorist's failure to understand learning. "Learning involves the reproduction of behaviors *whenever* and *wherever* those behaviors are functional for the achievement of systematically developed, personally relevant goals (Carkhuff & Berenson, 1976)."

In summary, behavior modification is a systematic effort to make an observable difference without learning anything in the process.

REFERENCES

AYLLON, T., & HAUGHTON, E.   Control of the behavior of schizophrenic patients by food. *Journal of Experimental Analysis of Behavior,* 1962, *5,* 343–352.

BACHRACH, A. J., ERWIN, W. & MOHR, J. P.   The control of eating behavior in an anorexic by operant conditioning techniques. Unpublished manuscript, 1963.

BANDURA, A.   Psychotherapy as a learning process. *Psychological Bulletin,* 1961, *58,* 143–157.

CARKHUFF, R. R.   The contributions of a phenomenological approach to deterministic approaches to counseling and psychotherapy. *Journal of Counseling Pychology,* 1967, *14,* 570–571.

CARKHUFF, R. R., & BERENSON, B. G.   *Teaching as treatment.* Amherst, Massachusetts: Resource Development Press, 1976.

DOLLARD, J., & MILLER, N. E. *Personality and psychotherapy.* New York: McGraw-Hill, 1950.

EYSENCK, H. J. (Ed.) *Behavior therapy and the neuroses.* New York: Pergamon, 1960.

FRANK, J. D. *Persuasion and healing.* Baltimore: The Johns Hopkins Press, 1961.

KRASNER, L., & ULLMANN, L. *Research in behavior modification.* New York: Holt, Rinehart and Winston, 1965.

LAZOVIK, A. D., & LANG, P. J. A laboratory demonstration of systematic desensitization psychotherapy. *Journal of Psychological Studies,* 1960, *11,* 238–247.

LOVAAS, O. Clinical implications of relationships between verbal and nonverbal operant behavior. In H. J. Eysenck (Ed.), *Experiments in behavior therapy.* New York: Macmillan, 1964.

MILLER, N. E. Liberalization of basic S-R concepts: Extensions to conflict behavior, motivation and social learning. In S. Koch (Ed.), *Psychology: A study of a science* (Vol. II). New York: McGraw-Hill, 1959.

MOWRER, O. H. *Psychotherapy: Theory and research.* New York: Ronald, 1953.

MURRAY, E. J. Sociotropic-learning approach to psychotherapy. In P. Worshell & D. Burns (Eds.), *Personality change.* New York: Wiley, 1963.

SALTER, A. *Conditional reflex therapy.* New York: Capricorn, 1961.

SALZINGER, K. Experimental manipulation of verbal behavior: A review. *Journal of General Psychology,* 1959, *61,* 65–95.

SHAFFER, G. W., & LAZARUS, R. S. *Fundamental concepts in clinical psychology.* New York: McGraw-Hill, 1952.

SHAW, F. J. (Ed.) *Behavioristic approaches to counseling and psychotherapy.* University of Alabama Studies, 1961, No. 13.

ULLMANN, I., & KRASNER, L. *Case studies in behavior modification.* New York: Holt, Rinehart and Winston, 1965.

WATSON, J. B. Behaviorism and the concept of mental disease. *Journal of Philosophical Psychology,* 1916, *13,* 589–597.

WILLIAMS, C. C. The elimination of tantrum behavior by extinction procedures. *Journal of Abnormal and Social Psychology,* 1959, *59,* 269.

WOLPE, J. *Psychotherapy by reciprocal inhibition.* Stanford, California: Stanford University Press, 1958.

WOLPE, J., SALTER, A., & REYNA, L. *The conditioning therapies.* New York: Holt, Rinehart and Winston, 1964.

YATES, A. J. The application of learning theory to the treatment of tics. *Journal of Abnormal and Social Psychology,* 1958, *56,* 175–182.

section four

LIFE, DEATH, AND TOUCHING:
CLINICAL APPLICATIONS

How the core dimensions and the different treatment modalities operate in helping and life—for better or for worse—is a function of the levels of proficiency that helpers have achieved in their helping and specialty-area skills. This means acquiring the attending, responding, personalizing, and initiating skills that facilitate helpee movement through the phases of helping: exploration, understanding, and action. It means understanding the urgency with which these skills are applied: every step moves us as well as the helpees, in a very real sense, closer to life or death. It means making the helping experience fully honest and treating the helpees differently according to their unique needs. It means recognizing that helping is, indeed, a way of life.

PHASES OF HELPING

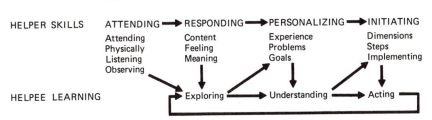

FIGURE IV   The application of helping skills leads to helpee change or gain.

*. . . the effective helper trusts the
known to enter the unknown.*

Beyond the Known

The Phases of Helping

Effective helping is possible. It depends upon many things (Cark-huff, 1969, 1972, 1973, 1974). Most important is the helper's ability to *respond* fully to the helpee's experience as well as the helper's ability to respond to his or her own experience. Responding only to what is presented by the helpee is not enough. The helper must be able to organize the resulting helping exploration to give the helping process direction. More specifically, the helper must make the process goal-directed. The helper's ability to appropriately *initiate* may be even more important than his or her ability to respond, in the sense that without initiating the helpee never gets to where he or she needs to be. Responding is critical to appropriate initiatives but by itself only facilitates the determination of where the helpee is. The determination of goals concerning where the helpee needs or wants to be, and getting there, wait upon helper initiatives.

Meaningful research in helping has remained in its infancy because of our inability to determine what is relevant to effective helping. In general, little if anything has been accomplished during the past decade to change this. Little has changed because we have yet to fully understand that the first goal of helping is to respond to the helpee's frame of reference in order to facilitate helpee exploration. The facilitation of exploration is not an end in itself and does not constitute a delivery to the helpee. It is, however, essential if goals are to be defined, changes are to take place, and the goals achieved.

All our statistical analyses, instruments of measurement, methodologies, and variations on basic conditioning techniques will not make a difference until we are able to train helpers to respond fully to the helpee's frame of reference. These responses need to be a great deal more than simple-minded reflections. The helper's ability to respond must take him fully enough into the helpee's experience, not only to facilitate helpee exploration but also to teach the helpee how to explore.

Providing helpees with high levels of conditions reflecting responding and initiating does result in three basic phases of helping that, over time, are recycled for new issues and increasingly more effective means of dealing with old issues. The "downward" phase establishes that the helper has attended well enough to listen and listened well enough to respond, at least at the level the helpee has presented himself or herself. The downward "phase," then, consists of better responses that facilitate helpee exploration. The "upward" phases consist of the helper's responses that personalize the helpee's experience in the form of relevant goals *and* the steps necessary to achieve those goals. During the early phase of helping the main objective is to engage the helpee in intensive and extensive exploration of himself or herself in relation to the problem situation. The main objectives during the middle and latter phases of helping are the determination of personalized helpee goals and the development of strategies to achieve them.

THE GOALS OF HELPING

The main helping vehicle to helpee exploration involves the helper's communication of high levels of responsiveness. It is important to note that responsiveness does not stop where initiative begins. The effective helper continues to be responsive throughout the helping process! The efficacy of helper initiatives is directly dependent upon the accuracy of his or her responding efforts. Responding skills initiate helping and serve to maintain helping on through the implementation of steps to achieve helpee goals. In addition, responding recycles exploration, understanding, and action.

The helper responds as often and for as long as it takes for the helpee to learn how to explore on his own. Her responses, when they contain feeling and meaning, elicit helpee behaviors that require additional helper responses. It is from this base that what is needed to give the process direction emerges in the "upward" phases of helping. It is from this base of helper responding and helpee exploration that the initiative or delivery aspects of helping emerge, first as goals and then as steps toward goals.

Helpee exploration is the cornerstone of what is needed for responding to where the helpee is. Helpee understanding is the cornerstone of what is needed for determining where the helpee wants or needs to be. The determination of where the helpee wants or needs to be is the cornerstone of developing steps to get the helper from where the helpee is to where the helpee wants or needs to be. Thus, responding *and* initiating yield understanding based upon exploration—understanding in terms of specific goals. The appropriateness of the goals is dependent upon the accuracy of the helper's responsiveness. The accuracy of the helper's responsiveness is dependent upon the helper's listening skills. The level of the helper's listening skills is dependent upon the helper's observation skills and the level of the helper's observation skills is dependent upon the helper's attending skills. Responding is more, much more, than a verbal exchange. Responding incorporates the complexities of attending: attending involves physical, emotional, and intellectual attending, observing, and listening.

The upward phases of helping—goal determination and developing steps to achieve goals—constitute initiative skills. Initiative skills make it possible for the helpee to act upon his or her world efficiently, effectively, and personally. The inability to act efficiently, effectively, and personally probably constitutes the reason(s) the helpee sought assistance in the first place. Helper *and* helpee action is based upon understanding.

The first goal of helping is helpee exploration.

The second goal of helping is helpee understanding.

The third goal of helping is helpee action.

Together, exploration, understanding, and action constitute the fourth goal of helping: helpee learning.

When helping is successful, the helpee learns what the effective helper can do: functionally blend a large repertoire of responsive and initiative skills in order to discover accurately what is needed to respond, personalize, and initiate steps to achieve goals. When this is learned, the helpee becomes a helper.

The outcomes of helping must be measured in terms of the growth or lack of growth of the client's repertoire of high-quality physical, emotional, and intellectual responses. It is this repertoire of high-quality physical, emotional, and intellectual responses that enables the client to relate to others effectively, learn effectively, and work effectively. *Exploration, understanding and action* are the dimensions of the learning process involved in acquiring new and effective responses.

The process of learning begins and ends with exploration, understanding, and action. The efficacy of any act depends upon its efficiency in achieving a goal or facilitating progress toward achieving a goal. Full understanding depends upon the degree to which goals can be operationalized so that they reflect personal needs and experience. The detailed definition of a goal and actions to achieve the goal rest on exploring fully where the learner starts. Learning can occur at higher and higher levels.

We may offer a set of propositions relating helper skills to the helping process.

Proposition: The responsive skills of the helper facilitate helpee exploration.

> *Helpee:* I don't think I can handle my daughter. She is only eight and she rules the house.
>
> *Helper:* You feel anxious because things are getting out of control.
>
> *Helpee:* They are out of control and I don't know what to do.
>
> *Helper:* It's a desperate feeling when you are not in control of your children or yourself.
>
> *Helpee:* I know it's me, nothing is right—home, the children—I feel stupid.
>
> *Helper:* You feel scared because you cannot handle things you were able to before.
>
> *Helpee:* It's like I used to be smart, now I'm dumb. Even the kids are smarter than I am.
>
> *Helper:* You're afraid for yourself and the children because you can't do what a mother should do.

The helper is communicating that she listened and understands at the level the helpee presented herself. The helpee began to examine the implications of her feelings—lack of control of self, home, children—and began to explore feelings of failure in her function as a parent. The introduction of mild helper initiative in the last helper response began to personalize the problem.

Proposition: The responsive and initiative skills of the helper facilitate helpee understanding.

> *Helpee:* That's it, I don't think—feel like a mother because my daughter runs me.
>
> *Helper:* You feel helpless because you can't help your daughter or yourself.
>
> *Helpee:* I should be able to. I've tried everything. I hold the children. I spank them. Sometimes I just give up and they know it and it gets worse.

Helper: You get to feel overwhelmed because you cannot find any way to get back on top.

Helpee: I'm not sure what else there is—maybe there is no answer—but there *has* to be.

Helper: You're terrified because you can't be the mother you desperately want to be.

Helpee: I do, I do want to be a good mother—it is up to me—but how?

The helper initiated to the level of personalizing the problem by focusing upon the helpee and her role as mother. The helper in addition looks at the "flip" side of the problem and takes the steps toward defining a personally relevant goal for the helpee: wanting to be a good mother. The helpee began to entertain the goal and looks for more concrete direction.

3) *Proposition:* The initiative and responsive skills of the helper facilitate helpee action.

Helper: You feel angry with yourself because you cannot be the mother you need to be but you want to be an effective mother.

Helpee: Oh, yes! Yes! It's been the most important thing in my life. That's why I work so hard—in the house—even in my school work—I try to learn things that will help at home. I need to start somewhere, and soon—perhaps with me.

Helper: You're impatient to get something going because time is running out. Your goal is to get back on top of being a good mother to your children. Perhaps the first steps involve getting yourself together.

Helpee: I think so—I'm so exhausted most of the time. I don't have the energy.

Helper: The first goal is to increase your energy and the first step here is to look at how much rest you get and then plan a rest program related to other factors that influence your energy level.

The helper not only initiated to define a first goal that has relevance for the helpee's problem but begins to focus on the development of steps to do something about achieving the goal. Steps to a goal make client action necessary.

Proposition: Over the period of helping, from exploration to action, the emphasis of helper-offered behaviors moves from responding to initiating.

> *Helpee:* I'm getting the rest I need but I'm still not on top of my kids.
>
> *Helper:* You're still anxious because the basic issues are not solved. It's time now we started to define some other goals—like how you want to relate to the children and how you want them to behave. Your first step here is for you to respond to them as I have responded to you. They need to know you can crawl into their world and see it as they do.
>
> *Helpee:* I know that is what you did with me. How do I start?
>
> *Helper:* You start by attending to them physically. When you speak to them or they to you, make eye contact and face them directly so they know you are attending to them.

The base of responding has been established. Goals have been defined and some goals achieved. The focus is on doing and acting systematically. The helpee learns to move from the simple to the complex because the helper initiates that way. Most importantly the helper initiatives are based upon her understanding of the helpee. The initiatives are relevant because they are personalized. There may be failures along the way and if they occur the effective helper recycles the process.

Proposition: Over the period of helping the helper will recycle the responding, responding plus initiating, and initiating plus responding process of helping many times.

> *Helpee:* I tried to teach the kids to respond to me like I have learned to respond to them, but it didn't work and I reverted back to my old ways.
>
> *Helper:* It was frustrating because the kids could not or would not do it.
>
> *Helpee:* Yes—I got angry.
>
> *Helper:* You were furious because you could not make it work but want to very much.
>
> *Helpee:* It would have meant a lot—you know—for them

to learn something like that from me—but it was too hard for them.

Helper: Remember we started with some very simple attending skills, Start there with them. Make sure they can attend, observe, and listen before you ask them to respond. Let's review the steps to learn how to attend.

When confronted with strong helpee feelings, the helper returned to responding in order to define a new goal and a new program. The helper, because he has a large repertoire of both responding and initiative skills, may appropriately select one or the other or any combination at any time during the helping process.

The three basic laws of helping are:

I.   Exploration makes it possible for learners (helpers and helpees) to determine where they really are—physically, emotionally, and intellectually.

II. Understanding makes it possible for the learners (helpers and helpees) to determine where they want and/or need to be—physically, emotionally, and intellectually.

III. Action makes it possible for learners (helpers and helpees) to get from where they are to where they want and/or need to be—physically, emotionally, and intellectually.

THE CYCLE OF HELPING IS RECYCLED

The helping process, for better or worse, begins before the individual is born. The world into which he or she is born prepares for the birth physically, emotionally, and intellectually. Those preparations can be effective or ineffective. Those preparations can be designed to facilitate the newborn's exploration of himself or herself in relation to the world, understanding that relationship in terms of positive goals and supporting actions to succeed in achieving goals or they can be designed to discourage exploration, understanding, and constructive action.

For many, the world they are born into is prepared with an impoverished, disease-ridden environment. Emotionally, the expectations involve crime, violence, and little chance to reach maturity. Intellectually, many are born into a world where it is expected that children will progressively deteriorate in performance with each passing year. For others, the environment and the process are more subtle but the results are the same. For the fortunate, there are expectations of excellence within a setting of attractive, stimulating surroundings supported by social stability. Many are destined to die young or die slowly, however, unfulfilled and hungry while the privileged grow to their fullest. The predictions can be made before they are born with frightening accuracy. The predictions and the bases of those predictions are the same for helpees of effective helpers and ineffective helpers with the same accuracy.

"For better or worse," child-rearing conditions are shaped by how families relate to the newborn. For better or worse, helping is shaped by the way helpers relate to their helpers. For most helpers, the new helpee is an additional factor that contributes to ever-increasing physical, emotional, and intellectual disorganization because the helper does not know what is important. The helper has no skills with which to organize the helping experience. More basically, the helper has no skills with which to organize a cry for help. There is no effort to enter the helpee's experience because such a reaching out must take place from some semblance of a constructive structure or system.

For the effective helper, the new helpee is welcomed as a person first and then as a potential source of a learning experience. The helper prepares by being rested and vigilant. The helper greets the helpee and moves to make the helpee emotionally and physically as comfortable as is functional. The helper who is effective is organized enough in his or her life so that he or she can set aside personal needs to attend fully to another person. The effective helper is fully aware of the existence of the helpee. The ineffective helper is only aware of his or her own rather miserable existence. The effective helper trusts the known to enter the unknown.

REFERENCES

CARKHUFF, R. R. *Helping and human relations* (Vols. I and II). New York: Holt, Rinehart and Winston, 1969.
CARKHUFF, R. R. *The art of helping*. Amherst, Massachusetts: Human Resource Development Press, 1972.

CARKHUFF, R. R.   *The art of problem-solving.* Amherst, Massachusetts: Human Resource Development Press, 1973.
CARKHUFF, R. R.   *How to help yourself: The art of program development.* Amherst, Massachusetts: Human Resource Development Press, 1974.

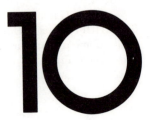

10

. . . the helper handles the crisis or not as he or she is a whole person or not.

Crisis Therapy

The Crossroads for Client and Therapist

Every step the individual takes toward making a decision moves that individual toward or away from life. As helpers or helpees, we resolve our crises by defining a goal. The goals we select reflect what we have learned and the methods we use to make choices. If our learning is limited to reacting to predetermined stimuli, our choices are only apparent. If our learning was and is the product of extensive and intensive exploration, comprehensive understanding, and the skills we need to plan and implement strategies that take us toward growth goals, then our choices are real choices. If the methods we employ to make choices are random and/or based on irrelevant factors, then the choices we make are likely to be irrelevant and therefore not functionally related to growth goals. If, on the other hand, our methods function to organize and personalize information and that organization requires some action, the choice we make is likely to be functionally related to growth goals. The nature of the choices made is only apparently complex. The common denominator cutting across all choices is life and death. A choice to learn a new skill to meet a crisis is clearly a life choice. A choice to continue to do only what we have done in the past is clearly a death choice. The choice to do nothing but observe and judge during a personal crisis or another's crisis is a death choice—nothing more!

A crisis requires new learnings that culminate in new responses. New learnings (crises), if they are to be physically, emotionally, and intellectually functional, require the input gleaned from extensive and intensive exploration, full understanding, and orderly, systematic goal-directed action.

The question we must ask of each step selected to disengage us from a crisis is: does this step get me closer to a growth goal?

The pattern of helping, as of life, is comprised of a series of interrelated crises. We benefit or not as we act constructively or not. Put another way, each crisis encapsulates a process leading to constructive change. In a very real sense, the rest of helping and indeed the rest of life is at best supportive and at worst irrelevant or even destructive.

Today it is in vogue to talk about "crisis therapy." Talking is precisely what most helpers do. When they talk about crisis therapy, they talk about the helper in some way intervening at a crisis point in the helpee's life. They consider this intervention and talk about it as if it were a bold, new step in counseling and therapy. To be sure, for many it is a bold, new step; but as always it does not go far enough.

When we write about crises, we are not simply concerned with the crises in the past or the present of the client. We are writing about crises that occur for the helper as well as the helpee, and between helpee and helper, both in and out of helping.

The obvious example of crisis therapy involves some critical moment in the life of the helpee where what he does or does not do will lead him toward more full emergence or deterioration. Thus, in the following excerpt the male client, who is an executive in his forties functioning at approximately level 2, presents the very real and immediate crisis of his life:

Helpee: I just can't go on anymore. Oh, no! I just can't go in each day.

Helper: You're down because you don't see any way up or out.

Helpee: I've had it. I think it's going to end each day. I live in fear of not making it through each day. It's unbearable.

Helper: It's so hopeless you're not sure you want to face another day.

Helpee: It's too much, I don't think I can take any more. I'm out of it already.

Helper: You're scared because you don't think you've got what it takes to make it through.

Helpee: I know I don't. I'm more than scared I'm all the way down.

Helper: You're beat because life is just too much for you and you can't handle it all.

Helpee: I can't handle anything, my wife, family, job. Can't even talk to people and they don't understand.

Helper: You feel alone because you can't reach those who mean the most to you.

Helpee: I used to—I want to but I just hurt them then feel guilty and ugly.

Helper: You're frightened because you can't maintain contact with those you love and you want to tell them how much they mean to you. Let's consider some ways to reestablish contact and plan how to do it. I think the first step is learning how to select a way to communicate again—how to solve problems.

In this case, when the helper realizes that his helpee is "at the end of his rope," the helper responds fully to that experience first. Then the helper identifies what the helpee experiences as missing and moves the helpee toward filling the gap with a skill. Crises are crises because the individual has no response to deal with a situation. The larger the repertoire of responses available, the fewer the crises the individual experiences.

What constitutes a crisis for some may not be for others. The external crises for the helpee may range from something as apparently innocuous as concern for an impending classroom presentation to the moment of contemplating suicide. For some the most innocuous may merge with the most serious. Thus, for example, the severe stutterer who has had a traumatic experience in a previous presentation and who in some way sees his or her future resting upon his or her next performance may consider the very serious consequences of a disastrous classroom experience. We can see most clearly the essential character of the crisis: whether physical or psychological, it is of life-and-death urgency.

In addition, there may be crises that occur during the helping process itself. During the initial phase of therapy, the helpee's growing feeling that the helper cannot understand him or her may constitute a crisis of minor or major proportions, depending upon the desperateness of the helpee's situation and the ability of the helper to handle the crisis. For the deteriorated schizophrenic who is the product of a series of severely retarding relationships, the helping encounter may offer the last promise of hope. He or she may make a feeble attempt to reach out for help. Whether or not the helper can understand him is indeed of life-and-death urgency.

An example of a potentially critical moment during helping might involve the helper's inability to enable the helpee to find direction; that is, having explored intensely and extensively as far as he can go, the helpee is not able, in his relationship with the therapist, to establish a meaningful direction for his life's activities. Again, depending upon both the helpee's and the helper's levels of development, the consequences may be constructive or deteriorative.

Also neglected are the crises that occur both in and out of therapy for the helper, both alone and in his interaction with the helpee. Thus, occurrences in the helper's own life situation and experiences in his relationships may constitute crises for the helper. For example, marital difficulties or a lack of sexual fulfillment might have a critical effect upon the helper interacting with a sexually attractive helpee and could create a crisis in therapy. Within the helping process itself, the moment when the helper has "lost" the helpee, when he or she is no longer in communication with the helpee—perhaps at a difficult moment for the latter— constitutes a severe crisis point for the helper.

AN HOURLY INTENSIFICATION OF LIFE

The only real helping takes place at the crisis point, most often with the focus initially upon external crises for the helpee but eventually upon crises involving both the helpee and the helper, both in and out of helping. At the crisis point, both helpee and helper are stripped of all facades, which is indicated by what they do or do not do. This communication is the most intimate person-to-person communication there can be. Although there are no fixed "rules" for responding at the crisis, the helper's goals are the same as when he or she is learning; explore in order to fix a goal and develop an efficient means to achieve the goal. Often developing a personalized goal with and for the helpee is enough to gain the time needed to increase the quality and quantity of the helpee's repertoire of physical, emotional, and intellectual responses. The helper's response reflects her recognition of the life-and-death urgency of the situation. *She responds the way she lives her life and she chooses life in her response.* In his or her "being" and acting he or she discloses the meaning and efficacy of his or her approach to life.

The first stage in crisis helping is an acknowledgment of the crisis by the helper. He cannot turn away from the crisis. Yet many helpers do turn away from the crisis point. Those helpers functioning below level 3 cannot clearly see the life-and-death urgency through the helpee's eyes. They cannot experience his or her desperation. They cannot allow themselves to do so. Perhaps most importantly, they are not aware that anyone at a crisis point can choose life. In their deterministic view of man, they do not, in effect, believe in the possibility of change. These people do not understand the privilege of helping another because they no longer believe in the possibility of change or growth. They deny change and growth because they are so caught up in their own needs that they can no longer act but can only react.

The helper functioning below level 3 does not approach being whole himself. *He is not and cannot be aware.* He emphasizes in helping, as he does in real life, the irrelevant details, the "in-between" stuff. The implications are profound. *If* helping begins at the crisis point and *if* the helper functioning below level 3 can neither acknowledge nor cope with the crisis, then *with the helpee functioning below level 3 there is no real helping.* While there may be helpee movement from the absence of effective communication to distorted communication from a distorted perceptual base, there is no real self-sustaining and effective communication.

If there is time at the crisis point—and often there is not—the helper may choose to proceed cautiously, and rightfully and meaningfully so. If there is little time, as is most often the case, the helper must move in quickly to clear away the "crud," the irrelevancies that cloud the critical issues for the helpee. In any event, whether there is time or not the helper must ultimately "touch" the helpee, letting him know that he is with the helpee in the helpee's deepest, most desperate moments.

Touching is, in effect, accurate responding to the feeling and the content of what the helpee communicates. Touching is relieving the confusion by providing a personally relevant goal for the helpee.

If the helpee cannot communicate his desperate circumstances or if he cannot allow his full experience of the crisis to emerge within him, the whole helper may precipitate the crisis by confrontation or other means. *The whole helper can experience the helpee more than the helpee can experience himself.* The whole helper can enable the helpee to face squarely the life-and-death issues before her and thus enable the helpee to take her first steps toward or back to life. *If both helper and helpee allow it to happen, helping represents an hourly intensification of life in all of its crises and all of its fulfillment.*

TO INCORPORATE OR BE INCORPORATED:
THE FIRST CRISIS

The physical prototype for the life-and-death crises is the birth experience, where the movement toward life involves the risk of death. Similarly in helping, the helpee seeks his or her fuller emergence or reemergence, or life, at the risk of death. This can be most clearly seen during early encounters with relatively pathological clients where in very direct or very subtle ways the helpee attempts to undermine the helper and the power implicit in his or her role. In a very real sense, although the helpee is drawn to helping, he finds himself quickly attempting to "take the measure" of the person sitting across from him. The issue, like all issues in the lives of many helpers, is one of destroying or being destroyed, of incorporating or being incorporated. Thus, in the following example a young man in his twenties functioning around level 2 is confronted by the helper with his engagement in a number of destructive activities. The helpee directly and explicitly describes his motives and intentions:

> *Helper*   John, you really want to destroy our relationship here.
>
> *Helpee:*   It's more than that.
>
> *Helper:*   You want to kill me.
>
> *Helpee:*   No, not really. I. . .
>
> *Helper:*   John, you want to kill me.
>
> *Helpee:*   Yes, I want to kill you. I know you haven't earned it but I want to kill you, maybe for everyone I hate.
>
> *Helper:*   That's too easy. You can't.
>
> *Helpee:*   I can! I can! One way or another I will. So I can't take you this way, but I'll find another. I'll fail you. I'll lead you astray. You'll think I'm improving but I'll fail. I'll be your failure case. You'll be responsible.
>
> *Helper:*   You'll do anything you have to, to undermine me, to destroy me, even something that hurts you.
>
> *Helpee:*   Yes. Yes.
>
> *Helper:*   If you can in some way defeat me, you won't have to change your way of living. You do stupid things to protect a stupid way of living, and that's stupid.

Helpee: Oh, I want to change. I do. I can't help it. I can't help it. God, I've been wrong to hurt you.

Helper: You had to find out whether you could take me. If you could, I couldn't help you, and I can.

It is almost as if the helpee, in his attack, is saying "overwhelm me and give me hope." The helper responds firmly to the helpee's desperate attempts to threaten the helper and to defend his way of living but, most importantly, he responds to the helpee's deepest need to lose in this encounter and to win in his life. He confronts the helpee with what the helpee is doing but reassures him that there is hope.

Having been unable to overwhelm the helper, the helpee is now confronted with a deeper, even more disturbing motive, that of wanting to give himself fully to this strong person. His dependency needs threaten him even more than his destructive impulse. It is as if he is saying "How can I trust that you will not abuse me if I commit myself to you?" Thus, in a later therapy session the issue of being incorporated arises.

Helper: You're really saying you don't know if you can trust me.

Helpee: Why should I? How do I know you're not really a neurotic? How do I know that I won't tap in on your need for power or something like that?

Helper: Will I do what you would do in the same circumstances?

Helpee: Will you destroy like I would?

Helper: The question is, "Am I the guy who can help you make it?"

Helpee: Can you help me change?

Helper: You've been led down a lot of primrose paths before. That's all over now, though. You've got to know this time.

Helpee: There's no more time. I'm running out of it.

Helper: It's pretty terrifying. This is your only hope. . .

Helpee: But I don't know if I can make the commitment.

Helper: You've got to ask that question—at the deepest level. I'd be worried if you didn't. Your life is at stake.

Helpee: If I commit myself, can I make it? Will you help me?

The question of trust comes up over and over again at deeper and deeper levels of helping. Many helpers are misled by a once-over-lightly on trust and confidentiality. The helpee's real question is whether he can trust the helper with his life. He asks "If I can upset him, intimidate him, and destroy him, I cannot trust him. If I cannot destroy him, will he destroy me?"

At another level the helpee is asking if he can trust himself with his own life. Because the helper sees the helpee's world better than the helpee and enables the helpee to understand his or her world better (goals), the helpee is faced with the first real choice: live or die. Up to the point the helper defines a goal and the means to achieve it, the helpee experiences only the choice to die.

DISTANCE AND EXPERIENCE

Throughout the early phases of helping, the issues of all phases of the helpee's experiences come up over and over again at deeper and deeper levels. The helpee who has had a meaningful helping experience may come to doubt the experience after a lapse of time. It is as if the helper's acknowledgment of the experience and its full implications would commit the helpee to further investments of himself without knowing the implications. Each step along the way commits the person to further steps and the direction cannot always be anticipated. In the following example, the client, a woman in her thirties functioning at around level 2, had a deeply meaningful experience with the helper at a moment of terror in her life. This was a moment in which she did not know if she could live or would die, a moment in which the therapist held out his hand to hold hers through the crisis. During the next encounter the client questions the meaning of the previous encounter:

> *Helpee:* You paw me just like all of the rest. You're just like the rest, you just want something from me.
>
> *Helper:* You question the whole experience and all of my motives.
>
> *Helpee:* You want the same thing they want—me.
>
> *Helper:* You don't trust that it happened.
>
> *Helpee:* It couldn't have happened.

Helper: There are implications either way.
Helpee: What do you mean?
Helper: If it didn't happen, then you can't trust all of this
             as real and you don't have to commit yourself.
             If it did, well. . .
Helpee: If it happened, it's the first time that anyone ever
             cared for me, without wanting something in
             return.
Helper: You feel insecure because you have never been
             here before.
Helpee: It's sure different and I'm different.
Helper: You've changed but you're not sure how.
Helpee: I've changed, yet I haven't. I'm still me but I
             can, I can—begin to see who you are. . .maybe.
Helper: You feel stronger because you have room for
             someone else now and you have always wanted
             to.
Helpee: That's it, I've never really left room for others.
             It's always been just me—and what *they* want.
Helper: You are larger and stronger and want to keep
             it that way.

The helpee wants to believe but has to doubt. If the previous experience were illusory, it cannot be made real. If the previous experience were real, the helper cannot allow the helpee's analyses to make it illusory. The neurotic's ambition is to make the real illusory and the illusory real. The helper must be deeply in the moment in the encounter or he cannot later trust his experience of the encounter any more than the helpee's later expression of his or her experience. Only if the helpee is not allowed to destroy what must live can she enter and trust later life experiences. In addition, the helpee may have a tendency to deny growth because with it comes more work, reevaluation, and responsibility—the very things the helpee has avoided.

THE HONEST CONFRONTATION

Throughout each of these examples, the helper has in the end relied upon his or her experience of the helpee. At the crisis point, the helper must rely upon his experience with helpees functioning below a minimally facilitative, self-sustaining level. Usually at this point the helper's most effective mode of functioning may involve an honest confrontation with the helpee. This is often because of the time limitations that an unresolved crisis places upon therapy.

Although an honest experience with a constructive person is precisely what has been missing in the low-level functioning person's life and is exactly what brings him to therapy, he will often do everything possible to prevent it's occurrence. He prefers his fantasies to reality. Even for the level 2 helpees, acting and doing cannot compete with insight and talking. The destroyer of his illusions is his murderer. He holds the helper off with intimidation, threatening to make the helper fully responsible for anything deleterious that happens to him. He defines an honest confrontation as a "hostile act." Indeed, any action by anyone is an attack. *Life is death and death is life.*

If, as is the case in most forms of traditional therapy, the helper does not acknowledge the crisis, confront it, and in so doing confront the client and himself, the helper's passivity reinforces the client's passivity. The only real change that might then take place is in the modification of the helpee's perception and the expression of his crises. The consequent insight gives him in helping perhaps the feeling or illusion that he is on top of his situation when in reality (and he finds this out when he returns to real life) he is not. He cannot act just as his helper could not act; a real helper is only acting in an honest encounter involving himself and the helpee. Providing high levels of facilitative conditions does not in itself constitute an act but rather, if effective, only increases the probability for action on the part of both helper and helpee. The crises in helping precipitate honest confrontation between helper and helper. Traditional forms of therapy neither recognize the crises nor acknowledge the necessity for confrontation for constructive purposes (Berenson & Mitchell, 1974).

A whole helper brings his whole person and all of his accumulated store of knowledge to bear at the crisis point. His very acknowledgment of the crisis dictates his full employment of himself. If the helper is able to "touch" the client, letting him know that he is with him in his deepest moment and that he will do whatever he has to do to free the helpee to choose life, then the closed cycle that disallows action is broken. Instead there is an opening movement toward emergence which will, in turn, involve other crises in life. Again, *life is a process of interrelated crises and challenges that we confront or not to live or not.*

Confrontation may never really be absolutely necessary and it is never sufficient. Confrontation within the context of high levels of responding by a whole helper may be efficient (Berenson & Mitchell, 1974). In the following example the helper precipitates a crisis:

Helper: We've spent several sessions together and I think I have some feeling for who you are.

Helpee: I've really appreciated your understanding. You have been very helpful.

Helper: Not exactly. Are you familiar with the details of the referral?

Helpee: Well, I didn't get along with Dr. S———and I guess I still have problems with other people.

Helper: JoAnne, you were labeled a psychopath. Do you understand what that means?

Helpee: I guess so, like criminal or something.

Helper: Sort of. For you it means the way you manipulate everyone without concern for their welfare.

Helpee: I guess that's what I did with Dr. S———.

Helper: . . . and others . . . and it's what you'd like to do with me.

Helpee: (Begins to cry.)

Helper: But I am different.

Helpee: I can't believe that I matter that much to you. I know you're different but I can't help acting that way. I can't help it. I can't help it. (Cries fully.)

Helper: You feel good—in one piece because you really make a difference to me.

Helpee: I don't think anyone ever felt I was important.

Helper: You were angry because you could not make people like you—respect you, but you want to make them respect you.

Now the helpee can choose a new and relevant goal with someone who can help her achieve it. The helpee is on the way to accepting some real measure of responsibility. The helper created the crisis and provided the means to resolve it. The helper, in his living embodiment as well as in his words, confronts her with her choice to destroy others as well as herself. In so doing, he holds out his hand to offer her a chance to choose life.

In the following brief excerpt, a juvenile delinquent, into whom a great deal of effort had been put, was about to make a break with her foster parents and reenter the "jungle" from which she had come:

Helpee: What does it matter?
Helper: It matters.
Helpee: You don't give a damn.
Helper: I'm here.
Helpee: (Yelling): You don't understand me. None of you. You don't know who I am, where I came from.
Helper: (Yelling): I don't want to understand one damn thing more about you than I know and I know who you really are.
Helpee: (Makes no reply.)

No more words were exchanged. The helper met the helpee's challenge more loudly than it was issued. He reaffirmed her human value and made it possible for her not to be bound by her past any more than he was. "I don't need to know any more about you. You are you and, as such, I value you." This encounter, brief as it was, marked the turning point in the girl's life.

Traditionally, confrontation has been employed only with delinquent or psychopathic clients. It seems as if only this population gives the helper license to return the "hostile act." In the following example, a young man functioning at around level 2 threatens one last potent act, suicide, and the helper responds:

Helpee: . . . you've pushed me too far, that's why.
Helper: You're really saying that if you die, I'm the murderer.
Helpee: You'll have my blood on your hands for everyone to see.
Helper: You've been pushed so hard that you've reached a point where it seems the only thing you can do.
Helpee: That's all.
Helper: That's honest.
Helpee: (After a pause): What do you mean?
Helper: *Well, it's either that or choosing to act to live.*
Helpee: (After a pause): I've had everything taken from me—all my dreams—I'm back at the beginning, with nothing.

Helper: There's just you, and either way you act, it's got to be for you—just you.

If the helper is indeed guilty, he cannot confront the helpee at this crisis point. The helpee's crisis becomes his and, if he cannot acknowledge the crisis for himself as well as the helpee, constructive change for either cannot ensue. Of course the helper must, as we have emphasized throughout, do more than confront the helpee. He must be willing to accompany the helpee ino the deepest, unexplored caverns of the helpee's behavior. The helper is the guide; it is her willingness to accompany that reflects her concern. It is his or her effectiveness in living that allows him or her to bring all of his or her resources to bear at the crisis. It is his honesty of communication and skills that allows him to "touch" the client at the deepest level and make a difference.

THE HELPER'S CRISIS

The crisis for the helpee, as can be seen, becomes the crisis for the helper. Whether or not the helper acknowledges it and attends to it does not make it the less so. If he can handle these crises, both he and the helpee can arrive at new levels of understanding and action. In the following excerpt, a 20-year-old male helpee functioning around level 2 confronts the helper with the product of his fantasies. During the previous session, in a moment of panic for the helpee, the helper had reached out both of his hands to hold the shaking hands of the helpee. The helpee, now distant from the earlier experience, denounces the helper:

Helpee: You . . . you're a dirty . . . seducer.
Helper: It's worse than that, isn't it?
Helpee: Yes! A homo! You're a dirty homosexual. (Silence) Well, I don't know. Maybe I want to seduce you.
Helper: You want to make a connection in some way.
Helpee: (Weeping) I never could love anyone. They wouldn't let my love in and now I have no outlet for my feelings.
Helper: Except now—with me.
Helpee: Maybe you're strong enough to accept it.
Helper: You want my strength—my potency. You want so much to be able to live, to act, to love. You want to choose life.

Because the helper is unafraid to enter forbidden areas about forbidden impulses, the helpee is able to express himself fully. Together they are able to arrive at the meaning behind the impulses, meaning that can be translated into constructive action.

Although the crisis that initiates the helping process is the helpee's, many of the crises along the way will be shared by both the helper and helpee. Depending upon the wholeness of the helpee, the helper may carry the major part of the burden in many instances. Consider the moment when both the helper and helpee are richly laden with emotional insights but have not yet discovered the essential, final direction of helping. The question for both is "What are you going to do with the insights?" or "What are we going to do with our insights?" It is the neurotic hope that insight is sufficient and that action is unnecessary. It is the neurotic desire to rely upon constructs rather than construction. It's the helper's crisis as well as the helpee's.

Similarly, the termination of helping is frequently more of a crisis for the helper than it is for the helpee. Or, put another way, it is as much of a crisis for the helpee as it is for the helper. The termination of effective helping should involve handling no different from the handling of any other crisis. The helpee must go out into the real world and the helper must let him go. Most often, this is difficult for the helper who has not given fully of himself, who has not discharged all of his responsibilities to the helpee. It is very difficult for the helper who does not trust himself or herself and does not trust what he or she has done in therapy. It is even more difficult for the helper who is not himself living effectively, for he cannot trust the helpee to live effectively upon leaving therapy. He fears for the helpee as he fears for himself, for he, the helper, cannot choose. Most often, whereas the first crisis is the helpee's, *the last crisis is the helper's.*

HELPER-INTRODUCED PROCESS CRISES

In the final analysis, then, there is no growth without crisis and the learning the crisis precipitates. The effective helper grows at the crisis point as well as the helpee, and while he may not be prepared for the particular crisis involved, it makes him tap his own resources and push out his own boundaries and skills. Within the crisis the helper, in effect, goes "all of the way" with the helpee and struggles in order to facilitate directionality for the helpee. The implications of not acknowledging and addressing the crisis are critical. The implications of "techniqueing it" are profound.

In this regard, a number of research projects (Carkhuff, 1969; Truax & Carkhuff, 1967) are relevant. In order to study the effects of the manipulation of therapeutic conditions, what were, in effect, "crises" were experimentally introduced; that is, during the first third of the therapy hour, high levels of facilitative conditions were offered the helpee by the helper. During the second third of therapy, the conditions were lowered when the helper selectively withheld the best possible responses that he might otherwise have made. The helper's responses tended to be innocuous rather than precipitously lowered. Finally, during the last period the conditions were raised again to a highly facilitative level. The sessions were taped and rated. The client, then, received low levels of facilitative conditions during the middle period; he was not understood with any degree of sensitivity. The therapist's regard and hovering attentiveness were not available to him and the helper was, to some degree, ungenuine. In effect, the helpee experienced a therapeutic crisis in the sense that he was attempting to communicate himself but did not receive in return facilitive communications from the helper. The findings are striking. The depth of self-exploration engaged in by both psychotic inpatients and low-level-functioning students was found to be a direct function of the level of conditions offered by the helper; that is, when the therapist offered high levels of conditions, the low-functioning clients explored themselves at high levels; when the helper offered low levels of conditions, the low-functioning helpees explored themselves at very low levels.

The following excerpts are drawn from the three periods of one of the studies of the experimental manipulation of therapeutic conditions. During Period I a highly resistant young female helpee functioning between levels 1 and 2 comes gradually to explore herself through the strenuous efforts of her high-level-functioning helper:

Period I

Helper: You keep staring at the tape recorder. Does it make you nervous?

Helpee: No, it's the only thing to look at in here.
Helper: You don't want to look at me.
Helpee: No, that's not it. I bought a tape recorder two years ago. (Pause) I can't think of anything else to say.
Helper: Maybe you'd just like to get out of here.
Helpee: I just wish I could think of something to say.
Helper: It's not easy to get started.
Helpee: It never is. I guess I can't help the way I am. But I'd like to change some of my ways.

The helper goes on to become more and more involved in process movement. However, during the experimental second period this movement ceases, and the exchange, which was dependent upon the helper's level of functioning, deteriorates to a level of everyday functioning:

Period II

Helper: I guess we're both kind of tired.
Helpee: I've been keeping late hours, working weekends, not getting any sleep. I have to rest to catch up on my studies.
Helper: Studies are hard.
Helpee: Yeah, but I like them, too, only not too much.
Helper: Too much is too much.
Helpee: Yeah, sometimes I just get tired, not enough sleep, I guess.

The process is an almost circular one that leads nowhere. It must be reiterated that the helper's responses during the middle period were not negative or destructive in nature but rather reflected the selective withholding of the best possible responses. During the final period, the helper again provides high levels of conditions and the client comes to explore herself at a very deep level.

Period III

Helper: What you have hidden from the world is pretty precious to you.
Helpee: I don't think the world could care less.

Helper: They don't really give a damn.
Helpee: I can't help feeling this way, but they always leave me out.
Helper: They're all wrapped up in themselves. Even if you did open up . . .
Helpee: They wouldn't hear me or see me because they don't care. (Sob) So I guess I hide the real me from them.

Thus the helpee proceeds to invest herself further in working out her identity, particularly in relation to others. With the helper tuned in, she can make amazing strides of progress. With the helper functioning at low levels, she cannot take a baby step.

To summarize, when the crisis involving low levels of communication is precipitated with low-level-functioning helpees, the communication process breaks down totally; the helpee collapses unless there is a facilitative person around to put the communication process together again. On the other hand, when high-level-functioning helpees are seen by high-level-functioning helpers the crises have less disastrous consequences. Thus, during the middle experimental period the high-level-functioning helpees continue to explore themselves independently of the helper's lowering of conditions (Carkhuff, 1969). It seems that, once the high-level-functioning helpee is aware that the helper whom he or she is seeing is tuned in on his wavelength and genuinely concerned for his welfare, he continues to function independently of the level of helper-offered conditions. Following the initial period of high-level conditions, the higher the level of helpee functioning the greater his or her independence of the high-level-functioning helper's conditions.

Another study (Carkhuff, 1969) with high- and low-functioning helpees supported these findings and established the differential effects of the manipulation of conditions by a low-functioning helper, where both the low- and high-functioning helpees demonstrated progressively lower depths of self-exploration; that is, having experienced the low-functioning helper's level of conditions, both the high and low helpees demonstrate less and less constructive process movement. The implications for the differential effects of high and low helpers upon high- and low-functioning helpees are compelling.

HELPEE-INTRODUCED PROCESS CRISES

Another type of crisis might be one introduced by the helpee. In a series of experimental studies (Carkhuff, 1969), unknown to the helper involved, a female helpee was given a mental set to explore herself deeply during the first third of an interview, to talk only about irrelevant and impersonal details during the middle third, and to explore herself deeply again during the final third of the interview. Thus, the helpee experimentally introduced a "crisis" for helper. After the helpee was exploring herself deeply and meaningfully, she suddenly "runs away" from therapy and the helper loses contact with her. Whatever he does, he cannot bring her back to high levels of therapeutic process movement. The communication process, for which he is largely responsible, has broken down.

The results are thought-provoking. In a way similar to the pattern of the high-level-functioning helpees, during the experimental period of the helpee-introduced crises the helpers functioning above level 3 functioned independently of the helpee during the middle period. There was a tendency for those functioning at the highest levels to increase the level of conditions that they offered when the helpee lowered her self-exploration. On the other hand, those helpers functioning below level 3 dropped their conditions precipitously when the helpee experimentally lowered her depth of self-exploration. However, unlike the pattern of the low-level helpees in the experimental manipulation of helper-offered conditions, during the final period when the helpee again explored herself deeply the helpers never again offered conditions even close to the level of those they had offered initially.

Perhaps many of the significant results of the study (Carkhuff, 1969) may be best portrayed by the helpee's illustration of her experience and her character sketches of the helpers involved:

> Recently I took part in a fascinating research project involving the manipulation of several helpers by a helpee. I was the helpee who attempted the manipulation by presenting a problem and exploring as deeply as possible for the first twenty minutes of the hour, then suddenly switching off to irrelevancies such as the weather, the decor of the office, and again after twenty minutes of chit chat,

suddenly going back into deep exploration of my problem. The object was to test the ability of the helpers to bring the helpee back in the middle section into contact with the emotional implications of the problem.

To give a clearer understanding of the project, I am a middle-aged woman who recently decided to enter the field of counseling. I had enrolled at a large university as a graduate student, and during the first semester I had had a brief chance to counsel an undergraduate student, with the sessions taped so that they might be a learning experience for me. My reaction upon hearing the tapes was not the expected one of hearing missed cues, but rather one of surprise and dismay at the personality I heard when I listened to myself. This, then, was the problem which I presented to each of the eight helpers whom I subsequently saw. Since none of the helpers had ever seen me before (except one whom I had met several months earlier in a casual setting), I was, for them, apparently just another helpee coming for help. Each session was taped, and this was accomplished in a routine way (it was fairly common at the Center for some member of the department to request that the next session be taped for training purposes). Thus, a real problem was presented by a legitimate helpee, and it was a genuine test of what happens to the helper when the helpee attempts to control the hour.

The following excerpts typify the functioning of the high-level helper during the three periods of the research:

Period I

Helpee: As you may know, I'm in counseling and I heard my first tape and it threw me for a real loop as to whether I should go into counseling because I came across a different person from what I ever thought of myself as being. I came out a weak, defensive, whiny old lady, and what worries me is, am I this person to begin with or is this just something superficial in my way of projecting myself? Or, you know, am I fit to counsel,

	because I wouldn't go to anybody who sounded like that myself?
Helper:	Are you saying, "My God, is that the real me?"
Helpee:	Yeah, that was exactly what I said.
Helper:	Sounds like it was something that, bang, hit you, and almost knocked you down.
Helpee:	For about two weeks it really threw me, but then I got to thinking, well, maybe it was a habit, some way of speaking that I'd learned and that it was interfering and was not the real me. And I don't know whether that's rationalizing, you know, or whether—I'm in a quandary now whether I continue counseling—it has a lot to do with it—you know, if something's there I can unlearn and project in a different way, O.K., but if I'm weak I have no business counseling others. And besides, I don't want to think of myself as this kind of a person because it's the kind of person I don't like.
Helper:	I get two messages from you. One is that this thing was a helluva shock to you, to hear your own voice, to hear what you thought you were in this interview, and I get another message from you, which, at another level, you're not really a weak, whiny old lady.

Even during the second period, the high-level-functioning practitioner was able to relate seemingly irrelevant material to personally meaningful experiences of the helpee. After all, her choice of irrelevant and impersonal material was in some way personal, and the helper stretched to tune in on its meaning. It was very difficult indeed for the helpee to maintain her mental set.

Period II

Helpee:	That reminds me, there's something about this town. It's an awfully cold town. Northerners are so blasted—uh—indifferent. Or I don't know, they're certainly not very warm or easy to know.

I've been here since last summer, and I swear I don't know anybody at all.

Helper: It's hard to know where you stand, at some deep level you feel very much alone, or cut off.

Helpee: Well, I think these professors particularly have their own little circles and nobody, you know . . .

Helper: There's no room . . .

Helpee: And nobody entertains much apparently, except within the department or something of that sort, and they have their own interests, the townspeople have their own interests, and the kids are busy studying and they have their little group, and I'm a grandma to them. And still there's not much you can do about this, but it is different from Washington. I was in this house here for two weeks before anyone even said, "Hello, you know, I'm a neighbor. How are you?" And finally one neighbor stopped in to borrow a stick of butter and then I didn't see anyone else for another two weeks.

Helper: I wonder if you're not really asking, "Does anyone around here really care?"

Finally, during the third part of the session, the helpee returned again to explore herself at relatively high levels.

Period III

Helpee: I did that for years and years, trying to be what someone else wanted me to be, but I thought I was over that . . .

Helper: You keep telling me "I'm not what my voice is. I'm a volcano."

Helpee: But I never associated my voice as being anything but . . .

Helper: You keep telling me you're not what you appear to be. You know what you've told me this hour— you've told me, "I look like I'm meek, but I'm not."

Helpee: I'm a lion, not a mouse.

Helper: Your voice changed a little bit when you said that. It was looser.

Helpee: Uh hum . . .

Helper: You could get pretty angry at that. "I'm not a mouse." What did you feel when you said that?

Helpee: I felt like roaring.

Helper: You're damn right you did. Wish you did—for you I wish you did. "Don't you call me a mouse." Do you ever feel like that?

Helpee: Oh, yeah, many a time.

Helper: I'm a mouse and a mouse can't help anybody. Lions can. Oh, I don't know—constructive lions can, lions who can make discriminations about when it is appropriate to raise your voice.

Helpee: Humm, I hadn't thought of that.

Helper: I don't come across like a full person if you always see me at my best, and in this society at my best means controlled, calm, polite, thoughtful, but never human. To be human I have to be able to communicate my anger *and* my joy and everything in between. And inside I know these things. I know these experiences inside. Huh? I've got to make discriminations about when it's appropriate to show these feelings, and by God counseling is an appropriate place.

With the low-level-functioning therapist, the results were quite different. Again, during the initial period, the helpee presented essentially the same difficulty.

Period I

Helpee: I have a problem. My problem began some time ago. I'm in the counseling program in education.

Helper: Say, I don't believe I got your name.

Helpee: Oh, Janie, Janie Clark.

Helper: Janie Clark. Thank you. You know who I am?

Helpee: Yeah, Dr. Jones.

Helper: Yeah, Dr. Jones, yeah.

Helpee: Anyway, I had my first client and it was taped, and when I turned on the tape to hear the cues

I'd missed and things, and I didn't hear anything except my voice and the way I came across as a person. And at the time it really threw me for a loop because I'd never thought of myself as the kind of person that I came out on the tape. It wasn't just, you know, the different sound of the voice, or anything like that. It was a whole new me, you know, a different me, and I didn't know whether it was just that I'd picked up ways of expressing myself, which I told myself at first, but I didn't like what I saw obviously. I came out a very weak, whiny, pathetic little old lady, and I'd never thought of myself that way. And there it was just clearly, that was all that was coming across.

Helper: This is your interpretation of the—uh—your listening to yourself on the tape. You thought you were not as strong a character perhaps.

Helpee: Nothing!

Helper: In other words, a difference in yourself.

Helpee: A blobby sort of a—no personality, no umpf, no nothing which you could relate to.

Helper: And you, you think this is—and what do you think, perhaps, the tape is a true indication of the—of your interpretation . . .

Helpee: Yeah, my first reaction was that maybe I'd learned to express myself poorly but then finally I realized that no, this was a part of me that I just never had recognized that was coming out and, this is a very recent thing for me to be willing to admit that, you know, that this is me. (Silence)

I have talked about it with a number of people and that undoubtedly has helped me to recognize that—I'm still pretty hung up on some of it, though. I'm so used to thinking of myself in certain ways—partly I can be totally unconscious of this and then afterwards I think, oh, there was that dear little old lady again, and, apparently there are some aspects of the dear little old lady that I still think I like.

Helper: Uh, huh.

Helpee: But I don't like the total picture at all, not at all.

Helper: So, you, now it gives you a sort of a negative picture of yourself.

During the second period, the client was able to manipulate the helper successfully. The discussion was on her terms, and, indeed, in many ways the therapist appeared to feel more comfortable.

Period II

Helpee: And I like the Northeast, and so they said, "Well, try this state," and so that's all I knew. And so then I came up here.

Helper: Now you're enrolled in the Master's program?

Helpee: Yes.

Helper: Are you teaching, too?

Helpee: No.

Helper: You have a teaching certificate?

Helpee: No.

Helper: What did you major in in college?

Helpee: Political science. Big help.

Helper: A general college education.

Helpee: Yeah. Oh, I love the weather up here now. I'm dreading the summer because someone told me it's hot. Part of the reason I came up here was because Washington summers are unbearable. But they tell me it gets real hot here. You probably would love some good hot weather, coming from the North, as you said.

Helper: No, I like cool weather.

Helpee: Yeah, I hate the thought of thinking of myself as the kind of person who anybody can say "boo" to and I'll turn around and run.

Helper: Yeah.

Helpee: I never understood how you guys got up here in this hall.

Helper: More room.

Helpee: Well, I thought it was because you guys must be in bad repute, and so they sent you to this old building.

Helper: I don't know about that part of it, but the ostensible reason is more room.

Helpee: It's pretty dilapidated, but it is kind of off to itself. The other building is so busy.

Helper: Yeah, it's crowded.

Finally, the client again returns to relatively high levels of self-exploration, but the helper does not quite return to the level at which he was functioning during the first period of the study.

Period III

Helpee: To me fighting is a dirty word—somehow it means hurting people, getting hurt, you know, there's nothing healthy or good about it—seems awful to have to fight.

Helper: When people fight you, you get hurt, so you don't want to.

Helpee: Well . . .

Helper: You don't want to fight other people so you won't hurt them.

Helpee: I don't want to hurt, or get hurt, it's a combination of all these things, and I don't want any part of it—but I don't like the other alternative which is to . . .

Helper: The reality I guess, in the best sense you'd like to avoid a fight, that is, if it's your way—but in real life people have differences of opinion and so this is where you're hung up so you'll either have to fight for your say or else you don't get it.

Helpee: You know I might just as well not have had the fight, you know. I would feel very defeated if I went in and fought and lost.

Helper: You mean you might feel more defeated than you feel now.

Helpee: Yeah, that's right.

Helper: You wouldn't feel that if you fought and lost.

Helpee: I identify fighting with losing.

Helper: I see. So you think you win a fight?

Helpee: When you get in a fight, you either win or lose, and I'm the loser.

Helper: Huh.
Helpee: I always have been, and I just always expect to be.
Helper: Which, in a sense, to me it seems sort of that in a sense you're defeated before you start. You're certainly not going to win the battle if you don't fight, uh, unless you're lucky, maybe, and it just sort of falls that way.
Helpee: But somehow it doesn't seem as much of a defeat if you, you know, I chose to walk off, and I haven't lost face, or something. I don't know, but if I fight, then my self-esteem goes down.

The declining pattern is one that (in contrast to the rising pattern of the high-level-functioning helper) most low-level-functioning helpers present over a number of sessions of therapy. That is, it would appear that following the exercising of the initial repertoire of responses during the early sessions, with the helpee's continuing presentation of crises, whether acknowledged by the helper or not, the low-level-functioning helpers deteriorate in functioning over therapy.

The helpee's impressions of her experience (Carkhuff & Alexik, 1967) are related as follows:

I must mention that as an inexperienced layman, albeit a beginning student in counseling, I had anticipated that I would learn a bit more about myself, particularly in regard to the techniques, from these experienced counselors. I had absolutely no forewarning that I would be so appalled at the destructiveness of some of the helpers nor that I would be so excited by the facilitative ones. I had not really envisioned that there would be a difference that I could so easily detect. After all, these were highly trained, experienced helpers, each of whom counseled several helpees daily. My first impressions were, in all but one case, validated by the replaying of the taped sessions. In this particular case, I think I was misled by the fact that this was a woman counselor, and being a woman, I probably unconsciously hoped to see a good counselor and therefore must have given her the benefit of the doubt. She also was bright and intelligent, and it was only after playing back the tape that I could see that her intelligence was misused and could not be trusted. But in all other cases, I sensed immediately whether a therapist was showing respect and genuine interest in me as a human being or merely reciting a litany, so to speak. With some, I came away feeling that I had had a glimpse of a real human being in a genuine encounter, and that this person had some understanding and appreciation of me as a human being. I felt that I had learned and could learn more about myself and life from this individual and was, therefore, hopeful of finding a better way of living. With others, I came away feeling that the helper had been totally indifferent to me and to my needs, either because of his own needs, or because he was incapable of feeling for me, that I had not only learned nothing from the encounter, but also that I left feeling very depressed and hopeless. This occurred with several helpers in a greater or lesser degree. With some of them, I felt sympathy—with others, I felt disgust and anger that they should be allowed to be in a so-called "helping" profession. I could only think of a really sick person who had finally worked up the courage to make perhaps one last attempt to find a human being with enough love and understanding to help him to find his way out of his misery. I was appalled to think of his winding up with some of these inadequate counselors who would surely destroy his last hope. It seemed to me criminal negligence on the part of society to allow this kind of helper to operate.

Concerning each of the experienced helpers whom the helpee saw in one study, she provided the following character sketches:

Counselor A

Counselor A walked in and I saw a man who looked shorter than he is with a brush of black hair tinged with gray, big wide eyes under bushy brows, the eyes the main feature. Something in those eyes makes you feel safe, and yet you know he can really think. But you know the guy has feelings by those eyes. None of those cold empty eyes. He talks in a voice so big it almost scares you, but not rough and not smooth, but gentle, though big. He could blast you right out of your chair, but he probably wouldn't. Somehow I know I could trust him. And so I started telling him how it is with me, and he seems to be right with me all the time. I don't know but it's as if he didn't even need my words and I didn't feel as if he was faking. Oh, some of the time I felt he was bored waiting for me to spell it out because he was ahead of me, not because he thought I wasn't worth his time. He had a way of putting my words into such specific and marvelous analogies that made me feel more deeply what it was I only vaguely was aware of before. He gave off vitality and allowed me to share it— not that I left him with less but that he had so much and he was allowing me to take what I needed. He made me feel as if I was OK and would be able to use it usefully and come out of it. He gave me hope, optimism, and a more clearly defined problem than when I went in. I left feeling that if anything else seemed insoluble to me, I'd must go in and see him again. And he left me feeling that he would be glad to help me again.

Counselor B

Counselor B was a slight, blondish, watery-eyed person whom you wouldn't ordinarily ever remember seeing. He has absolutely no presence. But he has a Ph.D. With this helper, within a few sentences I could hardly wait to get to the part where I could talk about nothing at all. He absolutely floored me when he asked a lot of irrelevant questions about my husband's salary, my status, and so on. I wanted to tell him what those questions did to me— I wound up just despising him, and unconsciously this came out. When I listened to the tape I heard myself give a very destructive laugh. I had definitely written him off within the first two minutes, and the only reason I stayed was to do the research, but I would never have returned to this man if I had needed help of any kind.

Counselor C

Counselor C is a big, blondish, sunny type of southern fellow. He is a genuinely warm guy and a very likeable one.

He exudes friendliness and his eyes sparkle. You have a feeling he could really enjoy a good laugh. I did not feel that he pressed hard enough on my problems, but that maybe he was just feeling things out the first session. I thought I liked him. He seemed too slow-paced and I didn't think his intellect was as sharp as some. But I felt that I didn't really know him in any sense and that he was holding back because he didn't know me yet.

Counselor D

I felt as if Counselor D was trying and wanted to be helpful, but I found it difficult to react to his personality. He was an older but sort of nondescript looking man, smoked a pipe, and looked possibly scholarly. He immediately indicated he was not feeling up to par and I felt I wanted to be nice to him because I felt sorry for him, but did not want to for my own sake. However, I felt he was reaching out to me, but sort of for my help. Was easy to talk about him as against myself but that seems a part of first-session getting to know rather than a definite lack of ability. Did not feel interested in going back to him, though.

Counselor E

Counselor E seemed pretty stiff and intellectual, and gave the impression of really knowing her stuff, and of having had to battle hard to wrench any of what she knew out of the men—almost a caricature of a career girl. But she had a soft voice and smiled brightly and made me feel as if she was on my side against the men in this world. She didn't actually say anything about men, so far as I can remember, but somehow I picked up the feeling that she was strange and different. It was easy to get her to talk about her pictures and books, which surprised me as I had expected her by her appearance to be tougher. I came away thinking she was really bright and knew about helping. After listening to the tapes, she came out the most boring, the least interested, and not very bright. I am still puzzled as to what made me think her bright as I am not usually fooled that easily. My only thought is that I projected my need to see a woman helper as good.

Counselor F

Counselor F was a big, burly, black-haired, beetle-browed, soft-fat foreign-looking man who might be a mechanic or farmhand rather than a Ph.D. in psychology. He was a typical client-centered therapist—fed me back my words until I wanted to say: "Haven't you any ideas of your own?" and "That's what I said, what are you saying them for?" It annoyed me very much, and I could hardly refrain from mentioning it. I felt he wasn't really very interested in my problem, but it was his job to sit there and be polite. My general feeling was one of annoyance with him. Would not go back if I had any problem. Came away from this interview feeling frustrated.

Counselor G

This poor lady surprised me in being better than I had anticipated. She looked like a tousled, slipshod sort of matron with no organization to her character or mind. She actually was a better helper than the neat, efficient lady I had seen before. She was touched by my problem because it coincided in some respects with hers, and soon I felt that I should be helping her. It was, in fact, very difficult for me to remember that I was there for research purposes and that I shouldn't, therefore, change roles with her during this hour. She made me feel very sad and depressed, and yet I liked her and wished I could cheer her up. She would not be able to help you grow, but could give directions for specific problems, and they would probably be oriented toward her own philosophy and her own problems. But she was herself more than some of the others.

Counselor H

Counselor H was a long, lanky, dark-haired, really blue-eyed, tall, stringbean of a man; young. Felt immediately a sense of intellect which was a relief after some of the others. Wasn't sure if he could be warm. As he talked he seemed warm, but I had a tiny part of me saying, "I'm not sure I'd like to get in a fight with him." I felt he might not be on my side if I didn't show up well. He was very sharp, and it was extremely difficult to pull him away from my problem. I was very depressed when I went in to see him, and he seemed to want to help me get over this depression and I felt that he probably could. During this hour, though, I was unable to shake off the depressions, which I felt was because I was unwilling rather than because he could not help me. Felt that if I went back to him and really put myself on the line, he could unravel a hell of a lot of my problems for me, but not sure I'd go back unless I felt especially courageous at the time. He might not go all the way with me if I showed something he didn't like or couldn't feel. He was very good, though; one of the best. I respected him and felt that he was good. It was just a matter of not feeling 100 percent safe. I felt him to be strong enough, but perhaps not tender enough.

These excerpts are classic in their depiction of many important aspects of helping. First, the dependence of the low-level-functioning, S-R reactor helper and the independence of the E-U-A actor helper (see page 285). Second, the helpee-manipulated excerpts and her descriptions place in sharp relief the difference between those who choose to die and ask others to die with them and those who choose life and ask others to choose life with them. Those who choose death at the crisis point do everything they can to make others choose to die. Those who choose life do everything they can to make others choose to live. Those who choose to die do so because they have closed themselves to new experiences. They live the same experience day in and day out because they cannot respond to anything or anyone. Those who choose life do so because they are open to new experiences. They live different experiences day after day because they can respond to anything or anyone when it is appropriate and they learn. Because they learn, they have fewer and fewer crises.

The helpee's descriptions of the helpers involved remains for us congruent with our experience and research as well as reflecting the helpee's experience. Those who can deliver results tell us early and sustain their efforts with energy, direction, and discipline. Those who cannot deliver results tell us early and communicate low levels of energy, lack of positive direction, and no discipline. Those who can help use time well, those who cannot help waste time. At the crisis, the low-level helpers lose all semblance of direction and never return to their previous levels of functioning, however brief and poor to begin with. The high-level-functioning helpers sustain their high levels, while the strongest of them actually increase their levels of functioning at the point of crisis.

SUMMARY AND CONCLUSIONS

Helping, if it is to occur at all, must be done by high-level-functioning people. What others do is some sort of twisted game without even the appearance of decency. It is sick and cruel. The low-functioning helpers are as much a failure in their lives as they are in helping. It can be no other way. They emphasize the irrelevant, personally and professionally, while they ignore the fabric of life woven from the learnings that emerge from the work and the skill it takes to meet and resolve crises.

Traditional psychotherapy is not helping. Helping provides the helpee with the conditions necessary for the acquisition of responses and skills the helpee did not have. Again, the effective helper provides the conditions necessary for learning. These conditions involve the appropriate use of responsive and initiative skills that, in turn, facilitate helpee exploration, understanding, and action. A crisis may or may not be a structure within which the helpee and helper can learn, grow, and initiate constructively. Whether it is or not depends upon the repertoire of skills the helper commands.

The helper handles the crisis or not as he or she is a whole person or not. There are rules for functioning in unknown areas and they involve energy, organization, direction, and systematic action as well as full vigilence from the helper so that he or she may explore, understand, and act.

Those who choose to die, helpers as well as helpees, have an incredible number of strategies designed to help them die and they all involve reacting. Those who choose to live have only one strategy to live and it involves learning.

REFERENCES

BERENSON, B. G., & MITCHELL, K. M. *Confrontation.* Amherst, Massachusetts: Human Resource Development Press, 1974.

CARKHUFF, R. R.   *Helping and human relations* (Vols. I and II). New York: Holt, Rinehart and Winston, 1969.

CARKHUFF, R. R., & ALEXIK, M.   The differential effects of the manipulation of client depth of self-exploration upon high and low functioning counselors. *Journal of Clinical Psychology,* 1967, *23,* 210–212.

TRUAX, C. B., & CARKHUFF, R. R.   *Toward effective counseling and psychotherapy.* Chicago: Aldine, 1967.

11

. . . What applies in an honest helping
effort applies in life. What applies
in life among growing and honest people
applies in helping!

In Search of
an Honest Experience

Confrontation in Counseling and Life

We have learned a great deal from our research and our clinical work (Berenson & Mitchell, 1974; Carkhuff, 1969). In many ways we have learned a great deal more in our efforts to be trainers and consultants. In many ways we have learned a great deal more listening to tapes of hundreds of helper–helpee interactions. Our experiential learnings, although they grow in scope, detail, and direction, are congruent with what we have learned from other activities. Our experiential learnings, however, put flesh on the bones, and too often we had to choose to laugh or cry. And too often we were furious. And constantly, consistently, we continued with our work. What made us furious was the repeated efforts of people to seek deeper levels of honesty with themselves and someone else only to become more dishonest. They became dishonest because helper and helpee lacked proper skills and/or the energy and discipline to learn them. Over and over again the pattern was the same: one of resolution to deterioration within a context of mutual self-destruction.

At the highest levels, a growing person and a growing relationship is highly conditional. Full honesty requires persons who are fully committed to personal growth at any cost. Full honesty, independent of anticipated responses, *except with the most fragile*, valid or invalid, sets the stage for greater self-definition, perhaps the most vivid aspect of growth. The resulting momentary closeness or distance emerges as an experience of knowing one's self at the deepest levels—alone and with others, free of the "should's" and "should not's," social-cultural myths, or injury and insult to one's basic commitment to grow.

There is a second assumption that aided us in the formulations of our research and generalizations. A person is often less than who he can be because others in his life could not or did not validate his experience; neither could they act on themselves or others constructively. A large number of people grow up starved for even minimal levels of understanding, genuineness, respect, and love (Carkhuff, 1969). Others who have become victimized are the products of much more subtle ways and means of denial and starvation. They have been exposed to parents, teachers, counselors, helpers, and employers who are themselves victims. These "helper-victims" excuse their inability to act constructively by postulating that each of us protects a core within that should not be shared or touched. Clinical experience teaches us that this inner, untouchable core is invariably something the person experiences as ugly, evil, and, hence, destructive. A few persons experience it as all that they have of what was once beautiful to them. This protection of or "respect" for the other person's inner core arises out of a pseudorespect rather than the basic ingredients with which people flourish. It is an appeal for a contract: I will not expose who you really are if you will not expose who I am (Berenson & Mitchell, 1974) and/or if I expose or touch you, I know I will act to destroy.

There is, however, another side of this. The healthier among us keep something of ourselves from others because we sense that they will use and abuse rather than respect and love. The lesson is simple; we have learned that there are too few whom we can trust with whom we really are at the deepest levels. For the most part, this may be adaptive in a cruel and neurotic world. It enables a person to experience deterioration at a rate slower than his more vulnerable brothers. With no interpersonal outlet for who we really are, even the more healthy enter into the "mutual nonexposure" pact in one way or another (Carkhuff, 1969). The deterioration for even the stronger comes in part from the fact that any such agreement does not allow for personal emergence or growth.

How then do we discriminate between those who confront to deny us our human substance and emergence, allowing us at best only to survive, and those who in confronting us share our experience and life by nurturing what is strong and attacking what is ugly and weak? What are the qualifications?

THOSE WHO ARE ENTITLED TO CONFRONT: QUALIFICATIONS

1. Only those who demonstrate deep levels of understanding that go far beyond what is being said are potential sources of nourishment and may be entitled to confront. There is extensive evidence that confrontation based upon deep levels of understanding results in a more full and immediate exchange between the parties involved. Confrontation without such understanding is not only more likely to be inacurrate in content and affect but is also more likely to be destructive (Berenson & Mitchell, 1974; Carkhuff, 1969). Only the deepest understanding will allow the helper to discriminate between what is destructive

in the life and phenomenology of the helpee and what is constructive. The foundation of trust does not come from confrontation
but from knowing that the other person truly understands and
can communicate his understanding and is willing to act when
the second party cannot act. Confrontation based on understanding serves as the basis for respect. It is also the basis for establishing the helper as a potent reinforcer (Carkhuff, 1969).

2. Only those who demonstrate deep and appropriate
    changing levels of regard and affect are potential sources
    of nourishment and may be entitled to confront.
Those who offer a steady unchanging level of regard and/or affect
communicate to the helpee that he or she, the helpee, cannot have
an impact on the helper (Berenson & Mitchell, 1974). The helper
in this instance serves as a model for not acting upon the world:
a condition that can only lead to experiencing the self as increasingly more impotent and, hence, cruel and destructive. Unchanging levels of regard and affect also suggest that the basis for the
relationship is "techniqued." The helpee consciously or unconsciously knows that his or her helper is a poor manipulator at
best. At worst the helper fears the implication of his own feelings
or is not in tune with them at all. The helpee comes to know that
the helper is himself a helpee. *Any ensuing interaction is a series*
of denying exchanges between two victims.

Helper affect must be at first suspended and then shared
as the helper gains in understanding of the helpee; and it must
be real. Helper respect moves from unconditional regard to conditional regard as his or her understanding of the helpee grows
(Carkhuff, 1969). Here the helper communicates that he never
acts independently of the helpee, that he acts and judges appropriately with growing direction, involvement, and demands upon
himself and the helpee. Increasingly and in a graduated way, the
helper respects that which commands respect. Increasingly and
in a graduated way, he is intolerant of anything in the helpee and
the relationship which does not demand that the parties involved
be the best they can be, helper and helpee. At the most intimate
moments of highest regard, the helper is a full participant with
joy and pain rather than an exploitive manipulator. The essential
message to the helpee is that the helper regards herself condi-
tionally and offers no less to those she is committed to serving,
even at the risk of losing the helpee.

3. Only those who are physically robust and live fully

from a high level of energy are potential sources of nourishment and may be entitled to confront. To confront and deal with the impact of constructive confrontation necessitates immense energy, durability, and size. Because confrontation based on understanding is a full and real experience, it must be met and dealt with fully. Fatigue and loss of persistence during what may be a lengthy encounter results in an abandonment, all too common, in the life of a helpee. The initiation of a confrontation offers promise; its premature conclusion is another in a long series of broken promises. The helper then becomes just another individual who has nurtured false hopes in the helpee.

By failing to deliver and follow through, the helper serves as a model who depicts the world as a place requiring only the appearance of delivery. He creates the impression that real delivery is unwanted and dangerous.

The helpee initially and periodically raises two basic questions: "Does the helper have anything I want?" and "Given my circumstances, could the helper make it better than I?" (Berenson & Mitchell, 1974).

If the helper presents an image of fatigue and physical weakness, the helpee knows the whole process is a lie. In other words, the helper in many ways is telling the helpee that, over a period of time, the helpee will look and live like the helper. At one level or another, the helpee decides whether he or she wishes to look and live like the helper. If the helpee chooses to stay with a sick-looking helper, the helpee chooses to die. We become physically what we are psychologically. To a large extent, the most effective therapies include a physical conditioning program.

4. Only those who love what they respect and respect those whom they love are potential sources of nourishment and may be entitled to confront.

Those who have become a party to the "mutual nonexposure" contract have agreed to ask others to be less than what they can be and, in turn, have agreed to be less than what they can be. In time, this conscious choice generates not only contempt for others but also contempt for one's self. Here we observe the basic source of the neurotic's cruelty toward others and himself. Anyone who accepts the neurotic's terms, to be less than what he can be, is loved for not growing and held in disrespect for entering the agreement in the first place. The neurotic knows that only a person reaching for his full potential would never become a party to the "mutual nonexposure" contract. Those outside the agreement are never loved by the neurotic but they are respected.

The helper, in the early phases of helping, has a choice: Be less than what he can be and win the love of the neurotic. Those who feel they can win the love and respect of the neurotic are themselves victims. Victims can only help others to become victims.

Love without respect is license to abuse. When the license is revoked, the neurotic is furious. He withdraws his love and in time his respect if the other party is resolute in not allowing anyone, even himself, the right to violate his constructive growth.

Only those who are themselves growing can experience genuine joy in another's emergence and growth. The growing person may at appropriate moments demand deeper and deeper levels of honesty in the form of confrontation from those significant to him. Such a confrontation comes from an intimate knowledge of who he is and who he is confronting.

The person who has ceased to grow himself knows he is deteriorating. The only thing he asks of others is that they deteriorate with him. He or she must then move to undermine, neutralize, slander, and destroy any growing person or any aspect of a person that is growing. His successful deleterious efforts produce the twisted rewards of nonexposure; his failure to undermine or destroy the growing is the only ray of hope for him.

Only those committed to their own constructive and creative personal emergence have the potential to confront constructively. Only those who act on themselves constructively are able to act constructively on others in the form of confrontation or in any other way.

THOSE WHO ARE NOT ENTITLED
TO CONFRONT

1. Those committed only to personal survival can only act destructively and are not sources of nourishment and are not entitled to confront.

Although they experience the full implications of living as a highly conditional existence, those committed only to survival do not understand or entertain the possibility of personal emergence. They have not enjoyed earlier periods characterized by understanding and unconditional regard from significant others.

For the underprivileged, the struggle for survival is familiar. The mysteries of growth are unfamiliar because the conditions for growth have been withheld. Promises of growth are held in distrust because promises in the past have not been fulfilled. Confrontation in this context involves little consideration for the consequences of what follows confrontation simply because there really is not anything to lose. For those who have enjoyed some measure of the conditions and opportunities necessary for growth and for those who have experienced fulfilled promises, embracing a survival state constitutes another strategy to avoid the exposure of their dulled affect, distorted motives, and lack of competencies. Their lack of self-regard convinces them that they are entitled to no more than survival.

When a person takes more or less than what he is entitled to, he is self-destructive and adds more refuse to that which he wishes not to see or have others see in him. Growth in others only forces him to anticipate that those hidden aspects of his nature and history may become public. Rather than allowing this to happen, he chooses neuroticism, undermining the growth of others, fear, cruelty, and even his own death. Those committed solely to survival experience anything of real potency as a threat to survival. Movement in life can, for them, have only the appearance of growth. Confrontation must also be an appearance of confrontation. It must be short-lived, weak, and self-neutralizing —leaving no tangible benefits or change.

The growing and whole person values another person's potential for growth more than the other person does. The final test of the helpee is likely to be an effort to turn this against the helper by withholding constructive behavior in order to place the helper on the helpee's schedule. This moment provides the effective helper an opportunity to risk the relationship and demonstrate in no uncertain terms that he will not and cannot become the helpee's victim if the helping process is placed on the helpee's terms and not the helper's. This is not to say that the helper ceases to respond to the helpee's needs. The helper spends the initial phases of helping doing mainly that—responding (Carkhuff, 1969). At a still deeper level, when the helper refuses to allow the helpee to turn his (the helper's) virtues against him, he is exhibiting profoundly deep levels of empathic understanding of the helpee. It is the helpee's failure to "take" the helper that provides the helpee with a real choice and a possibility to grow. It tells the helpee that there is, after all, a source of strength in the world that will not be employed to violate him.

2. Those who have lost contact with their own experience can only react and are not sources of nourishment and are not entitled to confront.

Confrontation, unlike the responsive dimensions such as empathy, emerges from the helper's experience of the helpee rather than the helpee's experience of himself. Confrontation gives the helping process concrete directionality by providing the helpee with a potent reinforcer who can and will act on another to achieve constructive ends. Beyond this, the helpee now knows that if he is to achieve more effective levels of living he, too, must learn to act on his world and his experience of that world.

The helper who offers confrontation without being in full contact with his experience of himself and the helpee can employ confrontation only as an impersonal technique. The resulting interaction is likely to be irrelevant and, therefore, destructive. Most typically, the confrontation by such a helper appears to focus on the real or fabricated pathology of the helpee. In reality, it is often a reflection of the pathology of the helper.

If the helper has no experience of his own to draw upon, he has nothing through which to filter the feeling, content, and experience of the helpee's life. At that moment, the helper as well as the helpee is exposed. If there is no delivery, both parties know it. At best it is another unfulfilled promise for the helpee, at worst a fixing of an inappropriate and maladaptive response: He agrees to agree.

At a deeper level, the helper without the sensitivities necessary for constructive confrontation hesitates to act in the first place. His confrontations of helpee weaknesses or pathology provide him with material that appears to be beyond the helper's control and/or influence and beyond the influence of any real intervention or action of a personal nature. The low-level-functioning helper is himself a victim and can only relate to and reinforce the helpee for being a victim. The victim knows that all acting on the world is destructive, for in the past all of his own actions have been destructive.

The entire experience, attempted confrontation by a low-level helper, brings both parties into deeper contact with their helplessness and impotence: the very reasons for seeking help in the first place. In this and many other ways, the helping experience is no different than the experience of their daily lives: constant and vivid reminders that they cannot function to service themselves or others constructively. Hence, they both develop behaviors that provide only the appearance of acting as well as philosophies that appear to justify not acting. The essence of what they are doing and saying is: "If I act, I know it will be destructive. If I only appear to act, I am only observing the pain I and others experience." They settle for the latter, of course: To be observers of human experience, nonintervening distorting observers, knowing full well that in their apparent action or nonaction they act to destroy. Characteristically, they will do anything to avoid being held responsible for not acting even at the sacrifice of their helpee, a constructive actor, or themselves.

Perhaps at a still deeper level, not being in contact with their experience is a sham. The fact is that they are aware that if they translate into action how they experience their world and themselves, they must destroy. *For them all action is destructive.*

3. Those who hold allegiances that are stronger than their commitment to constructive and creative personal emergence are not potential sources of nourishment and are not entitled to confront.

Behavior justified on the grounds that it serves an allegiance stronger than the commitment to creative growth and constructive personal emergence is too often the accepted basis for giving vent to injustice. It is merely another ploy of those not growing to act out their distortions with impunity. The less-than-healthy person all too often attempts to put his focus on what is right or wrong for society or an institution in order to divert attention from who he is. The healthy person, however, fully understands that few have the right to examine or judge him and that the great majority will distort what they see.

The emphasis for the helper is framed in the demand that those around him will not be accepted for less than what they can be. The helper's commitment beyond himself is toward persons, not depersonalized institutions.

In order to make this demand, the helper must understand the less healthy person more completely than the less healthy person understands himself. This is possible because the helper's self-understanding is free of distortions; hence, there is no contamination of his understanding of others.

Without this level of understanding and the ability to communicate it, confrontations initiated by the low-functioning helper and considered by the helpee confirm the low-functioning helper's conviction that the world asks only for cheap games and that, after all, there are no healthy persons.

It is a demand of the healthier person that the less healthy person not be accepted for less than he can be. The demand, if it is to be useful, must occur within the context of deep and full understanding. That is, the healthier person does have the potential for understanding the less healthy person more completely than the less healthy person understands himself. Without this depth of understanding and the ability to communicate it, confrontations in the form of demands are at best a hit-and-miss proposition. At worst, they are an experience confirming that there are no healthy persons in this world.

Confrontation without a base of deep understanding of the helpee sets the stage for the helpee to employ a wide variety of survival techniques. With only a knowledge of the techinques for survival and the lack of ability to tune in to other's experiences, the low-functioning helper, when he confronts, aids the helpee to employ a variety of diversionary tactics: (1) to avoid what he needs most: seeking a relationship with a high-functioning helper after leaving the low-functioning helper; (2) to destroy what he needs most: he will be more likely to distort the experience of meeting a real helper after his experience with the low-functioning helper; (3) to demand inexhaustible responsiveness from others while abusing most those who respond; (4) his last line of defense is to pose as a victim of a high-functioning helper.

These are some of the characteristics of the neurotic's style of life that brought him or her to helping in the first place. If like the great majority of helpees he encounters a low-functioning helper, these characteristics are confirmed and solidified. If he encounters a high-functioning helper, these characteristics are understood and confronted. The helpee's secrets are now public. His helper has provided him with an alternate style of life and, perhaps for the first time, the helpee has a choice.

GROWING SKILLS

In essence, then, only those who are committed to their own growth can experience genuine joy in another's emergence and growth and be a potential source of nourishment. The helper wants the helpee to live as he himself does; if the helper is growing, she will do all she can to promote growth. If the helper is deteriorating, she will do all she can to promote deterioration. Each kind of helper is fully aware of who she is and what she delivers to the patient.

There are other criteria that we have presented throughout. Here, however, we wish to explore the broader implication and meanings of this struggle to understand. Only the fully honest relationship can engender a full separateness in its closeness. That is, to leave the child, patient, spouse, or friend untouched communicates simply that there are parts of him and ourselves we cannot or do not wish to know more fully or to make public. But only by knowing fully and sharing our experience of the helpee can we validate his experience and existence. This confirmation of experience and existence constitutes the beginnings of self-definition, direction, and independent identity.

Only a person whose experience has been validated by a healthy person or persons early in life or at some crisis point can move on to meet the next crisis with greater courage and creative action. He has acquired the repertoire of response *skills* to do so. The others, like low-functioning helpers, have only a limited response available and are therefore less likely to cope with crises.

Facilitative confrontation is a set of skills. Like other skills, they must be learned. The honest and full confrontation initiated by a potent reinforcer (one who really understands) constitutes the conditions by which helpees learn these skills via modeling. *Self-definition and direction are directly related to the kind, quality and quantity of skills available in the time of crisis.*

Personal emergence starts when the child learns that he can contribute—*act*—physically, emotionally, and intellectually. These three sets of skills constitute the repertoire of responses he attempts to integrate in new ways to meet crises. The greater the number of skills in each area, the greater the probability of successful resolution of the crises. The high-functioning helper provides the helpee with a model of a person who can make such integrated physical, emotional, and intellectual responses, drawn from an ever-growing number of skills. His confrontations are new, unique to himself and the helpee.

The low-functioning helper with his limited number of poor-quality responses employs confrontation as an irresponsible venting of infantile impulses, stereotyped and unchanging from person to person.

Confrontation initiated by a healthy helper is a skill based on a large and growing repertoire of responses, integrated creatively. These responses are gleaned from his experience of the helpee, himself, training, and his own willingness to risk in order to grow and learn. Confrontation emerging from this broad base serves to set the stage for a fully immediate, intense, uniquely personal interaction. Within this context, the full experiential confrontation provides no protection from social-professional roles and games. The participants are exposed in all their strengths and weaknesses, all their constructive and destructive impulses.

CONFRONTATION AND THE WORLD
WE LIVE IN

Confrontation in life as well as in helping has become a verbal exchange designed to win a verbal game with the use of debate techniques. Rarely does it constitute an honest act. Even less frequently does confrontation constitute an effort to promote action for both parties. In more intense situations, confrontation is employed to expose and defeat so that the confronter experiences triumph and the person confronted experiences humiliation. For the most part, the constructive uses of confrontation are foreign. Confrontation may be acceptable as a defensive measure but it is completely unacceptable when a group leader gives permission to confront without regard to meaning, understanding, or outcome. This is most vivid in those forms of encounter or sensitivity groups where the leader encourages the venting of venom by middle-aged adolescents who appear much like young vultures experiencing their first taste of blood.

In more conventional forms of helping, helpers are allowed or encouraged to confront in only a few situations. For example, they have license to confront character disorders in short-term crisis situations, acting-out delinquents, and aggressive patients. Even in these situations, the confrontation is rarely honest or full. When it is employed, it comes off more like a game or gimmick. One must pause to wonder who is the real psychopath.

When employed consistently and used independently of high levels of empathic understanding, confrontation is negative and hostile. Within this context, the confronter is sick. Some even accept a fee for confronting like this and encourage others to do so.

SOME BROADER ISSUES OF PERSONAL
AND SOCIAL RESPONSIBILITY

Most experiences emanating from helping that initially began as an honest human experience are later transformed into a manipulative technique and a game. The employment of confrontation as a gimmick is amply illustrated in the writings and reports of T-, sensitivity, and encounter groups. Again, confrontation, when it does occur in and out of helping, is frequently implemented as a game independent of high levels of empathic understanding. That is what makes the use of these procedures a game in the hands of the average helper and they know it; they know they do not understand the helpee.

The most frequent tool of the low-functioning helper consists of a rather small set of questions. When he or she occasionally employs another technique, he or she presents that technique as his or her orientation.

The average helper cannot afford a full and open confrontation with his helpee because he cannot afford to expose the fact that he knows he has been cheating his patient. Thus his confrontations occur rather infrequently and when they occur they are not even related to the series of questions he has been asking. The confrontation has been, like the questions, formulated long before he ever heard of or saw the helpee. For most of these low-functioning helpers (those that employ confrontation at all) the incongruity between questions and confrontation are designed to make a desperate helpee think that his helper has something in mind that the helpee has not become aware of. From the low-functioning helper's point of view, the confrontation following his stereotyped questions is done with the hope of eliciting abnormal behavior (and it most certainly does) and of intimidating the patient so that he will not dare to confront his helper.

The average helper is convinced that if he confronts (or was confronted) fully, he would have to do so as a person. Without his armament of stupid questions, he, like the patient, will act destructively. What he settles for is a destructive approach he thinks will absolve him of his responsibility for destroying. He "sounds" professional. That is, without his role of expert and stripped of his status, when standing alone, he is—and he knows he is—a destructive person. In the hands of such helpers, roles and status are tools that assist him in his effort to avoid personal responsibility. From his vantage point, there is no consideration of the possibility that there are those who can risk full exposure in a full experiential confrontation. In addition, he does not entertain the possibility that such an encounter can be employed as a constructive experience for both the helpee and the helper. It is not possible for the low-functioning helper to entertain the possibility that another human lives honestly and lives more effectively than his helpee. The low-functioning helper is, and experiences himself as, a helpee—patient, victim.

Only when the helper knows he lives more honestly and effectively than his helpee can he, the helper, confront his helpee at the deepest and fullest level and deal fully with the necessary follow-through. That is, the aftermath of an experiential confrontation most frequently uncovers new material and, hence, there is a necessity for the helper to return to responding before reaching for new directions and more intense levels of immediacy.

A FEW ADDITIONAL POINTS

1. The less-than-effective person is essentially an observer and a poor one at that. He or she views confrontation as acting on impulse to defeat others. His impulses are largely dictated by fear and as a consequence lead to destructive action. He assumes this to be true for everyone else. The role of the observer-judge who never commits a direction of his own is adopted. The implication is that the observer- judge is superior to the doer. Thus the ineffective helper is convinced that in order to avoid being destruc-

tive, he or she must avoid acting, and he or she is correct in his or her case. His actions, based on little or no understanding, distorted perceptions, and the awareness that he cannot help anyone, even himself, are most likely to be deleterious. Yet his inability to act constructively is by itself destructive and he knows this too. So when she can, she will act to neutralize the efforts of effective helpers.

2. *The effective person is an actor, a doer, and understands and welcomes the responsibility for his or her action.* Because the majority of people are observer-judges, the effective person is ready to deal and live on the periphery of society (Carkhuff & Berenson, 1967). Unlike the observer-judge, he knows he must often pay a price for his growth and learning. He knows he often learns the most from acting on what he fears the most and learns the most from acting on what he loves the most (Carkhuff & Berenson, 1967).

3. *The effective person experiences no fear of exposure and is not motivated to seek exposure.* He or she can and must live in contact with his or her expanding experience and come into contact with the experience of another person. He does not question his responsibility for confronting and his obligation to follow-through with even higher levels of helping conditions. He is keenly aware of the role model he provides his helpees but is not dominated or neutralized by this awareness. He or she is thus free to make each encounter a new experience for himself or herself and his or her helpee.

4. *The effective person is not dependent upon others or society to define his identity or function in life.* His function and actions in life are defined in terms of how he experiences his world. He knows his perceptions are not distortions; and in a world largely governed by observer-judges, he has no alternative but to expand this experience and act on it in order to continue to grow. The effective person defines himself.

5. *The effective person knows he or she cannot live and grow while seeking approval and adulation from the large majority of observer-judges.* He knows the majority are not fit to judge or know him. He knows that to seek approval would put him on the others' schedules and hence render him as impotent and as destructive as they who withhold approval only for creative action and give approval for pseudo-action. He often

stands and lives alone, even at the risk of losing a relationship with a helpee.

6. *The effective person, while trusting his or her own motives, impulses, and actions, leaves room to trust the motives, impulses, and actions of other effective persons.* Because he seeks to learn and not distort, his accumulated experience and his ability to make appropriate discriminations allow him the time to continually increase intimate encounters with those who are also growing. He understands that such encounters will demand the full employment of his resources and the resources of the other person. By confronting a growing person appropriately, he offers full human equality and creates the conditions for even more intense encounters.

7. *At the moment of confrontation, the effective person communicates that he or she not only trusts himself or herself but is open to trusting the helpee.* He or she enables the helpee to experience his or her own potential for potency. The effective person may confront the helpee with what is constructive or confront to destroy what is keeping the helpee from growing. She does not confront merely to destroy the helpee or elicit pathological behavior. The effective person, while daring to confront, communicates that she does not fear what is destructive in the other person. The appropriate follow-through, higher levels of helping conditions, and persistence in the confrontation enable the helpee not only to experience his or her own potency, but also to let go of his or her attempts to defeat the effective person's efforts to help. The less-effective helper confronts to make the helpee experience impotency as he, the ineffective person, experiences it, and if he follows through, he does so to point this out in one way or another.

8. *By taking action, the effective person encourages helpee action.* There is the full realization that often nothing changes until both parties act on what they have come to understand. There is no learning without action (Berenson & Mitchell, 1974). There is no understanding without action. There is no growth without action. There is no hope for intimacy without action. Both parties grow from the feedback resulting from their acts and both become better defined as persons.

9. *After a full confrontation, both parties know that the helpee now has alternatives to his or her usual modes of respond-*

ing. He has learned to translate understanding into action. He has learned a new skill. He has also learned that as hard as he has tried he has not been able to injure or insult the helper's integrity and honesty. He has learned that, after all, it is possible to intervene in another person's life creatively and constructively and that he now has the skill to intervene in his own life. He or she has learned that he or she cannot destroy his or her helper. Both the effective helper and the helpee have put all of their constructive and destructive forces on the line and the constructive have outweighed the destructive.

10. *Helpee honesty, integrity, and growth can be encouraged only by a responsible and whole person.* Perhaps for the first time the helpee has experienced crises and has emerged more confident, more directionful, and more whole. He or she has come to know this because of the confidence and direction provided by his or her helper and the helper's ability to mobilize what was growing in both parties. Most importantly, such a relationship enables the helpee to accept responsibility for himself. The helpee knows he has been confronted and the confronter demanded change and that change occurred.

Confrontation is not a technique to be used by those helpers who have not or cannot master basic helping skills and who cannot manage their own lives with honesty, skill, and responsibility. It is not a technique to be used by helpers who move from one fad to the next and/or one extreme of orientation to the other.

Confrontation, although never really necessary or sufficient for effective helping, may be employed by a whole person (helper) to:

1. Address discrepant helpee behaviors.
2. Expand the helping process by creating various levels of crisis in the relationship and, thus, creating a need for the helper and the helpee to act.
3. Make the interaction between helper and helpee more immediate by dealing fully with the here and now.
4. Demonstrate that the helper not only responds but also acts on his or her understanding, even with some risk.
5. Uncover and open new areas to explore; recycle the helping process; re-explore previously discussed but unresolved problem areas.

REFERENCES

BERENSON, B. G., & MITCHELL, K. M. *Confrontation for better or worse!* Amherst, Massachusetts: Human Resource Development Press, 1974.

CARKHUFF, R. R. *Helping and human relations* (Vols. I and II). New York: Holt, Rinehart and Winston, 1969.

CARKHUFF, R. R., & BERENSON, B. G. *Beyond counseling and therapy* (1st ed.). New York: Holt, Rinehart and Winston, 1967.

12

. . . there are as many potential preferred
modes of treatment as there are helpees.

Differential Treatment

Other Sources of Gain in Helping

Differential treatment simply takes into consideration the levels of functioning of both the helpee and helper. Any program of treatment, teaching, or training must begin and end within the learner's frame of reference. The possibility of this occurring is directly dependent upon the level of the helper's responsive and initiative skills at moderate levels of functioning; initially, of course, helper characteristics such as age, sex, race, and social class are relevant. At high levels of functioning these personal characteristics become less and less important. There really is no substitute for skills. The effective helper needs no props such as special dress or hair styles "to make it with the kids" or "street" talk to make it with certain minority groups. The gaps between people are closed if one of the parties involved can provide the other with an experience that starts with relevant exploration and leads toward constructive and personally relevant action.

Most helpees bring with them a distorted frame of reference to their social encounters. Most of the helpee's communications are unrelated to what he or she is feeling in the moment. When helpees respond, the responses are most often negative and they are unable to use their responses for meaningful exploration. In general, helpees communicate little self-regard and deal with feelings in limited, vague, abstract terms, disorganized and with narrowly defined meanings. The same is true of the typical helper. What describes the helpee describes the helper and what describes the helpee describes the therapist. They are the same people, both in need of effective physical, emotional, and intellectual skills. The retarding parent, teacher, or helper is not merely different in degree from the facilitative parent, teacher, or helper, the structure and ingredients of their communications are different (Berenson & Mitchell, 1974).

LEVELS OF FUNCTIONING

The level 3 helper (person) responds to the feeling *and* the meaning of the other person's communication. The level 4 helper (person) responds to the feeling and meaning of the other person's communication, identifies a deficit, and defines a goal. The level 5 helper (person) responds to the feeling and meaning of the other person's communication, identifies a deficit, defines a goal, and provides a systematic program for achieving the goal, and then recycles the process. At level 5 the helper is responding to where the helpee is and where the helpee wants and/or needs to be, and develops means to get the helpee from where he or she is to where he or she wants and/or needs to be. This is essentially how level 5 people function in their lives.

Although we have described level 3 as the minimal level of facilitative functioning, it does not constitute a delivery. By itself, level 3 will not make a significant difference; it must be supplemented with goals and programs. As mentioned, level 3 responses communicate that the helper understands the helpee at the level the helpee presented himself or herself. In more broad terms, level 1 describes not only the retarding helper but also the severely disturbed helpee who is essentially insulated from constructive human encounters. Level 2 describes the more moderately retarding helper or distressed helpee who, unlike the level 1 person, lives in a world of distortion but does *live in the world* and is not oblivious to his world; level 3 describes the minimally facilitative helper or the situationally distressed helpee who, for all other purposes, is functioning at a minimally effective level. Level 4 may characterize the more potent individual who relates effectively and "makes things happen," whatever his area of endeavor but particularly in areas involving the facilitation of other persons. The level 5 person, in turn, is involved in a lifelong search for actualization for others as well as himself and is readily amenable to the sharing of his search with others. In summary, then, whether he is helpee or helper, student or teacher, child or parent, these (or similar) scales may be employed to assess the person's level of interpersonal functioning. The implications for a comprehensive model of facilitative processes are profound.

At each point of significant interactions in the individual's development, the consequences may be "for better or for worse"; that is, if we assume that the individual has the inherent capacity to be influenced in constructive or destructive directions, then each encounter with those significant persons designated by society as "more knowing" may have constructive or deteriorative consequences for the "less knowing" person. The assumption is that the individual does not begin with a disposition toward either constructive growth or destructiveness. Only as the child grows outward does he move in a positive or negative direction. Thus, the dominance of high or low levels of facilitative dimensions in relationships with parents, teachers, and other significant figures will contribute to effective functioning or dysfunctioning in the individual. It makes sense to say that helpers offering a continuation of the same levels of facilitative dimensions will continue to produce further constructive change or deterioration in the individual.

In addition, a clear implication of the model is that individuals are growing constructively when they move toward higher levels of functioning on empathy, regard, genuineness, and concreteness and are deteriorating when they move in the direction of lower levels of functioning on these dimensions.

Implicit is the assumption that the person in his relations with others shows the way he feels about himself. Again, only to the degree that he understands and respects a full range of experiences in himself can he understand and respect a full range of experiences in others.

Thus we can trace the development of individuals at any of the various levels. To be sure, we must acknowledge that the individual is not solely a result of a series of relationships or any other environmental factors. He is not simply "acted upon." Nevertheless, at this moment we can make a strong case for the critical and differential influences of the significant relationships in a given individual's evolution.

Only the whole helper can constructively intervene in the life of a helpee. He or she is in tune with his or her experience of the world and can discriminate between when his or her experience is congruent with or divergent from the experience of others. *The whole helper trusts his experience of the helpee more than the helpee trusts his own experience of himself. The whole counselor trusts his or her experience more than the helpee's expression of his or her's.* The ideal image of the counselor most usually supported in traditional training programs is that of an agent of change who does not interfere in the life of the client. He does not stray from an all-accepting attitude; he listens and understands the pain but *does nothing* active. At the other extreme we have behavioral manipulators who only apply predesigned programs related to symptoms. These helpers know how to act but not how to respond. They cite their success rates and admit to recidivism rates but are rarely specific in terms of total numbers. However, active intervention is frequently necessary. The helpee must make decisions. In addition, with any helpee functioning below a minimally facilitative, self-sustaining level, the helper must give helping a great deal of form and structure. The direction of helping is dictated by what is effective in helping the helpee to emerge with his or her own direction and skills. This direction must be based on the helper's skills and the appropriate use of these in the selection and implementation of a preferred mode of treatment. Furthermore, the selection and implementation of a preferred mode of treatment is viewed by the whole helper in terms of its *unique* contributions to the total treatment process, modified by the helper's experience wih the individual helpee. For example, this may lead to the interruption of a series of desensitization sessions by a confrontation between the helper and helpee concerning unconscious helpee or helper motives that lead to difficulty in the trials to extinction of anxiety. *A preferred mode of treatment may be employed by itself or in combination with other programs, depending upon how the whole helper experiences the client.*

Too often, counselors and therapists who do provide minimally facilitative levels of conditions are faced with the dilemma that the helpee, over the course of helping, has gained considerable insight into his dynamics yet can make no meaningful translations to action in his real life. The helper has learned to trust the words of the helpee rather than to evaluate and promote positive behavioral change. As is the case with restricting clinical practice to the tenents of any one school, *restricting practice to high levels of the core conditions has serious limitations.* It is the rare counselor who faces these limitations *with* the helpee, whether these limitations are due to the core conditions, the dictates of any one school, or the personal limitations of the counselor or helpee. Typically, counseling and therapy are honest *only* to a degree.

On the one hand, this may be due to the doubt the counselor has concerning what to do after being fully honest. On the other hand, for the less-than-whole counselor, honest expressions are often destructive. The gain is in the full honesty; there is no loss of face for honestly not knowing. The helper cannot and need not always be ahead of the helpee. The moments of "not knowing" provide the whole helper with opportunities to dig deeper into his or her experience of the helpee and of himself or herself in interaction with the helpee. These moments also provide the opportunity for the helpee to struggle for his or her own effective direction. *Whole helpers as well as their helpees often do not know where to go next; the whole helper has the resources to enter process without knowing outcome.* The effective helper can do this because of her winning record. More importantly, the effective helper knows there are few things in life for which he does not have a large and effective repertoire of responses. The helper knows how to define goals, knows what he or she needs to do this, and has the skill to use all this to get to the goal. In this moment the helpee comes to see something more of the helper's humanity with all its determination, strength, skill, and commitment in the face of doubts. *The periods of temporary loss of direction provide us with the needed clues as to the preferred modes of treatment.*

More typically, the helpee and the helper adjust to one another at a level that *appears* honest and fruitful but is in fact separate from life; it stops short of exposing what the helper does *not* know. The interaction is comfortable for each; but real helping begins when we face what we do not know. Any therapeutic relationship characterized by long periods of calm and comfort is only apparently helpful. The comfort merely communicates to both the helper and the helpee that each is willing to tolerate and accept the distance between them; after all, each means nothing to the other. Again, insights, high levels of core conditions, interpretations, and reflections are, for many helpees, not enough to promote constructive behavioral change. High levels of core conditions and insights do provide the helper with the experience he or she needs to determine how he or she can go about implementing the goals of helping; that is, the helper is committed to doing anything which will aid the helpee to translate his efforts into actions which will enhance personal emergence. Beyond the central core of facilitative conditions, the following general statement serves as an initial orientation for the helper. *Conditioning or direct management techniques are most effective with clients functioning at low levels; insights are most effective for those clients functioning at levels high enough to employ insights effectively in life.*

HELPING WITH THE LOW-LEVEL-
FUNCTIONING HELPEE

Helping for the high-level-functioning helper with the helpee functioning below level 3 must be on the helper's terms. Direct shaping and guiding are necessary and effective when provided within the context of high levels of responding. In the following exchange with a helpee functioning at level 1.5, after the first phase of helping the helper acts independently of the helpee's verbalization.

Up to this point the helper related to the helpee responsively to facilitate helpee exploration. The material explored was highly disorganized, often vague, and reflected high levels of helpee anxiety. Without direction the helpee would slowly deteriorate. More helper initiative was needed. Attempts to allow the helpee to direct the sessions led to increased confusion and disorganization as well as to both helpee and helper anxiety. The helper realized words about feelings were not enough and that unless the helping sessions translated into orderly action steps in the life of the helpee, things could only grow worse.

> *Helper:* It's like being buried under all the things going through your head.
>
> *Helpee:* I have a good imagination, it works by itself.
>
> *Helper:* It's confusing because there are so many things you think about.
>
> *Helpee:* Yes—so many—I get—they get me.
>
> *Helper:* It's like the thoughts control you.
>
> *Helpee:* I can't catch up—I go in all directions—I wonder if I'm crazy.
>
> *Helper:* It's frustrating because you can't control things.
>
> *Helpee:* I'm crazy, that's all—I don't have anything—or able—
>
> *Helper:* It's terrifying because you are not together inside —and you can't control your thoughts and feelings.
>
> *Helpee:* Everything happens without me—inside and outside, it's always this way—I don't get anything done and people know I'm strange.
>
> *Helper:* It's like being lost because you can't get on top of things—get them together but you want to—very much.

Helpee: If I don't—well—I'm out of it—out of it all.

Helper: You get so far down because your life depends upon getting yourself together and you can't wait to get started.

Helpee: Get started, that's all I try to do but I get lost.

The process was brought from almost complete confusion to the threshold of goal definition. The helper at this point knows he must take the process to more detail. The helpee was demonstrating stronger affect and more energy.

Helper: You get lost and scared because you don't know where you really want to go—except to get rid of those scary feelings.

Helpee: Guess I don't know why I do so many things—I try—to do what I'm asked to—but . . .

Helper: You feel mixed up because you can't tune in on what you are missing but you keep trying. I think the first step is to organize each day. We will meet, develop goals for each day and plan the details for accomplishing each goal. Our first goal is to get organized. The first step is to list what you do each day.

The helper became more and more active as it was appropriate, but always from the helpee's frame of reference first, then his. Active intervention began with the identification of why the helpee felt the way he did, then moved to the identification of a deficit, a personally relevant goal, and the first step toward reaching the goal. Implicitly and explicitly, the helper communicates a willingness to follow through. The whole helper can see the world through the eyes of his or her *helpee better than the helpee who is functioning at low levels; he or she can determine what is good and bad in that world better than the helpee.*

All helpees, high- or low-functioning, in their own way ask these questions:

1. "Is this person sensitive, perceptive, and strong enough to enter my world deeply without being destroyed himself, in which case I get worse?"

2. "Is this person sensitive, perceptive, and strong enough to warrant my full trust, so that I can follow his lead without the fear that I can destroy him or that he will destroy me?"

Helpees want to know if the helper has anything the helpee wants and needs. Helpees want to know if the helper can make it in the helpee's world better than the helpee can. Helpees want to know if the helper has a means to deliver what he or she has for the helpee in a form the helpee can use.

If the helper in any way avoided the full responsibility or avoided a full effort to determine an appropriate direction for himself in interaction with his helpee, there would have been no hope that the helpee would have answered these questions in such a way that helping would have occurred. This helpee could not take the chance of being let down after finding some hope. High levels of core conditions did not alone provide the impetus for real helping. Real helping is specifically made up of responding *and* goal definition *and* program development (Carkhuff, 1973, 1974).

THERAPEUTIC CONDITIONING

In other instances, the core conditions may offer the helpee *hope* that the helper may be able to help; they provide the foundation for effective helper intervention. In the following case, conditioning procedures were introduced in order to free the helpee of burdensome aspects of selective but basic social functions so that he could act with confidence upon his newly acquired insights.

In the following excerpt a 20-year-old college junior functioning at level 2 and achieving well academically is certain that he will, at some critical moment in life, fail an important challenge. In addition, he had been a stutterer for about 16 years and had undergone long periods of speech therapy. The following exchange is after summer vacation during which the apparent gains of counseling of the previous spring had been lost:

> *Helpee:* The first part of the s-s-summer was great—ah— pretty good. I came back, and oh, hell, it's the same—I'm going to bust.
>
> *Helper:* Whatever we did last spring was *not* enough, Lee —guess we start from that.
>
> *Helpee:* Oh, you did help—a—lot—it's just that, well, I could not keep hold of it—you did help, honest.
>
> *Helper:* No, I don't need that—you don't either. I missed the boat—I need only to look at you—to know.

Helpee: Don't blame yourself, maybe that's the way—or
this is the way I will be—I let you down—I
always felt good for a few days after our sessions.

Helper: Look, we're not going to pass credits back and
forth—and we're not going through old stuff. But
you are a big, strong guy and I'm going to make
you work.

Helpee: I'll try anything.

Helper: There's a set of procedures and techniques I've
been studying. I've never tried them out but from
what I've read and observed, I think we can
profit from giving them a damn good try.

Helpee: What's it like?

Helper: I'll be learning as you learn, but the first thing
we'll do is train you to relax.

Helpee: If you could j-j-just do that—it would be *something*.

Helper: I want us to do a lot more. Give us a couple of
months. We'll meet about three times a week and
I'll share—explain everything to you as we go
along.

Helpee: Sounds kind of mysterious right now.

Helper: Guess it does—but in a nutshell—I'm going to
get you to think about, with me, things that get
you nervous—until the thoughts don't bug you
anymore. Then we will practice things, like
speaking before a group, until that gives you no
trouble. We'll work it through from easy stuff to
the more difficult—step-by-step. Look, give me a
few days to work it all out, then you and I will go
over the entire program—I think you're a natural
for this—I'm comfortable about the whole thing
and pretty confident that it's what we need.

It is obvious that there is a deep level of respect and trust
between the helper and the helpee. The helper shares fully how
he experiences the helpee and, once again, takes over the direction of the course of helping. Counterconditioning is dictated.

The helper, in conjunction with Lee, works out a hierarchy
of meaningful stress situations involving both school and home

and the significant people in both settings. For example, at the bottom of the hierarchy—the stress situation first worked upon—we find Lee under conditions of deep relaxation conjuring images of both (1) walking to a critical class where he must, later in the year, make an important presentation and (2) walking toward his house where he must make explanations to his father of his week's activities. When Lee felt anxiety, he let the helper know. In small but distinct gradations, he moved into the classroom (home), at first when the instructor (father) would not be there and then when he was present. Finally, Lee made his classroom presentation in imagery. In addition, in each case a transition was made from imagery to role-playing and then actually acting. However, even the behavior therapy did not always go smoothly. After ten sessions of relaxation and desensitization training, a seemingly impassable plateau was reached. During these sessions, another experienced counselor was employed to role-play critical adult male figures in the helpee's life: father, high school football coach, and ROTC commanding officer.

The client, although a person of superior talents and physical resources, was shaped from early childhood to seek the approval of others. He had learned that to do *his* best alienated others because his superior performance was a threat. Approval from critical others was always held back and, in his desperate search for acceptance, he geared his efforts to a mean or modal level of output. He settled for the "nice guy" role, never threatening, never challenging, always walking a tightrope between failure and a minimally acceptable performance. At the time of these early conditioning sessions, Lee had lost contact with experiencing himself as superior in any area of endeavor, even physically:

> *Helper:* Damn it, Lee, you let everybody judge you—
> you're always bound up with it—you even want
> to look good to us.
>
> *Helpee:* Wh-what do you mean?
>
> *Helper:* You know what I mean—they're not fit to judge
> you, damn it, you let yourself jump—for their
> approval. You'll end up like them. But you'll
> know, Lee—you'll know deep down—*jump!*
>
> *Helpee:* Go to hell!

There was a long pause while the helper and helpee looked

at one another and at the same moment exchanged big broad smiles.

> *Helper:* Now you look 6 feet tall and strong—and it feels *good.*
>
> *Helpee:* Ya-Ya—you're darn right.

The helpee was, for the first time, in contact with who he was. Someone actually approved of him when he was fully himself. He experienced some surprise and a great deal of pride: the monster he feared did not emerge and, in fact, was nonexistent.

At this point there is not only *real* hope but a growing sense of conviction that the helpee needs to *act*. Beyond this, the helpee began to experience a deeper and firmer awareness of his own values, his own integrity, and the initial experiencing of both fear and anger in the face of what had been fearful life decisions and circumstances.

At the twentieth session (the sessions having involved open honest confrontations and desensitization training), the helpee voices deeper doubts about the motives of the two helpers.

Time was running out and the helper knew it and employed confrontation as a tool to make the process more efficient. Within the context of the response base established during earlier sessions, the confrontations also provided more focused exploration. At this point the highly initiative confrontations became highly empathic responses. Although equally successful, interactions can take place without confrontation. In this instance it saved time, allowed the helper to explore using more initiative and cleared up any doubts the helpee might have had about whether or not the helper would go all the way. Alternative ways of dealing with the lack of progress would involve a broader base of responding, moving to more cognitive means for developing and to courses of action. Most of all, the helper knew that successful helping in this instance must culminate in training the helpee in the skills he needed as well as desensitizing him to anxiety-provoking stimuli.

> *Helper:* Lee, I sense your holding back again—not going all the way.
>
> *Helpee:* Ya, I can't help it but I keep thinking that in the end you will humble me—just like the rest.
>
> *Helper:* Maybe I'm no different, but you'll never know unless you go all the way, Lee, you'll never know.

There is little trace of any traditional helpee–helper roles. The helpee had come to view the two helpers on an equalitarian level. He refers to them by using their first names, not as a gimmick introduced by the helpers but coming from the helpee spontaneously.

Finally, having successfully made his classroom presentation and received a very high rating by his instructor, Lee presented the helpee's viewpoint of his helping experience to a class of graduate students. His presentation was spontaneous and unprepared. Indeed, the presentation was a commanding one. Following the presentation, there was an exchange among Lee, the helpers, and the students:

Helper 1: What set of things contributed most to where you are now?

Helpee: Getting bawled out—a couple of times.

Helper 2: I remember the day we said let's junk the desensitization today and get the bastard.

Helpee: Two weeks ago we just walked around the campus. It was a warm day, like today. You asked me about the talk I had to give to the ROTC class, and I began to say things that—I was sure the talk would go lousy, and you jumped on me. Little things help, like "to hell with what others think." I could tell the both of you were angry with me. You had a perfect reason to be ticked off at me. I was so foolish. We had some real good talks. I think that's the whole thing. As for (I don't know what it is called) desensitization, it's hard to say if it helps or not. It's been about a month. I think it helped a little bit. It's not the real thing. I used to picture scenes in my mind. I'd be asked if I was anxious, and raise my finger if I was nervous. I got to dislike it, after a while. It might have helped a little. I don't know if it worked. It isn't like being here talking to the class.

Helper 2: Somehow you have to translate the whole thing into action.

Helpee: Somewhat. I did notice that after picturing the ROTC, going there didn't seem to bother me as

much. It helps to a certain extent, not completely, though, because it is not the real thing.
. . . Ya, it gets you going. I used to picture classroom scenes; entering the class was a big thing.

Helper 1:   Are you aware of the resources you brought to
bear? What did you contribute here?

Helpee: When I first started, not much of anything
really. Later on, my first presentation to this
group, I was very embarrassed, everybody sitting around, knowing. It was very hard, very
hard, believe me. First, just because it was a
class, a group of people, and secondly, they did
not know the whole story. I think the hardest
part is going through these different things with
other people, *live.* I think I really had to push
myself. Had to push myself to come here for the
practice sessions. The thing that really did it
was sheer drive on my part to go through with
it. Now, today, when I first came here, it was
completely different. I was relaxed.

Helper 1:   What did you tap in on in yourself?

Helpee: Basically, I learned that what I feared, I *could*
do. Everything I feared I could not do, like
speaking before a class, I found I could do.

Helper 1:   The systematic part gets the helpee started
toward considering problem areas. After handling them in imagery, you have to tap in on
your own strengths. Maybe that's part of the
unique contribution of behavior therapy.

Helpee: Between sessions I used to try to put into
action what we talked about, like I'm doing
right now, here talking with you.

Helper 1:   Who are we to you now? (Referring to the
helpers collectively or separately.)

Helpee: Well, I don't look on you as being doctors. I
see you as, as friends. I almost think of you as
being one of the guys, just a friend. The professional role stuff is gone. You've become
people.

Helper 1:   (to the group) I think some of you have to
doubt.

> *Helpee:*   (looking at the group) If you want to ask me anything, ask me.

This experience was very important to the helpers. Their willingness to break with traditional roles and methods was possible because they really did understand the helpee better than he understood himself and the helpee knew it. The experience drove home several important lessons for both the helpers and the helpees: there needs to be goals, and they, the helpers, had to learn more systematic methods for achieving goals. In addition, it led to more highly developed responding skills so that the helpers found themselves confronting helpees less frequently. They found that responding culminates in systematic training programs for helpees that render confrontation unnecessary. In fact, they found that except for the very lowest-level-functioning helpee, the *general* program was the same for all levels of helpees: responding to feeling and meaning, then systematically adding the identification of deficits, goals, and individualized programs.

HELPING WITH A HIGHER-LEVEL HELPEE

The helpee initially functioning above level 3 affords the whole helper basically the same experience. That is, the helping process, if it is to succeed, must provide the helpee with the conditions needed for full exploration, understanding that culminates in goals, and action that takes the helpee from where he is to where he wants and/or needs to be. The helper's task is basically the same: the helper, regardless of the helpee's level of functioning, must respond, personalize, and initiate. The helper, during the middle and late phases of helping, organizes the emerging direction and gives it definition with a strategy that leaves the helpee with new responses.

If the helper is less than whole, then the level of the helpee's functioning is irrelevant. If the helper is whole, then the level of functioning of the helpee is relevant because it will determine personalized goals and programs. Helping starts with where the helper is and where the helpee is, for better or for worse. It is for better if the helper has a larger repertoire of physical, emotional, and intellectual responses than the helpee. It is for worse when the helper has no more (or fewer) responses than does the helpee.

A 32-year-old woman distressed about her relationships wonders if she will always be lonely.

Helpee: I've never been—say warm, open—always a bit careful, you know.

Helper: You feel different because it's been hard to make close friends.

Helpee: I've had a few good friends when I was in school but they were just like me—sort of square.

Helper: You've felt alone because you didn't do the same things others did.

Helpee: There was—is no one to really talk to—I didn't know if anyone would listen—guess I'd bore them.

Helper: You feel insecure because you don't know if you can make friends.

Helpee: I'm really worried—because I can't get close to people—or don't know how. I handle most things —but when it comes to people I don't know or trying to get closer to someone I end up making wisecracks.

Helper: You are really furious with yourself because you are not more comfortable with people and you want to be. Let's consider what you'd like to be able to do with someone you like.

Helpee: I'd like to ask someone to do something with me—show—concert—

Helper: OK—what's the first step?

The helper and helpee worked together to develop a program to make friends and do things with them that included steps to: greet people, react with polite responses, initiating simple kind acts, responding to other people's experience, selecting something to do together, issuing an invitation, and doing something together.

Helpers functioning below level 3 focus on irrelevancies. Helpers functioning above level 3 focus on what makes a difference.

Helping is skills training for the helpee. In this instance, the helpee learned some basic greeting skills, politeness skills, responding and initiative skills, including something about how to develop a simple program.

In another instance the helper may instruct the helpee in the skills needed to resolve problems of choice. The need of the helpee to understand his or her experience often dominates. The helpee, if he or she is to fully understand, needs more than psychodynamic constructs, whether they are psychoanalytic or based upon learning theory. The helpee needs to be able to organize experience so that something can be done.

> *Helpee:* I know it's a good chance to get ahead but it will leave me with less time for my family.
>
> *Helper:* You feel conflicted because both the job and your family are very important.
>
> *Helpee:* Yes, it's well—I want to be more than a house-wife—I need to get out—meet people—you can get a pretty dumb feeling talking only to children all day.
>
> *Helper:* You're feeling boxed in because work at home really doesn't tap all you can do.
>
> *Helpee:* I know I can do more—not run the world, but more—it's like—well—at home I'm always responding to what everyone else wants—and that's OK, but it sure isn't all. Yet I want my home to be a good place for my family.
>
> *Helper:* You feel torn because you can't do everything you want to do but you want to do as much as possible. I think we can try some problem-solving techniques that might help you decide on a course of action that reflects what is important to you. Then we can develop a plan to put it into action.

The helper and helpee continued to explore the problem until they were able to state it in very specific terms, such as: the time the helpee had was less than the time she needed to do everything she wanted or needed to do. With additional exploration they defined the goal as: the time available must become equal to or greater than the time needed and wanted.

The helpee learned how to define a problem in very specific terms.

The helper and helpee then moved on to develop possible courses of action that were relevant to the goal and workable. They then moved to identifying helpee values related to the goal such as: family, money, self-development. They rank-ordered the values and assigned them weights.

The helpee learned how to develop realistic courses of action and relate them to the values she had that were relevant to goals.

Finally, the helper and the helpee systematically evaluated each course of action in terms of her values. The helpee was able to determine, step by step, if a course of action would help or hinder her achieving her goal. Problem solving in a systematic way organized all the critical factors that had been scattered and confused. By exploring each step carefully in terms of the helpee's frame of reference, the helper was certain that the ingredients and how they interrelated reflected the helpee's experience and life. The helpee acquired a set of skills she could now use in a wide variety of problem situations at work, at home, with individuals and groups.

In summary, the sources of gain in helping above and beyond the central core of facilitative conditions involve the use of problem-solving technology and program development. Behavior modification and some aspects of trait-and-factor counseling constitute special cases of program development. The personalized program designed to guide helpee action is the preferred mode of treatment for that helpee.

If used so that it would make a contribution, psychoanalytic theory and practice would need to view helpee free-association as exploration. Helper interpretations would need to be developed to the point of specific goals, and therapeutic follow-through would take the form of personalized strategies to implement the use of the helpee's new skills. The first step in a program to be effective for the psychoanalyst would be to attend to the patient. The second step would involve observing the patient; and the third step would involve listening to identify the patient's feeling and the reason for the helpee's feeling state. It may take the form of this illustration:

> *Helpee:* No matter how much I do I never feel it is enough. I can't seem to satisfy anyone—even myself—it's just no good.
>
> *Helper:* You feel useless because what you do does not seem to make a difference to anyone.
>
> (Rather than a diagnostically oriented question

or even an interpretation about feelings of impotence after free association.)

Helpee: I do what I can and then more—sort of—I must do more than anyone else to feel I've done my share.

Helper: You feel insecure because you don't think others have left room for you—because you want a place in this world.

Helpee: I try to earn it—I try to make up for something about me—I want to feel as good as anyone—but I don't—because I've failed too often—no one really notices me—

Helper: You feel almost ignored because no one seems to appreciate you.

Helpee: I don't appreciate myself—well, yes I do—I don't know—I'd like to make them all pay—but then I could not live with myself if I really hurt them.

Helper: You're disgusted with yourself because you cannot live more independently of what others think and you do want to be more independent.

Helpee: I'm afraid—that's right—I don't feel like a man and I'm forty-three years old. I've spent my whole life trying to make people love me and I end up not caring very much for myself.

Helper: You feel weak and vulnerable because you cannot respond or initiate like you think an adult should and you want to feel like an adult. Our first goal is to develop a program to help you get yourself together physically. Then we will work on programs to put it together emotionally and intellectually. Your first step is to make an appointment to get a complete physical examination so we can begin by getting in shape.

There could have been interpretations of unresolved oedipal feelings, a castration complex, even an oral or anal fixation. Even with all these insights, correct or not, the helpee would still be an infantile, selfish person who is too preoccupied with his own needs to respond effectively to the world he lives in. He is angry because the world is not designed to serve only his needs.

If he is to change he needs to learn and develop other emotional responses. In order to develop a larger repertoire of emotional responses he must develop a larger repertoire of physical responses. Eventually, if change is to continue and be self-sustaining, this helpee must learn intellectual skills related to setting goals related to responding to other people's needs and acting to do so. His maturity and adulthood depend upon expanded skills, not insights that are as impotent as he.

A BRIEF OVERVIEW

Extensive research studies of helping developed and validated the methods illustrated in this chapter (Carkhuff, 1969, 1971). Specifically, helpees move toward their helper's level of functioning and these results lead directly to large-scale training applications with both credentialed and functional professionals in a wide variety of human service fields.

Effective living and helping are, in general, a function of two factors: the skills with which helpers relate to other people (interpersonal skills) and the skills they have in their specialty areas (program skills). The implications for the helping professions are important. With systematic selection and systematic training, helpers may be developed to effect significant and constructive change in individuals and communities.

The implications for individual helpers are even more critical. In order to accomplish effective helping, the individual helper must ensure his or her own effective development and translate his or her own offerings systematically into efficient programs. The most effective modality for our own development as well as that of our helpees is skills training.

Our goal in helping, then, is to populate the world we live in with helpers. The means to accomplish this are at hand: to develop our interpersonal skills and to complement them with a growing repertoire of effective programs as well as to master the technology needed to develop new programs. In this manner we can transmit to our future helpees the kinds of interpersonal and specialty skills they need to function as helpers. In turn, our helpees-turned-helpers can transmit the kinds of interpersonal and specialty skills that their children, students, and helpees need to function fully in their worlds.

REFERENCES

BERENSON, B. G., & MITCHELL, K. M. *Confrontation for better or worse!* Amherst, Massachusetts: Human Resource Development Press, 1974.

CARKHUFF, R. R. *Helping and human relations* (Vols. I and II). New York: Holt, Rinehart and Winston, 1969.

CARKHUFF, R. R. *The development of human resources.* New York: Holt, Rinehart and Winston, 1971.

CARKHUFF, R. R. *The art of helping.* Amherst, Massachusetts: Human Resource Development Press, 1972.

CARKHUFF, R. R. *The art of problem solving.* Amherst, Massachusetts: Human Resource Development Press, 1973.

CARKHUFF, R. R. *How to help yourself: The art of program development.* Amherst, Massachusetts: Human Resource Development Press, 1974.

13

Helping is as effective as the
helper is living effectively.

Counseling as a
Way of Life

Traditional psychotherapy is about many things. It is about sickness, theories, dynamics, insights, diagnoses, symptoms, the unconscious, interpretations, and even status. None of these things makes a difference to helpees; they don't even make a difference to the psychotherapist. Helping, too, is about many things that reflect the human condition. Helping is about human growth, personal responsibility, learning, and skills. All these things do make a difference to the helpee and to the helper; they make a difference to all people! Helping makes a difference because while it equips the individual with a larger repertoire of skills, helping translates to experiencing the strength and beauty in realizing human potential. Helping is about effective families, work, education, productivity, the individual, society, even politics and intelligence.

In the first instance and in the last instance, helping is about life and choosing to live it.

Helping has been learning for us: learning how to make a difference for the young and old, male and female, healthy and sick, strong and weak, courageous and cowardly, black and white, brown and yellow and red. Helping is learning how to translate our experiences of joy, anguish, anxiety, anger, digust, fury, and love into something that makes a difference: a product. A product, not fantasies filled with hopeless and distorted imagery. A product, not inactivity filled with a growing emptiness. A product, not lies filled with hate. Products that make a difference in the constant struggle to realize human potential emerge from those who can learn more than they know each day and minute they live and know they have learned something only if the experience translates to a product and more learning.

Helping is a search for truth and it is possible because some of us learn how to see and hear, and feel and understand and act beyond the boundaries of our own skin. Helping is learning to take only what you have earned and then working to earn more. More of what? Responsibility for more of yourself and more of the world you live in. Helping is freedom. The learning gives the growing the skills they need to understand what they did not understand. The growing person's constant learning and increasing responsibility sets him or her free.

Just about every person dreams one day about being fully human, strong, wise, powerful, just, tender, generous, loving, peaceful, warlike, directionful, demanding, generous, secure, courageous, calm, passionate, large, and committed. The gulf between those who are these things and those who are only caught up in their fantasies was created by a choice. Some have chosen to grow while others have chosen slow deterioration and the gulf grows wider and deeper. This chapter is about some of the things we have learned about those who do not yield to self abuse by only reacting rather than acting. It is about those who are resolved to realize that those who demand only comfort can be out-worked, out-lasted, surrounded, helped, or destroyed because they are stupid. When the growing person understands this, he or she simply moves on to create new levels of living. The growing experience life as full because they realize they are the unbroken promise of human potential, the hope, perhaps the only hope (Berenson, 1975).

Fraudulent living, supported and nurtured by social myths, can at best yield only theories and research of half-truths and ineffective clinical practice. The contamination seeded by social myths too often influences the direction of those with enough energy to attempt growth and constructive impact. Personal emergence is structured in terms of living up to the image of the perfectly acculturated individual: an individual trapped and held back by these half-truths, myths, and the characteristics of his ideal image. Striving to live up to an image denies the possibility of unique, fully creative personal emergence, for ideal images are only socially determined.

Attempts to emerge are easily neutralized by society's apparent value of the image and by those who have chosen only to die slowly. In addition, neutralization of potentially creative acts is accomplished by reminding the potent person that he is not altogether living up to his image—society's weapon of using his virtues against him. *The whole person needs no image to live up to and is not conflicted by the lack of perfect consistency.*

THE WHOLE PERSON

The whole person does not merely live in the external world. *The life of the whole person is made up of actions fully integrating his emotional, intellectual, and physical resources in such a way that these actions lead to greater and greater self-definition.*

Wholeness comes from the movement of the individual toward a larger and larger repertoire of physical, emotional, and intellectual responses of high quality. Obviously the rate of increase will vary from individual to individual, modality to modality, and situation to situation, as well as from their interaction. The direction of this movement, although influenced by individual differences and environmental differences, has essential common aspects. It is these *common* themes we have attempted to spell out.

More specifically and by way of illustration, the counselor and helper who is whole addresses his or her energies to a full synthesis of (1) research, (2) theory, (3) the creative consideration of all theories and research in order to develop preferred modes of treatment, and (4) the development of an integrative model of his own, consistent with who *he* is and one which he is able to employ with the totality of his being.

Although we stress the physical and experiential bases of life, ours is not an anti-intellectual stance. The full person who accepts the responsibility for having impact on others (parents, teachers, clergymen, spouses, counselors, and therapists) responds to make generalizations from stable bodies of phenomena in his life as well as to test, in experience and research, deductive hypotheses derived from his own and the theories of others. Constant qualification, modification, and movement into the unknown serve as the fabric for his growth. *Helping is as effective as the helper is living effectively.*

We, as a people, can no longer delimit ideally effective helping to the counseling and therapy hours. Those hours, on the average, are neither ideal nor effective. The implication here is quite clear: most counselors and helpers are asking their helpees to learn to live more effectively. In reality, they are asking "the less knowing" person to do something that they, the helpers, cannot do.

Effective helping is not separate from life but offers a unique and vivid contrast to the general life experience in society. This contrast cannot be experienced so long as the "more knowing" person functions within a socially defined role. Only by breaking free of roles can he give his fully integrated self to the experience, the learnings and relearnings. Only in this manner can he tap his own resources at a deeper level and hope to become an ever-expanding whole person.

Beyond these general statements and observations there are a number of specific points reflecting the implications of becoming whole.

1. The only consistency for the whole person is internal. The person who is in tune with and acts on the bases of his integrity is free to modify, incorporate, and learn from venturing into the unknown, with fear but with a knowledge that his inner being will not and cannot be destroyed. Furthermore, he is not neutralized when others demand consistency. The person who has reached society's limits of tolerance for personal emergence and stops has agreed not only to emerge no further but also not to upset social systems and not to expose others who have sold their integrity.

2. Creativity and honesty are a way of life for the whole person.

The whole person is fully aware that he is as creative as he is honest. Any semblance of trading or compromising responsible honesty results in attenuated creativity. The *real* risk for the whole person involves honesty *not* being a way of life, in all his actions, with and including physical implications. A dishonest act, for the whole person, results in a dysfunction of the basic physical foundations of life: eating, sleeping, elimination, and sex. Honesty in communication is not, however, without qualification, as in the case of the extremely brittle patient.

3. Although the way the whole person lives his or her life is seen by others to be too dangerous, too intense, and too profound, he or she is in tune with the fact that his or her real risk involves living life without risk.

Life has meaning in new discoveries, larger boundaries, deeper insights, more pain, more joy, and the realization that the whole person can only be as full with another person as he is full with himself *when alone.*

4. The whole person realizes that life is empty without acting.

The full person must discriminate among possible acts, make his choice, and ACT. The most significant learning comes from acting on those aspects of life the individual fears most. For the whole person there is security only in risks. In this way, and only in this way, can the individual gain or lose. In a life without risk, no one wins, no one loses, and *no one learns.*

5. The whole person realizes that whatever he or she does is worth doing fully and well.

Full emergence depends on a full and an integrated output of energy.

6. The whole and creative person functions at a high energy level.

He employs his energy fully, resting only as much as is necessary to restore his usual vigor so as to be able to bring to bear and tap his *talents fully* in dealing with crises and being productive in everyday life.

7. The whole person comes to the realization that few men or women are large enough or whole enough to nourish and love the creative person.

A full relationship, free of neurotic drainage, is only possible among whole people. Others functioning at lower levels cannot go beyond insisting that the creative person has been lucky enough to stumble on a new or novel gimmick.

8. The whole person is fully aware that any significant human relationship is in the process of deepening or deteriorating.

Stability in any relationship is only apparent. When it is not growing it undergoes changes that increase distance between those involved; this is true for parent–child, teacher–student, husband–wife, and helper–helpee relationships.

9. The whole person realizes that most men and women say "yes" out of fear of the implications of saying "no," and that most men and women say "no" out of fear of the implications of saying "yes."

The whole person can predict a great deal of behavior from this statement, knowing that the majority of people cannot see or respond to anything but the fear of the implications of their act at a choice point.

10. The whole person is fully aware that in order to live life in such a way that it is a continuous learning and relearning process, he or she must periodically burn bridges behind him or her.

The full life requires making discriminations. To leave room for everyone in one's life is only to leave room for one's self and, thus, to retard self-definition. Clinging to past associations that drain energies only nourishes neurotic needs and diminishes creative output.

11. The whole person realizes that he or she is, and must be, his or her own pathfinder, and travel a road never traveled before.

The whole person can be alone with himself. Creative acts by definition require new and untrod directions. If the person cannot live with himself, he cannot discover directions congruent with who he is; only when he does can he hope to reach for full fruition of his talents and person.

12. The whole person does not fear living intensely.

The whole person experiences greater joy and greater pain. He or she is aware that life is as full as it is intense. He or she can endure and even flourish as he or she lives intensely, because he or she has fully integrated the emotional, intellectual, and physical. It is only under extreme circumstances that the whole person taps deeper personal resources and significant new learning.

13. The whole person is prepared to face the implications of functioning a step ahead or above most of those with whom he or she comes into contact.

Knowing when not to act or to respond in terms of his or her deep sensitivities requires fine discriminations. These actions depend upon whether or not the second person recognizes that the whole person can be a positive and constructive influence. The whole person's insights, because they are so far beyond the obvious, are often interpreted as being psychopathic or paranoid. Further, he or she is often isolated and the subject of malicious gossip picturing him or her as an insensitive freak, or infantile. In other instances, the least fortunate of those exhibiting unusual talent are shaped up early in life. They are usually put on reinforcement schedules so that they provide entertainment for the less potent and the impotent.

14. The whole person is aware that for most people life is a cheap game.

Psychotherapy, as another social institution, is seen by most as a means for getting people back into the game. The whole person asks the question as to whether or not he or she wants to help them back into the game. Furthermore, she searches ways and means to bring the "less knowing" to fulfillment in a life without games.

15. The whole person is fully aware that many of society's rewards are designed to render the creative impotent.

Striving for and then achieving societal rewards traps the creative person into living his life so that he proves to others that he was, after all, worthy of such recognition: he can no longer make new contributions; he or she can rely only on old ones.

16. The whole person realizes that to emerge within the acceptable levels tolerated by society means institutionalization.

Institutionalization within society renders creative acts and persons neutral and keeps them from further growth by making them a part of *history*. Society, after a long series of trials, moves to institutionalize the creative person operating beyond its limits.

17. The whole person realizes that he must escape traps to render him or her impotent.

A few of the traps involve invitations to join society at considerable compromise, living up to images, rumors, and myths, and responding to all the efforts to discredit the whole person's work rather than continuing to produce.

18. The whole person is aware of the awesome responsibility that comes with freedom.

The whole person must do more than know all that there is to know about his or her life and work in order to stay whole and extend his or her boundaries. He must go beyond the known to meet his responsibilities to his own integrity, knowing that without this he cannot act responsibly, with and for another.

19. The whole person understands fully that unconscious motives are the inventions of the weak and cowardly.

The unconscious is a weapon of the clever but dying. They use it to avoid being held responsible for their destructive ways of denying responsibility and making others the negative focus of authority. The whole person knows that if anyone believes another person has acted stupidly or cruelly because of an unconscious motive, the destructive person knows the believer to be a fool and now both have license to perpetuate their cruelty.

20. The whole person knows that he or she can develop

> his or her own direction if he or she is willing to pay
> any price to grow.

The price is simply working with goals while foregoing personal comfort.

> 21. The whole person understands that most are con-
> ditioned to confuse process or promises with outcome.

The whole person knows that his or her ability to discriminate between pseudogrowth and growth as well as between use and abuse will enable him or her to focus on deliveries that make a real difference.

> 22. The whole person knows that cruelty is the result of
> being convinced that you cannot deliver anything of
> value to yourself or to others.

The whole person makes a difference by continually developing and refining his or her substantive skills and knowing the value of what he or she delivers. No one who has something that makes a constructive difference will tolerate its abuse.

> 23. The whole person understands that incompetence is a
> diversionary tactic to cover for childish impulses.

Maturity for the growing includes competence. For the immature, incompetence is a denial of all things that make a constructive difference.

> 24. The whole person knows he or she must nourish what
> is growing or he will not grow. He or she also knows
> that if he or she does not destroy when necessary, he
> or she will not grow.

There are conflicts, even wars, that a people have no right to lose. Only a whole person can decide to help or not help because the rest cannot help.

> 25. The whole person knows that if he or she falters or
> does not act upon his discriminations, the weak grow
> strong.

When the whole and strong act upon their discriminations, the weak grow weaker.

> 26. The whole person understands that the complete man
> can respond as fully as any full woman and a complete
> woman can initiate as fully as any full man.

A complete person is appropriately responsive and initiative. At the highest levels of maturity and effectiveness, responding and initiating are one and the same thing.

27. The whole person knows that we know all there is to know about psychopathy when we realize that it is the preoccupation with irrelevancies.

The whole person learns from other whole persons. Sick people make a sick difference. Healthy people make a healthy difference!

28. The whole person knows that honest work makes the irresponsible painfully anxious.

Most enemies are defeated by their own anxiety and fear. The psychopath avoids work at all costs. Even at the threat of death the psychopath would choose not to learn what he needs to learn in order to live.

29. The whole person knows that the work he does that yields a product helps him grow.

Those who choose not to work by only appearing to be working become victims. Victims are never to be trusted because they kill. Once victims kill they cannot stop killing.

30. The whole person values truth above all else.

Any person less than whole knows who he really is when he encounters another person who is committed to what is true.

31. The whole person understands the implications that crises often serve to assist efforts to avoid truth.

There are no crises in what is true. The less-than-whole person creates crises to divert others from the pursuit of truth. Truth will expose how evil the neurotic is. Not sick, evil.

32. The whole person knows that the first and last crisis for everyone is whether or not to work with the truth.

The choice to work with the truth is a life choice. The choice not to work with the truth is a death choice.

Whole persons have little use for the traditional theories about therapy because they are not prisoners of their own history. They are free of their history without denying their roots. On the contrary, whole persons respect and continue to learn from their parents for a lifetime. They do not avoid value judgments but make them with confidence because they, as persons, make a difference in their worlds. Most of all, whole persons do not need to help nor do they need helpees because they realize that effective helping requires helpers who can make it without helpees.

Only the fully functioning whole person has the *right* to be a helper, for only he or she lives in society yet is able to see society through the eyes of its victims; and only he or she can discriminate between the good and the bad. Those counselors and therapists functioning below this level have *no right* to offer themselves as helping agents and models. The fact is that most counselors and therapists cannot successfully meet the circumstances with which their helpees are failing to cope. The interaction between such a helper and his helpee can be nothing more than a fraud.

We present a stance calculated to encompass all aspects of life based on the interaction between a potent helper and his helpees; that is, the helper struggles to do what is most effective: ultimately, both helper *and* helpee are influenced by what is most effective for the other. Short of this, the relationship is a circle of mutual denial and deprivation of what constitutes the basic fabric of facilitative interpersonal relationships: *responsible honesty.* Typically, the counselor assumes a facade of honesty so that the client can sound honest. In other interactions both parties operate from the following base—"You fool me and I fool you"—which leads to greater and greater accumulation of hate. In the context of a significant relationship, if one party is able to fool the other there is nothing to respect. In more general terms: neurotics respect strength (those who cannot be fooled) and love weakness (those who can be fooled as he or she is fooled). Their tragedy is that they encounter so few who deserve both respect and love, and that they, the neurotics, cannot combine love and respect in any instance.

The whole person makes a choice to be a full participant in life. In this way, his life is not only intense—he is testing limits, learning, confirming, and expanding—his superiority becomes a way of life. For those who only observe or selectively participate, life is a series of competitive engagements, often without a winner or a loser. Above all, the selective observer is careful not to engage those who can expose him or her, and he or she cannot or will not see others to expose. What does grow in the observer and selective participant is despair, despondency, and self-contempt in his or her pseudosearch for an honest experience. In order to experience some semblance of stature and potency, the observer surrounds himself with others who fear exposure as he does. Collectively, they can make efforts to stifle the personal emergence of those outside the agreement.

Any full, open, honest, and growing interpersonal relationship begins with at least one party who can be whole and the other with the potential to become whole. The relationship is further characterized by dignity, decency, and vitality. Each wants challenge from the other. The less-than-whole person demands unconditional positive regard and the whole person demands positive regard that has a base of *conditionality*. The whole person does not expect to be accepted at less than who he or she is and seeks relationships with others who will respond to him fully *only* when he or she is whole. *The psychological distance between people is in inverse relationship to the wholeness of the parties to that relationship: the more whole they are, the closer they can be.*

In order to live the life of a whole person, the individual believes deeply that even major adversities will not destroy his inner core. The emotionally and physically impoverished live life carefully avoiding all major risks, convinced that if they are hit they cannot get up again. If the helper cannot get up after being hit, he or she cannot help another off his or her back. *Denial of the physical base of life is a reflection of the stance of those who have learned to view emotion as weakness and intellect as a weapon.*

If helping is not a way of life, then it is a game. In this view (aside from superficial behaviors) helping is irrelevant or destructive insofar as it reinforces the notion that the successful life is the one which you "technique" best: it becomes just one more of many selfish and cruel manipulations.

REFERENCE

BERENSON, B. G. *Belly to belly, back to back: The militant humanism of Robert R. Carkhuff.* Amherst, Massachusetts: Human Resource Development Press, 1975.

section five

TOWARD A
TRAINING MODEL

The helping process is in the end a skills-acquisition model: a learning process by which the helpee with a limited repertoire of responses is transformed into a person with an extensive repertoire of responses. He or she is equipped to help at least himself or herself and in that respect is a helper. By the same token, the training process is also a skills-acquisition model with the end being to produce helpers who can help other people. This means acquiring all of the subskills that comprise the attending, responding, personalizing, and initiating skills that enable helpees to explore, understand, and act upon their worlds. It means the commitment and discipline that enable people first to learn and then to teach what they have learned in the most efficient and effective manner: training.

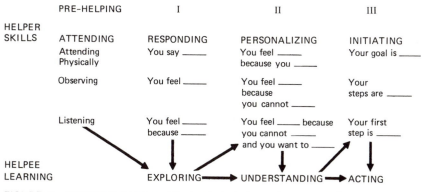

PHASES OF HELPING

	PRE-HELPING	I	II	III
HELPER SKILLS	ATTENDING	RESPONDING	PERSONALIZING	INITIATING
	Attending Physically	You say ____	You feel ____ because you ____	Your goal is ____
	Observing	You feel ____	You feel ____ because you cannot ____	Your steps are ____
	Listening	You feel ____ because ____	You feel ____ because you cannot ____ and you want to ____	Your first step is ____
HELPEE LEARNING		EXPLORING →	UNDERSTANDING →	ACTING

FIGURE V   Training in helping skills leads to helpee change or gain.

14

We can never settle for less
than a whole person in training.

Training as a Way of Life

The ultimate goal of both training and counseling is a whole person. In counseling and therapy, we often settle for less, much less, than the whole person. We are often misled by the apparent needs and resources of the client. Thus, in being guided by what is effective we may facilitate the client in a direction that will leave him far less than whole. Nevertheless, for those clients with the necessary emotional, physical, and intellectual resources, the whole person remains our goal.

We can never settle for less than a whole person in train-ing. Indeed, our helper graduate must be more, much more, than a whole person. He must be a whole helper—a constructive human with a high energy level and vast resources, with the knowledge of system and technique and verbal and research tools: the system and technique in order, at a given point in time, to bring the most efficacious practices to bear; the verbal and research skills in order to articulate and understand the practices.

The whole person must be able not only to perceive and discriminate differential levels of facilitative conditions but also to communicate at high levels, all of which raise the question of the selection of therapists.

We could make graduate training a long-term experience for those who cannot discriminate levels of conditions related to constructive client change. Thus, in offering high levels of conditions over an extended period of time and in emphasizing the personal experience of therapy, constructive change may be as possible as it is in formal therapy. Then, however, we are involved in the total reconstruction of the communication process, just as we are in working with low-level patients. The investment is tremendous on the part of all persons involved and, again, we must ask what it is that indicates to these persons that they are potential counselors and helpers. In some way, we must be able to discriminate those who can perceive and discriminate various levels of interpersonal functioning from those who cannot. Unlike the client whose communication process has broken down, we simply cannot take the time in training to reconstruct the trainee's assumptive world and perceptual system. *Distorted perception necessitates therapeutic personality change. Distorted communication necessitates training.*

This is not to say that trainees cannot benefit from personal therapeutic experiences, whether individual or group or both. Nevertheless, our research and training efforts suggest that those who are functioning at the highest levels—those who are closest to being whole—can benefit the most from the training experience. Those who are functioning at low levels are the least likely to benefit, and *those who are functioning at low levels following training simply cannot be turned loose on an innocent public.*

THE TRAINING PHILOSOPHY

It is important to remember that training in helping is another instance of interpersonal learning processes in general (Carkhuff, 1969). Graduate training in the helping professions as well as the training of functioning professionals at different levels is not an isolated process but, rather, another instance of interpersonal learning or relearning—as is the therapeutic processes for which it is intended. The same variables that operate effectively in any learning process, whether parent–child, teacher–student, or counselor–counselee, will be effective in all of these processes.

In this context, either we "hook" the trainee in a lifelong learning process or we have failed him or her and ourselves. The helping professions have not yet faced up squarely to the criteria problem in assessing our training programs. We busy ourselves with predicting success in graduate school (grades), which bears no relationship to the contribution a graduate will make in real life. We have settled too early for indices such as publication lists, which themselves present quantity–quality problems. We have not learned how to measure the contribution of the university professor or the practicing clinician who facilitates the development of any number of persons who go on to make their own contributions.

Implicitly, we are asking for constructive change or gain on the part of the trainee. Just as in helping, our goal in training is to facilitate this change in the direction of the optimal personal development of a "whole" person. We are asking the trainee to become an everchanging, ever-evolving person in the process of becoming more effective in his or her world. We are, in effect, asking him or her to become a person who lives, learns, and works effectively in his or her world, facilitating both his or her own efforts as well as the efforts of those with whom he is associated in an attempt to make life more worthwhile for himself and those around him.

We are attempting to involve the trainee in a lifelong learning process. In this regard, the trainer has not simply an opportunity but a responsibility to expose the trainee to his or her own orientation to helping. This orientation must be based upon the best available evidence at that point in time. The trainer must ensure that the curriculum culminates in skills objectives that are achievable by the trainee and that translate predictably, within limits, to human benefits. In other words, the trainer must glean from his or her experience what he or she has found to be helpful in translating to helpee change or gain. And then he or she must transmit this to the trainee in the most efficient and effective manner. That is the nature of training.

The purpose of the training is to build the helping-skills repertoire of the trainee so that he is capable of effecting helpee change or gain. The trainee will ultimately be able to utilize his basic skills or develop new combinations or new skills needed to meet the criteria of human benefits.

In this context, the training program must integrate all those elements that are most conducive to learning. Training in helping skills would seem to offer at least three primary sources for effective learning: (1) the conditions or atmosphere that afford the trainee an experiential base calculated to nurture the trainee's self-development; (2) the trainer identified as a model for effective functioning; (3) what is taught and reinforced didactically in an attempt to develop trainee skills. The learning process takes place most effectively when all elements are present and integrated in a way of living and learning effectively: an interactional process in which the trainer offers to the trainee what has proved meaningful and effective in his or her experience in the context of a facilitative relationship that provides the trainee with the conditions that facilitate his or her own exploration, understanding, and action. In short, the trainee can find out who he or she is and what he or she has to offer in conjunction with a trainer who makes known who he or she is and what he or she has to offer.

In relation to all of these things, helping training must be designed to stay in the forefront of meaningful and significant current research, theory, and practice in human learning. The training program is seen as only one phase of a continuous cycle of (1) researching the processes leading to human resource development; (2) applying the effective ingredients to training; and (3) researching the human resource development process subsequent to training. This cycle reflects the belief that research, training, and practice are not just complementary but that the efficacy of each is integrally contingent upon the other. Each is a particularly rich source for the other. Our most effective efforts can be brought to bear by those involved ultimately in the soil of practice and research, those who actually work with helpees whose needs constitute the basis for the helping professions, and those who, in turn, can explore those dimensions that offer the prospect for best serving those needs.

The training program itself must be researched to determine its own efficacy. Priority, it can be seen, is given to the production of new knowledge concerning effective interpersonal learning and relearning processes. To the helper "on the line"—the counselor or therapist—falls the chief responsibility for conducting and disseminating to the helping professions the research upon which depends the possibility of more effective helping. To the person who wants to be primarily a helper, we suggest only that he or she must wear "blinders"—looking neither left nor right nor back—not to find daily new and researchable problems and dimensions in his "routine" practice. It is not that he himself must spend long hours implementing replicated Latin Square designs. Rather, he must consider his practice a wealthy source of ideas. And in the necessary spirit of inquiry concerning the discovery and transmission of more effective modes of practice, he or she has a responsibility to frame as systematically as possible his or her ideas in order to stimulate the efforts of others as well as his or her own.

THE TRAINING EXPERIENCE

In training as in counseling, we work toward constructive change and increased levels of interpersonal skills. In both training and counseling we draw upon the same basic sources of learning in an integrated approach.

Thus training, counseling, and all other interpersonal learning exepriences involve an interaction between a person designated by society as "more knowing" and one designated as "less knowing." The "more knowing" must have the complete freedom and feel the heavy responsibility to pass on to the "less know-ing" all that he or she has learned in his or her experiences in the relevant area. In effective learning experiences, however, she does so with an openness to the trainee's response to her con-tribution. Thus, she is open to potential learning in the process. If the trainee's response makes more sense than his or hers, or if it can be incorporated in an integrated formulation more mean-ingful than his or hers, then the teacher becomes the learner. In educational and training settings, the "more knowing" person may actively teach; in counseling and therapy, the therapist may actively give direction or even "shape" the client's responses to the outside world. However, the effective learning process always takes place in and is modified by the experiential context.

Both training and counseling are experientially based; that is, as in all learning processes, what is critical is the trainee's experience of the process. There are a number of relevant ques-tions here: Does the trainee feel truly understood? Does the trainee experience himself or herself as benefiting from this process? Does the trainee's experience have a place in the learning process? Does the trainee feel free to act, qualify, and modify the learnings that are passed on to him or her? Does the trainee have the experience of a second, real party to a real relationship and truly meaningful interaction?

Finally, the trainer or counselor acts as a role model for effective training and counseling. This significant source of learn-ing is very often ignored. Thus, the whole helper or trainer is not only offering high levels of facilitative conditions and didactically teaching about facilitative conditions and their effects in living, but he or she is also a role model of a person who is living effectively. Again, the training process is as effective as the trainer is whole.

Because of inadequacies in all these sources of learning, the trainee will be limited by the low-level trainer's level of func-tioning (Carkhuff, 1969; Pierce, Carkhuff, & Berenson, 1967); the trainee cannot go beyond the level of functioning of a trainer who cannot add to the level of the trainee's response and who cannot give him or her more meaningful direction in life.

The effect of the training experience is not dependent solely upon the therapist-trainer's level of functioning. The trainee must be open to the possibility that the trainer can have a constructive impact upon the trainee's life; that is, she must be open to the possibility of change. In our experience, some trainees are not open to change, most often those who need it the

most. Rather, they tend to see their roles as counselors and therapists and guidance and social workers as "just another job." They
do not understand the privilege and responsibility of the helping
role. In some strange way, they are "entitled" to influencing the
lives of others. Unfortunately, we know all too well, from research
and experience, the two-edged effect of "helping." Students are
often vociferous in their calls for meaningful experiences; so
long as their experiences are not meaningful, they have an
excuse for not reaching into themselves. When a meaningful experience is offered them, some cannot deliver; the most destructive among them will seek to undermine the experience in order
to maintain their identities. *They cannot help others!* Just as the
trainee who is a mature adult cannot emerge in a program where
trainees are treated like children, so will "the child" have difficulty in a program where trainees are expected to be adult and
professional.

Other trainees will test early, *make a commitment to themselves,* and become, early in their careers, creative and productive
contributors in all of their efforts, whether interpersonal or otherwise. For still others, the process of testing is longer and repetitive
and the experience of "rebirth" more agonizing.

Thus, in order for effective training to take place, the
trainee must be initially open and ultimately committed to *his
or her own constructive change.* In addition, the trainer must
be whole or in the process of becoming whole, for his limitations
place limitations on the growth and development of the trainee
and his fullness makes fullness possible in the trainee.

In one very real sense, the functioning of the whole counselor may differ from the functioning of the whole trainer. A
whole counselor alone can provide her clients with a real choice.
The whole counselor can choose to move clients in the direction
of either (1) greater individuation and personal emergence or (2)
conformity with a societal model of the modal man. The ultimate
direction of the therapy process may depend upon the level of
development, the resources, and the needs of the client. In many
cases, it simply makes more sense in terms of the investment of
both the client's and the therapist's time and energy to move the
individual client toward more socialization. This may be tem-
pered, however, by training in a variety of more effective modes
of functioning, such as teaching the client to assert himself or

herself so that the client can share more fully in the rewards of the relevant social system. In some cases, the two directions are not mutually exclusive. The concept of living independently of society suggests that, at many points, societal and individual goals are quite compatible; at other points they are not. In any event, only the whole therapist can move the client in either direction.

The trainer's task is a more difficult one. If we accept the proposition that only the whole therapist can offer the client the possibility of movement in either direction, then the less-than-whole therapist can only offer movement in his or her direction, usually that of the totally socialized man. If this is so, unless we are dealing with extremely limited population samples, we must train only those therapists who can offer the client movement in either direction. *We can only train therapists who are committed to becoming whole themselves.*

The training situation must be a living, flourishing, productive pocket of health within a neurotic environment. As a marriage between two whole people provides a pocket of health for the children involved, so must a training program in the helping professions do similarly. In this way, the training program becomes something more than the sum of the whole people in it: *a pocket of health in a resistant world.*

Just as in a healthy marriage, there is room for direction imposed by the "more knowing" person upon those less experienced. The following is an example of a practicum classroom exchange following a role-playing experience involving John (as helpee), Joan (as helper), and a helper trainer—an experience that, as so much meaningful role-playing does, became quickly more real than role for both parties.

> *Helper/Trainer:* John, did you get a feeling like you were going round in circles?
> *John:* A little bit, yeah.
> *Helper/Trainer:* Where did that leave you?
> *John:* Right where I began.
> *Helper/Trainer:* I think this makes a point. Level 3 responses are essentially interchangeable with the client's. They don't help the client to go further.
> *Joan:* I wasn't able to say some things that I wanted to.

Helper/Trainer: Right. You get a piece of the feeling and right away you look for the dynamics behind it. You try to get handles on it.

Joan: I felt the feelings.

Helper/Trainer: But you won't let the whole feeling come up inside yourself.

Joan: It frightened me.

Helper/Trainer: It's a pretty desperate feeling. If you let it in. He was saying, "I can't touch other people. I can't touch other people. I can stay with them—and be with them—but I can't touch them."

Joan: I wouldn't know what to do with it.

Helper/Trainer: John couldn't let it seep in all the way. If you could let it come up inside of you—it's there in you—he might have a chance. You're carrying him away when you look for handles. It's even hard to pick up because he doesn't have the feeling full. John, you feel it now, physically, you're flush.

John: Right on it.

Helper/Trainer: Joan?

Joan: More work for me.

The direction derives from a commitment to those who are once-removed from the immediate setting, the helpees for whom we serve. The commitment to the welfare of our helpees implies a commitment to our own welfare. Again, role-playing and other classroom changes may evolve into an intensive, personal experience not unlike the therapeutic process leading to constructive change.

Tom: I feel that I get hung up when I have to put forth when there's a group, and I felt anger and hate for everybody here, and I feel like saying I didn't want to do it.

Roy: Maybe it's not all fear, though. Gee, I'm anxious now, too. In a way I'm angry with the group, too. We're revealing ourselves to the group, but maybe it's for us.

Tom: I want to please but I'd still like to say "No."

Roy: In a way you'd be getting out of it. You're still hung up with them—you're still living in a way for them. That is what you want to break.

Tom: Right. It's what I want to break.
Roy: Maybe bringing it up now will get it out and put it out.
Tom: That scares me, though. They won't like me then.
Roy: You don't want to be alone.

While the emphasis is upon training and constructive change, the whole therapist is incomplete without the tools of inquiry and formulation. Within the training program, the search and research stress the criteria of meaning, although not to the exclusion of rigor. The whole person must be equipped to make enlightened inquiries into his efforts, whether in therapy or in training. In our attempts to become increasingly more effective individuals, we simply ask questions concerning what we are doing or professing to do; in the case of the trainees, we ask questions concerning what they will actually be doing when they leave the program. In this way, and only in this way, can the student become involved in a lifelong learning process. Most important, the search and research is geared toward asking questions, *the answers to which translate in some way to human benefits.* The therapist is dedicated to integrating his clinical and research learnings in coherent theories and testable models, the implications of which will point not only to new areas of research in therapeutic processes but also to all areas of human relations. In addition, these efforts will afford the therapist a clear perspective of history and human society.

THE TRAINING CONTENT

The content of the training is the content of helping (Carkhuff, 1972; Carkhuff & Pierce, 1975). Training simply means training in the helping skills needed to facilitate the helpee's movement through exploration, understanding, and action (Carkhuff, 1972). This means learning the details of the attending, responding, personalizing, and initiating skills necessary for helping (see Figure V).

Attending Skills

The attending skills are calculated to involve both helper and helpee in the helping process. The content of the attending skills involves at least three sets of skills: attending physically, observing, and listening (Carkhuff, 1972). Attending physically involves organizing the environment in a functional way to facilitate the movement of the helpee through helping. This means organizing the setting in such a way as to insure access and retention at a minimum and involvement and motivation at a maximum.

Attending physically also involves posturing the helper so that he or she is fully attentive to the helpee. This means that he or she is squared with the helpee, his or her right shoulder to the helpee's right shoulder and vice versa. Also, posturing means that the helper is leaning forward or toward the helpee and making eye contact with the helpee. By giving the helpee his or her full attention, the helper increases the probability of observing the relevant dimensions of the helpee's presentation.

Observing includes observing the context, the appearance, and the behavior of the helpee for clues to the helpee's physical, emotional, and intellectual state. The helper knows most of what he or she needs to know about the helpee's resources through observing him and his behavior. In addition, he or she increases the probability of listening and hearing the helpee accurately.

Listening involves suspending judgment and focusing upon the helpee in order to hear the content, the feeling, and the reason for the feeling (meaning) of the helpee's expression of his or her experience. Listening offers the helper the cues she needs in order to respond to the helpee's inner experience.

The attending skills involve the helpee in the helping process. The test of the helper's attending is whether the helpee begins to share personally relevant material. The attending skills lay the basis for the responding skills, which facilitate helpee exploration.

Responding Skills ✓

The responding skills involve responding to the content, feeling, and meaning of the helpee's expression of his or her experience (Carkhuff, 1972). Responding to content is based upon listening for content. Where the expression is not too lengthy, the helper may repeat verbatim the content of the helpee's expression. Where it is lengthy, the helper may attempt to reconstruct the content with the following format:

You say ——————— .

The content lays the basis for responding to feeling. The helper learns to ask the following question: "If I had said what he said, how would it make me feel?" The answer to that question is the feeling word the helper would employ in the feeling-reflection format:

You feel _____ .

The communication of feeling to the helpee requires the meaning or the reason for the feeling in order to relate the expression to the real-life world that the helpee can do something about. In so doing, the helper uses the following format for making interchangeable responses to the helpee's experience:

You feel _____ because _____ .

The helper learns to create an interchangeable base of communication with repeated responses so that both helper and helpee can be sure of the accuracy of the helper's responses. The ultimate test of the helper's responsiveness is the level of self-exploration in which the helpee engages. The helper responds to the helpee at the level that the helpee expresses himself or herself in order to facilitate the helpee's exploration of where he or she is in relation to his or her world. Helper responsiveness and helpee exploration lay the base for helper personalizing, which leads to helpee self-understanding.

Personalizing Skills ✓

The personalizing skills involve personalizing the meaning, problems, feeling, and goals of the helpee's exploration of his experience (Carkhuff, 1972, 1973). Personalizing meaning involves individualizing the helpee's role in the experience which she is exploring. Personalizing the meaning makes the helpee directly accountable for the reason for his experience. In personalizing the meaning, the helper may use the following format:

You feel _____ because you _____ .

Personalizing problems means developing the response deficit or vulnerability that the helpee experiences. Personalizing the problems makes the helpee directly accountable for the problems he is having. In personalizing the problems, the helper may use the following format:

You feel _____ because you cannot _____ .

Personalizing feelings means developing the new feelings that may attend the personalized problem. In other words, the question for the helpee is, "Now that I am accountable for the problem, how does that change my feeling?" In personalizing the feelings, the helper may use the same format as he did for personalizing the problem with a new or different feeling:

You feel ——————— because you cannot ——————— .

Having personalized the problem, the helper is now able to help the helpee to personalize the goal. The goal is simply the flip-side of the problem. The helper may simply append the desires of the helpee to the format for personalizing problems and feelings:

You feel ——————— because you cannot ———————
and you want to ——————— .

The helper personalizes the goal for the helpee so that the helpee can understand where he or she is in relation to where he or she wants to be. The ultimate test of the helper's personalizing skills is the level of self-understanding the helpee achieves of where he or she wants to be in his or her world. Helper personalizing and helpee understanding lay the base for helper initiating, which leads to helpee action.

Initiating Skills ✓

The initiating skills involve initiating the goal, initiating the steps to the goal, and implementing the first step (Carkhuff, 1974). The goal is developed from the personalized understanding phase. The goal must be objectified in observable and measureable terms. The goal may be presented to the helpee in the following format:

Your goal is ——————— .

A goal is operationalized by the steps needed to achieve the goal. The goal is the final step. The first step is the smallest step that can be taken toward the goal. The primary steps are the major steps sequenced toward the goal and the secondary steps are the sub-steps leading to the primary steps. The steps may be presented to the helpee with the following format:

Your steps are ——————— .

When all the primary and secondary steps to the goal are developed, the helpee sets out to implement the first step. At each stage of implementation of each step toward his goal, the helpee masters the steps by repeating, reviewing, rehearsing and reinforcing the steps he takes. The first step may be presented to the helpee with the following format:

Your first step is ——————— .

The helper learns to facilitate the helpee's action by helping him develop an action program. The ultimate test of the helper's initiative skills is the level of action in which the helpee engages.

The action on the part of the helpee, in turn, elicits feedback from the world in which he acted as to its degree of effectiveness. This feedback stimulates expanded exploration which, in turn, facilitates more accurate understanding and ultimately more effective action. The cycle of helping is the cycle of learning.

In summary, then, training as well as helping are instances of learning or relearning processes. As such, the purpose of training is to effect lifelong learning for both trainer and trainee. In this regard, the training program must implement fully what is known of these processes in their effective instances and be prepared to research what is unknown in order to remain itself "in process." In short, training as well as helping is another instance of living effectively, including especially the involvement in the interpersonal learning processes that are facilitative of the development and growth of all persons involved.

Training is a way of life. That is the way it must be or it is not at all.

REFERENCES

CARKHUFF, R. R.   *Helping and human relations. Vol. I: Selection and training.* New York: Holt, Rinehart and Winston, 1969.
CARKHUFF, R. R.   *The art of helping.* Amherst, Massachusetts: Human Resource Development Press, 1972.
CARKHUFF, R. R.   *The art of problem-solving.* Amherst, Massachusetts: Human Resource Development Press, 1973.
CARKHUFF, R. R.   *How to help yourself: The art of program development.* Amherst, Massachusetts: Human Resource Development Press, 1974.

CARKHUFF, R. R.   *The art of helping training* (videotape series). Amherst, Massachusetts: Human Resource Development Press, 1976.

CARKHUFF, R. R.   *The art of helping communication and discrimination* (audiotape series). Amherst, Massachusetts: Human Resource Development Press, 1976.

CARKHUFF, R. R., & PIERCE, R. M.   *The art of helping: Trainer's guide.* Amherst, Massachusetts: Human Resource Development Press, 1975.

PIERCE R., CARKHUFF, R. R., & BERENSON, B. G.   The differential effects of high and low functionary counselors upon counselors-in-training. *Journal of Clinical Psychology,* 1967, *23,* 212–215.

The healthy person demands of himself
. . . and others no less than they can be . . .

A Statement of
Training Values

The critical ingredient in the training process, just as in the help-ing process, is the person conducting the process. Who is the per-son of the trainer? What are his values? How does he translate them to his own learning? How does he translate them to his own learning? How does he translate them to human benefits?

The helping professions need—even demand—a statement of values that blends the objectivity of established technology with the subjectivity of human experience (Carkhuff in Berenson, 1975). Such a statement must reflect individual experience as well as be responsive and responsible to the world beyond the individ-ual. Above all, it must be militant about human values and the means to translate these values into action.

The fundamental assumption of any teaching or learning stance is this: the only reason to live is to grow, and, therefore, growth is worth any price. It is the "growth" part that makes us humanists. It is the "price" part that makes us militant.

It is with this feeling knowledge of growth and price that we submit our own credo of militant humanism—a dozen prop-ositions that guide our movement into the world and our emer-gence and growth within it. The first proposition has to do with understanding, an essential beginning point in any humanistic credo. Thereafter, the propositions depart substantially from other humanistic positions, becoming progressively more initiat-ing and militant in tone.

PRINCIPLES OF MILITANT HUMANISM

Proposition 1: Understand What Is There in Ourselves

This is the easiest proposition for humanists to incorporate into their credo. The essential beginning point in all human relations and human resource development is with ourselves. We must be able to understand our own experiences. We must be able to understand and respond to the experiences of others. If we are not aware of the variety, the depth, and the intensity of our per-sonal experiences, then we are not in touch with ourselves. If we are not in touch with ourselves, we cannot be in touch with others.

The role of understanding and responding to what is there

has typically been assigned to the stereotype of the mother in the Western world: the mother responds to the needs and feelings that are present in her child. The picture of the mother holding and feeding and loving her child—independent of his or her behavior—is a familiar one. In order to respond effectively to what is present in her children, she must be able to respond effectively to what is present in herself.

Our communication with others, then, begins with our communication with ourselves. However, we must be able to do more than respond to what is there. We must learn also to respond to what is not there. Responding to what is there prepared us for this. Our own growth, we have found, has been a process of learning and responding to what is there, realizing what is missing, and then searching or building to meet the needs.

Proposition II: Understand What Is Not There in Ourselves

Our ability to understand what is there is limited by our ability to understand what is not there. We can only understand fully what is there when we have grown to understand what is not there. We can nourish, nurture, and respond to an individual in terms of what he or she has expressed of his or her experience but we can never understand him or her fully until we know what he or she has not experienced. If, for example, he declares his philanthropic disposition toward the world but does not act on it, then we will not fully understand his expressions of responsiveness until we understand the absence of his initiative. If we, in turn, respond to ourselves only in terms of our intentions, then we will not hold ourselves accountable in terms of our behavior.

The role of understanding and responding to what is not there has typically been assigned to the stereotype of the father in the Western world; the father responds to the dimensions that are absent or missing in his children but that are, in his estimation, necessary for their adulthood. We are reminded of our Chicano friend's father, who never held or responded to his children with warmth and understanding, not because he could not or did not want to but because in his own way he meant to prepare them for the very difficult life that lay ahead of them. (By the way, he is now free to respond warmly to his grandchildren, because he feels the danger in their world less intensely than he did in the world of his own children.)

Proposition III: *Understand the Need to Act*

Understanding the need to act is a natural extension of responding to what is not there. If we understand what is absent, we
understand what is there. If we understand what is there at the
deepest levels, we understand the need to act on what is not
there. A growing person is as much a function of what he or she
is not as of what he or she is. It is what he or she is that he or
she builds on. It is what he or she is not that he or she reaches
to become. Effective helpers understand these needs in their
helpees. It is what motivates the helpee to act—the experience of
having been understood fully by a helper who models behaviors
that the helpee wants to incorporate into his own way of life. It
was this consideration that led us in our early work in counseling
to extend the helping model from one using responsive dimensions only to one incorporating the initiative dimensions of
problem solving, program development, and other kinds of skills
programs. It was this consideration that led us from the romance
of the one-to-one rehabilitation scene to the hard work of preven-
tive and educative activities of large-scale social action. Indeed,
there is no rehabilitation without prevention. At the deepest
levels, there is no understanding without action. But constructive
action is not possible without the persons necessary to discriminate and model such behavior.

Proposition IV: *Make Value Judgments*

Making value judgments is the heart of militant humanism. A
fully functioning person is capable of making value judgments
concerning what is there and what is not there. The basis for his
or her value judgments is simply this: the behavior is either helpful or harmful to himself or others. If it is helpful to himself and/or
others, it is "good." If it is harmful to himself and/or others, it is
"bad." If it is helpful to himself and not harmful to others, or not
harmful to himself and helpful to others, it is "good" but capable
of improvement. As parents, we know we will never allow our
children to do anything destructive to themselves or others and
we will always encourage them to do things that are constructive
for themselves or others.

   A further differentiation regarding helpfulness and harmfulness must be made. Helpfulness and harmfulness must be dis-
criminated solely and exclusively by tangible evidence of physical, emotional, and intellectual growth. There are criteria of

growth that are observable and measurable. For example, we must be judged by our own continuing growth in these areas and by the continuing growth of the people around us who are most intimately associated with us—our family, our friends, our colleagues, our helpees, and our trainees.

Proposition V: *Act on Value Judgments*

Acting on value judgments is the natural extension of making them. It is not enough simply to make value judgments concerning what is helpful and what is harmful; we must also act on them. We are committed to nourishing the forces of life and growth wherever and whenever we find them. Again, if we have not understood what is not there, we cannot respond to what is there.

We cannot nourish life forces if we do not also destroy death forces wherever and whenever we find them. Many of us in the so-called human services are content to attempt to provide a haven for a few; together we huddle against the storms of a cruel and destructive world. This huddling is out of cowardice. We are the victims of the same vicious machine that produces the victims we would help. With our arms around each other we will drown—together. The commitment to life must be reinforced. The eager vitality of the young and innocent student must be nourished, as must the tired vitality of the battle-weary veteran teacher. If there is no justice for the parent, there is none for the child. The commitment to death, however, must be extinguished. The second grade teacher who achieves only seven months' reading growth in one year in his or her class or who develops seven stutterers a year must be trained or retrained, treated, reassigned, or fired. Persons paid to discharge responsibilities in developing the resources of others must be held accountable. The effective helper knows that her essential task in helping is to nourish the life forces and destroy the death forces within an individual. The effective person knows that his or her essential task in life is to nourish the life forces and destroy the death forces within his or her world.

Proposition VI: *Follow Through in Achieving Values*

Just as it is not enough to make value judgments, so also is it not enough to act on them. The goals are achieved in the follow-

through, not in the initiation. Successful treatment is accomplished in the after-care programs and not in the counseling
hour.

Realize that there is a war! The war is between those who
are effective in developing human resources and those who are
not. This war is won in its day-by-day battles and not in its
declaration. In this regard, we have seen little evidence demonstrating the effectiveness of the so-called humanists. We have
seen even less evidence of the disciplined existence necessary for
the achievement of valued goals. When the major issue of a
humanistic conclave is whether or not therapists should sleep
with their clients—and most of the disagreement is not over
whether it should be done but over establishing the conditions
under which it should be done—then the humanists have failed
to demonstrate either the helpfulness of their value system or
their ability to achieve more worthwhile goals. There is no room
for self-indulgence in the lives of people who are about something
important. This is brought home most vividly by the contrast of
the pseudogrowth concerns of those who search for such "freedom" in their lives and the survival concerns of those upon whose
slavery these "freedoms" are predicated. People who do not have
themselves and their families "together" have no right to intervene in the lives of others. Too few humanists we know can claim
this right.

Proposition VII: *Demand of Ourselves No Less than We Can Be*

This is a point of significant departure from humanistic principles
as they are espoused in their most popular form today. The
humanist tends to assume a consistent stance of "unconditional
positive regard" or "nonpossessive warmth" or "nonretaliatory
permissiveness" or some other such tongue-twisting nonsensical
attitude. Of course, he or she can only do so in role relationships,
particularly in the very early stages of human relationships. With
intensity and intimacy come demands. The healthy person demands of himself or herself no less than he or she can be. The fully
functioning person demands of others no less than they can be at
their developmental level. In order to make demands of others,
the fully functioning person must make fine discriminations. In
addition, he or she must make a transition into the demanding
phase. The fully functioning person will indeed find that he is

most effective initially when he is unconditional in his regard for the other person. This nonretaliatory attitude, to be sure, encourages free experiencing, free expression, and free experimentation in behavior.

With the base of behavior, however, the fully functioning person will encourage the other person to establish a base of positive behavior at the next level. Again, she will make fine discriminations in communicating her positive regard for those behaviors that move the other person toward constructive development and growth. Finally, with the base of positive behaviors, the fully functioning person will become differential in his or her regard, communicating positive regard for positive behaviors and conditionality or negative regard for negative behaviors. In the highest level relationships, each party accepts the other at no less than he or she is capable of being and thus impels both himself and the other to increasingly higher levels of functioning. Good marriages are predicated on this principle: when either party would settle for less, the other asks for more.

✓ Proposition VIII: *Get Ourselves "Together," Physically, Emotionally, and Intellectually*

In order to make demands of ourselves and subsequently of others, we must have ourselves "together," physically, emotionally and intellectually. Functioning on any one of these dimensions is ultimately related to functioning on the others. At the highest levels, these dimensions are integrated in a fully functioning person who is more than the sum of these dimensions. He or she is a full and moral being who is buttressed by a working cosmology that guides his or her development and predicts his or her world. If he or she is not physically strong, he or she cannot protect his or her loved ones. If he or she is not emotionally sensitive, he or she cannot stand for what he or she believes. If he or she is not intellectually acute, he or she cannot advance his or her cause for the actualization of all people's resources.

The years spent in physical, emotional, and intellectual development are not wearying years for the fully functioning person. They are fulfilling and energizing years, because he is about what he is about and he has increasingly larger resources to be about it.

Proposition IX: *Acquire and Develop
Substantive Skills*

It is not enough to be together, physically, emotionally and intellectually. The fully functioning person must also acquire the skills necessary to develop, sustain, and complement his or her efforts. This principle is particularly noxious for many "do-your-own-thing" humanists because it requires work. Without work there are no skills. And without skills there is no delivery. Our degrees of freedom are a function of the discriminations we can make; and our discriminations are a function of the responses we have in our repertoires. We are as effective as the quantity and quality of skills we have in our response repertoires. No more. No less. Indeed, we are as spontaneous and creative in an area as we have responses in our repertoire in that area, for spontaneity and creativity are not possible without the basic responses in the repertoire. In addition, we are as effective as the repertoire of programs we can call upon to systematically fill an existing human need. And where there are no programs, we will develop them because, as part of our commitment, we have learned the skills necessary for such program development. A person without skills is not trustworthy, for he or she must live by guile.

Proposition X: *Concede to People More
Functional than Ourselves*

When we walk onto any field of endeavor, we attempt to discover those persons who have the most to offer. We will make every effort to influence the situation so that the most effective members of a team will be appointed "quarterbacks"—not to exclude input from the team but to direct the team's activities, because the most effective are best equipped to teach the members what they need to know in order to produce a winner. This is a very important principle of militant humanism, for demands, resources, and skills are not enough. The person who is functioning at his or her fullest, at whatever his or her level of development, must learn to concede to those who are functioning more fully than he or she. This is the source of his learning! This is the source of his growth! This is the source of his life! This is the cornerstone of learning.

In this manner, based on functionality, we develop a hierarchy of effectiveness in which those functioning at the highest levels guide and develop the resources and skills of those functioning at lower levels, perhaps even enabling them to grow beyond the level of the teacher. The higher the level of functioning of the helper, the more trustworthy he or she is in this regard. The basis of trust comes in experiencing the understanding of the fully functioning person. The basis of motivation comes in experiencing the skills of a fully functioning person. The basis of learning comes in learning with the fully functioning person. The basis of growth comes in growing with the fully functioning person. The basis of life comes in living with the fully functioning person.

Proposition XI: *Develop Skills-Acquisition Programs for People Who Are Less Functional*

It is not enough to elicit trust through responsive behavior, nor is it enough to elicit motivation through initiative behavior. The fully functioning person must also provide the opportunity to close the gap between himself or herself and those who are functioning at lower levels and who acknowledge him or her as an agent of their change. She can provide the opportunity to bridge this gap by developing systematic programs that take the learner, in a step-by-step fashion, to or beyond the level of the teacher. This is the cornerstone of training. In other words, the ingredients in the learning organization are the trainer and the trainee. The modality is the program that relates these people to each other in the most efficient and effective way. In our own work in social action, we have found that we are only as good as the skills we have to offer the community we service. Indeed, we are only as good as the skills in which we can train others to service themselves. Our contract with a minority group is a simple one: "Here is a set of skills we have that you can put to your use. We will be here for a limited period of time and will attempt to train ourselves out of our jobs."

Proposition XII: *Commit Ourselves to Living at Any Cost*

This is the place to end as well as begin. In every moment of every day we make life-and-death decisions. Some are small, some are large, but each leads toward its final culmination. We used to remind ourselves of these decisions several years ago, before we stopped going to faculty meetings and finally quit the collegiate scene in order to do the things that we are about: research, training, and practice. We asked ourselves, "How would we feel if we spent our last moments here?" Put another way, "Of what relevance is this for life—ours or anyone else's?" And we got up and left and returned to the work of life.

The choice is ours—to concern ourselves with the irrelevancies that lead to deterioration and death or to commit ourselves to the relevancies that lead to growth and life. The choice is ours and we must accept the responsibilities for ourselves and for others, for when we choose for ourselves we choose for all mankind. If the only reason to live is to grow, then growth is worth any price—even work! The militant humanist trains for life, not only with specific goals in mind but also in preparation for meeting any moment in which he or she might be able to grab life more fully in whatever form it shows itself or any moment in which he or she must be able to wrestle down death in whatever form it shows itself.

It is not enough to be willing to die for the cause of life. We must also be willing to live for the cause of life.

A training stance holds a number of implications for ourselves and others. It means that we are committed to sharing everything that we know with others. It means that we are committed to learning everything that we can from others. It requires a militant humanism where the goals or ends are humanistic and the means are disciplined and militant to achieve those ends.

Perhaps the thing that differentiates the training stance from all other helping processes is the dimension of conditionality. Ultimately, the trainer demands of himself or herself and others that they be no less than they can be. This is a cornerstone principle of training: where each pushes the other to function at the highest level; where competition and cooperation converge to produce human resource development.

REFERENCE

BERENSON, B. G. *Belly-to-belly and back-to-back: The militant humanism of Robert R. Carkhuff.* Amherst, Massachusetts: Human Resource Development Press, 1975.

section six

TOWARD A TEACHING- LEARNING MODEL

If training is the preferred mode of teaching the *trainee* the skills which he or she needs to live effectively in his or her world, then the skills which the helpee needs to live effectively in his or her world. Training is the preferred mode of treatment.

If learning is the preferred mode of acquiring the skills in training, then learning is the preferred mode of acquiring life skills in helping. In other words, learning is the preferred mode of *treatment.*

Together, teaching and learning are the preferred ways of living. That has personal implications for you, the reader, and for us, the authors. For we have served as teachers and you as learners. It remains for you to acquire the skills to become our teachers. And for us to acquire the skills to become your learners.

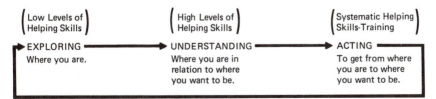

FIGURE VI   Learning leads to personal change or gain.

16

... he or she uses every precious moment to move
on to the next level of learning as if his or
her life depended upon it. Because it does.

Beyond Counseling
and Therapy

Summary and Overview

We began our search for the effective ingredients of helping with a single dimension. We believed that since all learning must begin with the learner's frame of reference, this dimension of empathy cuts across all orientations to counseling and psychotherapy—indeed, across all helping and human relationships.

We have spent the last decade filling out the missing ingredients in an equation for human resource development. Each time we have added and tested a new dimension, we have found that it was neither necessary nor sufficient for the change or gain of our helpees. In addition, we have found that often its contribution was accounted for by a common factor.

We have analyzed and then tested the possible contributions of potential preferred modes of treatment. We, ourselves, have attempted helping in nearly every form known to man.

We have concluded that most of what is done by the typical counselor or therapist in the typical counseling and therapy session is, at best, immediately irrelevant to human benefits and, at most ultimately harmful to human growth and development.

In each moment in time, we are either growing or dying. With each step we take we are moving toward either life or death. We can do a dance around the choice point—for awhile. But sooner or later, we must choose to accommodate and adjust to the sickness around us or to free ourselves and those we serve to become more fully functioning human beings (Carkhuff, 1976).

In Chapter 1 we explored the facilitative and retarding effects of helping and human relationships and studied the helping skills that relate to these effects. We found that the helping dimensions of empathy, respect, genuineness, and concreteness related to the helpee's movement in the helping process: the phases of exploration, understanding, and action leading to helpee change or gain. These phases of helping serve as the process criteria that guide the helper's utilization of helping skills. Both within sessions and between sessions, they provide the helper with the cues he or she needs to facilitate the helpee's movement toward change or gain. The phases of helping are the cornerstones upon which we build effective helping programs.

Chapter 2 gave us an opportunity to do our own needs assessment, to look at the levels of helping skills available from the general public as well as those provided by professional helpers. They are low levels of conditions and they produce low levels of results. Whereas the mutual nonexposure contract between counselor and client maintains the appearance of nourishment, the counseling relationship is, in fact, a debilitating experience for both parties.

In Chapter 3, we began to understand the helping skills we need to have in order to effect helpee change or gain. We factored the helping dimensions into responsive and initiative factors and developed the factors to facilitate the helpee's movement through the phases of helping: *attending*, facilitating the helpee's involvement; *responding,* facilitating helpee exploration; *personalizing*, facilitating helpee understanding; and *initiating*, facilitating helpee action. We understand where we are and where we want to be in the development of our helping skills.

In Chapters 4 through 8, we took a further in-depth look at five of the major helping approaches in order to determine what additional benefits might accrue from any one or more of these positions. Client-centered counseling, we concluded, is a historical footnote to the development of the empathy training which it has by philosophical disposition resisted. In emphasizing the frame of reference of the helpee, it marks the point where the exploration phase of helping begins. In negating the systematic development of action programs, it marks the place where helping fails. Its sole contribution is the skill of reflecting feelings (Chapter 4).

Existential therapy is a play on words about human interactions. The behaviors of its promulgators in emphasizing exploration are most discrepant from its lofty ideals of enabling people to act and to accept the responsibility for their action. It contributes no skills, only concepts emphasizing license for genuineness in the therapeutic interaction (Chapter 5).

We concluded that there is nothing to gain from psychoanalytic psychotherapy other than fantastic concepts which can never serve to bridge the gap from human exploration to human understanding, let alone human action. It offers no skills that translate reliably to helpee change or gain—only the fantasies of very fertile imaginations—and fantasies are goals without steps (Chapter 6).

The trait-and-factor orientation offers the means to operationalize goals in terms of the dimensions that constitute the goals. As such, it contributes an understanding of the goals for where the helpee wants to be. Unfortunately, while it contributes to goal definition, it does not contribute to the exploration process by which goals are developed. In addition, it does not help to develop the action steps to get the helpees from where they are to where they want to be in their world. In sum, the trait-and-factor approach is an early stage of program development (Chapter 7).

Behavior modification approaches are more fully developed instances of program development. They develop goals, usually the flipside of the stated problems or symptoms—in other words, the elimination of the problems as symptoms, and developing the action steps to achieve the goals. They do not offer any special skills for facilitating the helpee's exploration and understanding of the goals but usually draw from a limited repertoire of symptom-reducing programs to define the problems. As an instance of program development, however, the behavior modification approaches are potential preferred modes of treatment (Chapter 8).

Chapter 9 teaches us that the heart of helping is the helping skills that the helper uses to facilitate the helpee's movement through the learning process: the attending skills that involve attending physically, observing, and listening; the responding skills that incorporate content, feeling, and meaning; the personalizing skills that personalize feeling and meaning, problems and goals; the initiating skills that help to develop the program steps to achieve the goals.

Chapter 10 teaches us that the person who is less than whole is aware only of the death choices at the helpee's crisis point. Because there is no life choice, there can be no behavior change: "The helpee can certainly not have anything that I cannot have." The helpee chooses life because the helper chooses life and has the skills to implement his or her choice and to help the helpee implement his or her choice.

In Chapter 11, we learn that confrontation is never necessary or sufficient. But in the hands of a whole person, it may be efficient. It facilitates the helpee's choice of life at this crisis point by providing the helpee with a fully honest encounter and personalized choices as well as the life-and-death implications of those choices.

In Chapter 12, we learn that all helping has a common core of learning: exploration, understanding, and action; and that all helping culminates in preferred modes of treatment, which are operationalized by personalized goals and individualized learning programs. The effective ingredients of helping are the core of interpersonal helping skills that facilitate exploration and understanding, and the program development and implementation skills that operationalize the action phase of learning. There are as many preferred modes of treatment as there are people.

Chapter 13 teaches us that any system is only as good as the helper is whole. Even the whole system is only as good as the helper is whole. The goal of learning is to become a whole person. The goal of helping is to help someone become a whole person. The goal of living is to be whole.

In Chapter 14 we learn that training is the preferred mode of becoming a whole person. Training is the most efficient and effective modality for transforming helpees into helpers. Training is a way of life. That is the way it must be or it is not at all.

Finally, Chapter 15 teaches us that it is not enough to set humanistic goals. We must pay the price to achieve these goals. At the most basic level we must develop programs to achieve these goals. And we must be disciplined in the implementation of these programs. We must be militant humanists or we are not humanists at all.

TRAINING AS A PREFERRED MODE
OF TREATMENT

We have concluded that training is the preferred mode of treatment (Carkhuff, 1969; Carkhuff & Berenson, 1976).

There are several assumptions which we have made in drawing this conclusion.

The first is that human beings are inherently neither good nor bad. The history of humankind is a chronology of the extremes of building and destroying. People are what they are taught to be. And they are taught through the experiences that they have had—helpful and harmful. They are taught through the models which they have had—good and bad. They are taught through the direct teaching they have had—for better or for worse. The fact that most people do not fully develop their resources and exhibit the extremes of constructiveness—or, for that matter, destructiveness—is because they have, for the most part, not been taught.

The second assumption is that the only way to really teach

people how to grow, how to be effective, how to be constructive, how to be good, is through skills-development. Skills are observable, measurable, achievable, teachable, and their translations to human benefits are, within limits, predictable. We learn through helpful or harmful experiences according to the skills our teachers had or used. We learn through good and bad modeling and imitation as a function of the skills our models exhibit. We learn through direct teaching—for better or for worse—according to the skills that are taught us. The only way to develop human resources is through skills-development.

The third assumption is that the most efficient and effective means for teaching people how to develop their resources is through training. Training is a systematic means for increasing the quantity and quality of responses in a skill area. In training, the trainer uses his or her other skills to develop the experiential base for learning—in a helpful way. The trainer presents himself or herself as the model who exhibits the skills the trainee is to emulate—for the trainee's good. Finally, the trainer presents the skills to be learned in the most direct teaching fashion—for the betterment of the learner. The only way to ensure human resource development is through skills-training.

Training is the preferred mode of treatment.

Training as a preferred mode of treatment involves at least three phases.

The first of these phases we may consider to be a needs-assessment phase. A needs assessment is conducted both internally and externally. This means that we begin with the helpee's frame of reference in order to determine the needs that he or she experiences himself or herself as having. In some way, we have to relate the helpee's frame of reference to whatever it is we have to offer him. In order to do this, we need to utilize our best interpersonal skills to facilitate his or her exploration and understanding of where he or she is in relation to where he or she wants to be. A needs assessment also means that we assess the helpee from our own frames of reference. In order to do this, we need to have specialty-area skills that enable us to diagnose and set goals to help him or her to further explore and understand where he or she is in relation to where he or she wants to be.

The second of these three phases involves developing the programs and curricula to meet the needs of the helpee. In other words, when we find out where the helpee is in relation to where the helpee needs to be, we develop a program or curriculum to get him to his goal. This program or curriculum must culminate in a skills objective that meets the needs of the helpee. Once we have developed the program, we can refine our diagnosis of where the helpee is and set more precise goals for where he or she needs to be. In order to do this, we need program- and content-development skills that enable us to operationalize our skills objectives for where the helpee needs to be in order to get to where he or she wants to be.

The third of these three phases involves transmitting the skills to the helpee in the most efficient and effective manner. We simply call this training. Again, it involves the trainer delivering to the helpee the skills the helpee needs to get from where he is to where he wants to be. In order to do this, the trainer must have all of the teaching methods, learning strategies, classroom management and differential reinforcement procedures necessary to make the skills delivery.

The trainer trains the helpee in the skills the helpee needs to serve himself or herself. The skills the trainer transmits to the helpee transforms the helpee into a helper.

It is not enough to offer the helping skills to the helpee in order to facilitate the helpee's movement through the phases of helping—although this is where we begin the helping process. Ultimately, we must teach the helpee all the skills he or she needs to service himself and others. In addition to the specialty-area skills he determines that he wants or needs, this means that we train him in the very helping skills that we first offered him.

In order to train the helpee, the helper must first be trained himself.

LEARNING AS A PREFERRED WAY OF LIVING

If we are to teach, we must first learn.

A while back, the senior author had a conversation with Rudolph Dreikurs. In it, he was asked by Dreikurs whether man was determined or free.

The answer was this: "I believe that a person who believes

he is determined is determined and a person who believes he is free is free."

Let us explain.

In our experience there are two basic kinds of learners: the Stimulus-Response or S-R Reactor types and the Exploration-Understanding-Action, or E-U-Actor types. The first is a determined person because someone else has set the goals for him or her, set up the stimulus complex, and administered the reinforcements. That someone else manipulated him in such a way that he can produce the behavior, but it is not under his control. He or she is not an actor. He or she is a reactor. Given that the controller reinstitutes the stimulus complex and the differential reinforcements, he reacts appropriately. Unfortunately, without the complex or the reinforcements, he cannot even react.

The E-U-Actor type, on the other hand, has made learning a way of life. In every situation, old or new, he or she is investigating the nooks and crannies of experience by maximizing input: he or she is exploring where he or she is. Within the ever-expanding limits of his experience, he or she is narrowing or choosing the goals that are most meaningful for him: he or she is understanding where he or she is in relation to where he or she wants to be. Finally, he is planning and preparing and then implementing his program to achieve his goal: he is acting to get from where he is to where he wants to be. Indeed, he or she can learn to act in any situation.

The S-R Reactor type is a prisoner of his or her environment. He or she is determined by forces outside of his or her control.

The E-U-Actor type is in control of his or her role in the environment and ultimately, perhaps, of the environment. He or she is free within the limits of the environment.

The one knows only what he or she is conditioned to know and reacts only when he or she is conditioned to react.

The other learns in the true sense of the word.

The E-U-Actor is constantly searching out new arenas of learning. He or she is constantly acquiring new skills within each of these arenas.

He recognizes that his freedom, his spontaneity, his creativity are dependent upon the skills he has and the discriminations he is able to make about where and when to use them.

The E-U-Actor lives efficiently. Given its predetermined time-limits, she fills it with as much learning as is needed to increase her effectiveness in her world.

Indeed, the E-U-Actor knows that the development of his or her human resources is a function of his or her skills development. Accordingly, he or she uses every precious moment to move on to the next level of learning as if his or her life depended on it. Because it does.

So does ours. And so do the lives of our children.

REFERENCES

CARKHUFF, R. R.   *Helping and human relations* (Vols. I and II). New York: Holt, Rinehart and Winston, 1969.

CARKHUFF, R. R.   *The promise of America*. Amherst, Massachusetts: Human Resource Development Press, 1976.

CARKHUFF, R. R., & BERENSON, B. G.   *Teaching as treatment*. Amherst, Massachusetts: Human Resource Development Press, 1976.

INDEXES

Name Index

Subject Index